S0-CBL-516

# *M*odern Thoughts, *Wise Mentality*

**A Collection of BLIA General Conference Keynote Speeches (1992-2006)**

*by* VENERABLE MASTER HSING YUN

國家圖書館出版品預行編目資料

當代人心思潮＝Modern thoughts, wise mentality／
星雲大師著；妙光法師等翻譯. --初版.--臺北市：香海文化,
2006[民95] 面； 公分 --（人間佛教叢書）（人間論叢）
中英對照 ISBN 978-986-7384-54-6(精裝)
1. 佛教-語錄
225. 4
96000174

人間佛教叢書
人 間 論 叢❶ | **Modern Thoughts, Wise Mentality**

Writer／Venerable Master Hsing Yun
Publisher／Venerable Tzu Jung
Chief Editor／Meng Hua, Tsai
Main Editor／the Office of the Founding Master
Executive Editor／Po Jung, Chen
Book and Cover Designer／Po Jung, Chen
English Translators／Venerable Miao Hsi, Venerable Miao Guang,
Amy Lam, Jeanne Tsai, Raymond Lee, Shirley Hsueh, Tom Graham

Published by Gandha Samudra Culture Company
9F., No.327, Songlong Rd., Sinyi District, Taipei City 110, Taiwan
(R.O.C.)
TEL: 886-2-2748-3302     FAX: 886-2-2760-5594
Postal Order／19110467    Gandha Samudra Culture Company
http://www.gandha.com.tw
http://www.ganha-music.com
e-mail:gandha@ms34.hinet.net

Dealership owned by China Times Publishing Co.
and Gandha Samudra Culture Company
No.16, Lane 134, Liancheng Rd., Jhonghe City, Taipei County
235, Taiwan (R.O.C.)
TEL:886-2306-6842

Legal Advisor／Chien Chung Su, Ying Fu Mao
Registration No.／局版北市業字第1107號
Fixed Price／NT$280
ISBN／978-986-7384-54-6

# Contents

# Foreword

## One Theme, One Concept

The Buddha's Light International Association (BLIA) was inaugurated in Los Angeles on May 16, 1992. For over fourteen years, members of the BLIA have followed the founding objectives in propagating the Dharma for the benefit of all beings, and in establishing a Buddha's Light Pure Land through various programs in education, culture, charity and Buddhist practice. In 2003, the BLIA was also recognized as a non-governmental organization (NGO) with special consultative status in the Economic and Social Council of the United Nations.

Since the inauguration of the BLIA, I have delivered a keynote speech during the BLIA General Conference every time, as a means to provide members with spiritual guidance and direction for future development of BLIA. First of all, in order to spread happiness in society and to establish a world in which people of different races and ethnic groups can live together in harmony, I have proposed the theme, "Joy and Harmony". In addition, to enable everyone to understand that all sentient beings are interdependently in existence, I have introduced the theme, "Oneness and Coexistence."

In our modern society, it is essential to deal with people and their affairs with respect, and to benefit others with tolerance and open-mindedness. Hence, I have advocated the theme, "Respect and Tolerance." Abuse of power in politics, the uneven distribution of economic wealth amongst the human race, and discrimination amongst religions or ethnic groups are the consequences of inequality and conflict. Thus, I have advocated the theme, "Equality and Peace."

In life, there are many forms of imperfection, such as the sorrows of parting and the joys of union, sufferings and impermanence in life, or environmental pollution, affecting the body and mind of people. I thus raised the awareness of "Wholeness and Freeness," a condition which people of this world truly admire and pursue. Nature is the basis of all phenomena. Our mind

and life can only be set free when we respect and obey its laws. Thus, "Nature and Life" was delivered to awaken us, and to enable us to cherish our lives, so that no action be taken that is against the principles of nature.

Even though technological advances have improved the quality of our lives, they have also changed our values on life. Modern people tend to be unable to differentiate right from wrong; thus, I advocated the theme, "One Truth for All." Simply, "one truth for all" is the wisdom underlying the law of causes, conditions, and their effects, as well as emptiness and dependent origination. Similarly, the principles of "justice and morality", "non-self" and "altruism" are also "one truth for all." When everyone adheres to the morals of "one truth for all," justice and righteousness can be established in society.

"To resolve" is a very wonderful term in Buddhism; it refers to the development and active disclosure of our inner treasures. To be more explicit, I mentioned the following four necessary resolutions: resolve to be kind and compassionate, resolve to strengthen our minds, resolve to develop oneness, and resolve to achieve the enlightened mind. Other than developing our internal world, we should also resolve to develop our external world. Therefore, the above four resolutions should be complemented with the following four aspects of development: to develop truth, goodness, and beauty in human nature; to develop a wealth of blessings, wisdom, and virtue in this world; to develop harmony, joy, love, and respect in human relations; and to develop the future oneness between the self and the Buddha. To resolve is the construction of ourselves, while to develop is the construction of our world. Thus, "To Resolve and To Develop" is our mission to our family, society, country, the universe, as well as ourselves.

In order to apply the teachings of the Buddha to our daily lives, and to plant the seed of Buddhism in the human world, I have undertaken the following four transformations for Buddhism with the theme of "The Human World and Life:" transform the Dharma using humanistic qualities, transform human life through the fragrance of books, transform the monastic and lay communities with equality, and transform religious centers through localization.

Throughout the years, I am aware that Buddhist practice seems to be stagnated on aspects of Buddhist "faith," "worship," and "prayer." Hence, I advocated the theme, "Self-awareness and Practicing the Buddha's Way", with the hope that everyone will make a solemn vow and say: "I am a Buddha." Furthermore, one should resolve to elevate their spirituality through self-awareness and practice the Buddha's Way. A religion is accepted and sustained because of its effort to spread the right teachings to change the world for the better and to benefit humanity. Therefore, I propose "Change the World and Benefit Humanity" as the objectives for everyone who propagates the Dharma.

While the themes may differ every year, each of them conveys a concept of its own; therefore, One theme, One concept. These concepts are applicable across all time and space, and answer to the needs of contemporary human minds.

Oneness, coexistence, and nature are the fundamental phenomena of all living beings, while joy, harmony, respect, tolerance, equality, and peace are the essential guidelines for interpersonal relationships. Therefore, it is fair to say that "one truth for all" and "to resolve and to develop" are keys to the advancement of our society. When everyone has self-awareness and resolve to practice the Buddha's Way, change the world, and benefit humanity, then the state of "Wholeness and Freeness" can be attained through benefiting oneself and others.

In order to provide an integrative reading, Gandha Samudra Culture Company has compiled and translated my keynote speeches over the years into a book, entitled *Wise Thoughts, Modern Mentality,* I hereby, briefly introduce these themes along with their origin and morals.

*Hsing Yun*

At the Founding Master's Residence
September 2006

Foreword     vi

# Joy and Harmony

*We have to join the world rather than leave it behind; we have to substitute activity for passivity, replace pessimism with optimism, and transform an aversion of the world into genuine love. We have to express the dynamic and correct views of international Buddhism through joyous, altruistic givings.*

BLIA 1st General Conference
Los Angeles, USA
May 16-20, 1992
Edited by Robert H. Smitheram, Ph.D.

Now that the modern civilizations of the world are all in dialogue with one another and citizens of this global village can travel about with such frequency, Buddhism must also gradually overcome its traditional ways of doing things by coming out of the forest and joining society. It must expand the functions of the temple by entering into community service; it must reach out to families and be of benefit to the nation, and then by transcending national boundaries, it must spread around the world. The Buddha's Light International Association (BLIA) was established in order to effect this change by promoting harmony, compassion, and friendship among the entire human race. The BLIA is characterized by the following:

1. Faith: Having a devout faith in Buddhism is the foundation of this association.

2. Outreach: Serving the general public represents the goal of this association.

3. Modernization: Adapting to modern development forms the character of this

association.

4. International exchange: Increasing international exchange enlarges the spirit of this association.

Therefore, members of the BLIA should observe the following:

1. Realize that all beings on earth are interdependent.

2. Be compassionate and treat all beings as ourselves.

3. Have the wisdom to distinguish right from wrong.

4. Have the strength to be magnanimous towards everyone.

5. Make a positive connection with others by practicing generosity.

6. Follow the path with a pure mind.

As we take our place on the international stage, we must demonstrate to the people of the world that we are a joyous community filled with harmony and friendship, which is why the theme of "Joy and Harmony" is important. In the past, Buddhism often presented itself through misguiding images of passivity, pessimism, and as an aversion to the world that strongly emphasizes ascetic practices; a misunderstanding that led to the gradual decline of Buddhism. It is true that the Buddha taught the concepts of suffering, emptiness, and impermanence, but at the same time, he also taught us to seek joy and happiness in the Dharma. Thus, the reality of suffering in the world that Buddhism underscores does not fully represent all of the Buddhist teachings. The true picture of Buddhism is represented by contemplative happiness and Dharma joy. In Buddhism, we find the teachings of kindness, compassion, joy, and equanimity; the sacred path of bringing aid and comfort to the world; and the sublime happiness of the Western Pure Land and the Pure Land of Crystal Radiance. Those who attain enlightenment through the Dharma always joyfully call out: "Dharma joy! Liberation! Contemplative happiness! Serene bliss!" These examples illustrate how, in all respects, Buddhism leads one to joy and happiness.

The establishment of the BLIA is an expression of the joy and happiness that is experienced through the practice of Buddhism. We have to join the world rather than leave it behind; we have to substitute activity for passivity, replace pessimism with optimism, and transform an aversion of the world into genuine love. We have to express the dynamic and correct views of international Buddhism through joyous, altruistic givings.

Actually, being subject to the endless cycle of birth and death already causes enough suffering, so why would we want to increase the level of sadness and suffering in the world? The "medicine of happiness" can cure the disease of suffering. We have to create a forward-looking view, one that brings blessings and happiness to others; one that enables others to share their joys and be filled with hope. The Buddha once said, "All phenomena are impermanent." We have to understand that "impermanence is a good thing!" For impermanence constitutes change, where good changes into bad, and bad as well changes into good. Because of impermanence, everything is subject to the principle of "cause, condition, and effect." As long as good causes and conditions are present, we can be sure that the final result will be good despite all the difficulties encountered along the way. This is why members of the BLIA must proceed from seeking their own Dharma joy to realizing the happiness that transcends time and space, but they must then go on to spread contemplative happiness to all sentient beings. We can offer the boundless happiness of our body, speech, and mind to all within the Dharma realms, and in this way, our fellow beings who have forgotten what it means to smile, or those who with a heavy brow have long felt uncared for, will be able to receive their share of the "happiness empowerment." Thus, we must uphold the motto of the BLIA:

*May palms be joined in every world in kindness, compassion, joy, and giving;*

*May all beings find security in friendship, peace and loving care;*

*May calm and mindful practice seed patience and equanimity deep;*

*May we give rise to spacious hearts and humble thoughts of gratitude.*

Implementing this joyous style of Buddhism will promote the growth and development of this happy Humanistic Buddhism, ensuring that those with joy will maintain their optimism, even when they are tormented by the Eight Sufferings. We must learn to liberate ourselves both mentally and physically, because wherever the Buddha's light shines, even the shadow of sadness and suffering will be completely gone.

At the entrance to Fo Guang Shan Monastery, there stands the Gate of Non-duality. The following couplet is inscribed on the gate:

*Non-duality originally has no gate. Duality is not really duality; it is our own, true self-nature.*

*The mountain is called a holy place. The mountain is not really a mountain; it is actually a manifestation of our own, pure body.*

The pure Dharma body of the Buddha is each individual's true nature; there is no distinction between them whatsoever. Equality, harmony, and perfection are already present in our Buddha nature, so there is no need to seek these things outside of ourselves. Besides the joy we feel, the chartering of the BLIA also means that we must uphold the inclusiveness of "harmony," which will attract new members and expand our service.

"Harmony" means an acceptance of others, an equality in treatment, and a respectfulness in word and deed. The future of the BLIA will only be assured by maintaining the spirit of accepting what is different from oneself. According to the Buddhist sutras, "When all the rivers flow into the ocean, they will only have one taste, the taste of saltiness;" and "upon taking the Buddhist path, all are equal as Buddhist disciples." In the past, Nanda and Ananda of the aristocratic caste honored the low-born Upali, the Zoroastrian Kasyapa, and the sophist Katyayana, as their brother disciples, due to the egalitarian ideal that "when members of the four castes join the monastic order, they all become part of the Buddha's family," clearly showing how from the outset, the Buddha overturned the racial and class distinctions. The Buddha's harmonious accommodation of all people contributed to the strength and propagation of Buddhism down to this very day. If it is to have a standing in the world, the BLIA must likewise endeavor to accommodate other people and seek harmony among all sentient beings; only then can it grow and flourish.

The ideal being advocated here is to accommodate diversity within commonality, and to seek commonality within diversity. In Buddhism, this means that the Theravada and Mahayana schools must seek harmony; the traditional and modern practices must be harmonized. This also means that harmony must be sought between Chan and Pure Land, the esoteric and exoteric teachings, the monastics and the laity, and between the mundane and the supramundane levels. Harmony is actually the Buddha's teaching of the Middle Path, which represents the true meaning of the Dharma.

Harmony is a necessary part of our world today. It is essential between countries, people of differing ethnic origins, differing communities, all sectors of society, and political parties. In future, only harmony can enable the people on earth to survive together. Members of the BLIA practice the Bodhisattva Path: "Though we practice in remote areas, we should have a concern for society; as citizens of the earth, we should still keep the universe in mind; and while staying at Dharma centers, we should benefit all sentient beings. Though heaven might be very appealing, we should beautify this human world of ours." Engaging in this practice of harmony encompasses equality and respect, and when both oneself and others are all actively involved, then there can be a robust benefit to both self and other.

Since its early development, Buddhism has placed supreme emphasis on assimilating the theories of those standing in opposition, as well as absorbing the reasonable arguments of different viewpoints. It has also continuously adopted many useful methods employed by other schools of thought and religious traditions. In so doing, Buddhism has been able to flourish by adapted to the various geographical, historical, cultural, and social conditions. Having such an open attitude towards their external environment, it is easy to see that internally, Buddhist harmony has maintained a sense of all-inclusive, open-mindedness. For more than twenty-five hundred years, Buddhism has continuously produced a profusion of dazzling lights, like a continent of floral blossoms or a flock of singing birds. Within the body of the Buddhist teachings, differences in theoretical arguments are not uncommon: instantaneous versus progressive enlightenment, delusion versus realization, reality versus phenomena, emptiness versus existence, and so forth. In Indian Buddhism, a split developed between the Mahasanghika and Theravada schools; while in China, there are the differences among the Eight Schools. Though the variations have been many throughout Buddhism's development, the teachings have never deviated from the fundamental concepts of the Three Dharma Seals and the Eightfold Noble Path. This is why the Dharma can be viewed as extremely profound and all-encompassing. It is exactly this harmonious quality of the Dharma that we hold dear to our hearts. We advocate the following:

1. Honor every religious tradition, both its teachings and its followers, by holding an impartial, respectful, and open-minded attitude, provided the tradition is righteous and does no harm.

2. Adopt the characteristics and methods of others in a positive, willing, and prudent manner, provided these are beneficial to the human race.

3. Nourish the world, the human race, and their universal interdependence, by understanding the richness and expansiveness of the Dharma, provided we possess an exalted aspiration.

4. Accept civilization and its advances that enlighten self and others, by taking actions that are harmonious, reciprocal, and communicative, provided we have a righteous heart and a sincere mind.

Therefore, the vow that all the members of the BLIA have in common is "We will live together in harmony with all the beings of the world!"

The importance of harmony was also made apparent by the recent racial riots that occurred in the Los Angeles area. This shows us how a lack of harmony and patience, a lack of mutual reconciliation and respect, builds barriers among races and generates racial discrimination; what follows in the end are these outbursts of violence. When we take a look at the ongoing racial disputes around the world and the endless entanglement of violence between nations, we can see how modern civilization has adversely affected peace and tranquility and created chaos around the world, greatly harming our natural environment. This is why "joy and harmony" are advocated by the BLIA not only as a hope, but most certainly as a need. This is why the "joy and harmony" as promoted by the BLIA not only constitutes a subjective hope, but a true, objective need as well. This holds a special significance for this epoch, in that we can play a role in putting an end to discrimination among races. In a sense, we are promoting harmony for the human race when we develop modern cultural ideals; we are bringing hope to the world when we advocate the propagation of the Dharma for the benefit of all living things; and we are arousing the conscience of all beings as we revive Buddhism and spread the Dharma. This represents the honor of the BLIA and its members, as well as an obligation.

The BLIA has many tasks ahead, and the spirit of the Association will be handed down from one generation to the next. We hope that through the blessings of the Triple Gem and the compassionate light of the Buddha, we can direct our faith, patience, and perseverance to prolonging the life of wisdom in the Dharma. Similarly, we can employ the Buddha mind and compassionate thought to dispel the ignorance of self and others. We can receive the infinite freedom of "harmony" and bestow the generosity of "joy," in order to fulfill the goal of the BLIA: to promote Humanistic Buddhism; to build the Pure Land of Buddha's light; to purify the hearts and minds of humanity; and to build world peace.

# Oneness and Coexistence

*Oneness is equality, and coexistence is compassion. Though there are various beings, all beings are equal elements within one embodiment of dependent origination.*

*Even though the forms of phenomena are different in myriad ways, all share the Buddha nature. Through compassion, we can accept and appreciate each other; through harmony, we can coexist.*

BLIA 2nd General Conference
Kaohsiung, Taiwan
October 16-20, 1993

BLIA 3rd General Conference
Vancouver, Canada
Sepember 23-27, 1994
Edited by Robert H. Smitheram, Ph.D.

The Buddha spoke the Dharma for forty-nine years, delivering over three hundred discourses. He never limited the focus of his audience to one locality, one nation, one time, or one congregation. With regard to locality, he would always speak of the three thousand chiliocosm of boundless lotus lands; with regard to living beings, he would describe them as infinite, for they inhabit worlds of the ten directions as numerous as sands of the Ganges River; and when speaking about time, it was always the three great incalculable kalpas. Buddhism speaks in terms of causality, regarding the whole world as one family and all living beings as existing through the combination of causes and conditions to form a non-dual oneness. The sun, the moon, and stars in the sky shine upon each other regardless of luminance; mountains and valleys follow one another in endless succession regardless of their height or depth; and rare and unique flora and fauna complement each other regardless of how they vary. Thus, this universe is actually a perfect domain of oneness and coexistence.

"Oneness" means equality and tolerance.

For example, although the body's various organs of sensation such as the eyes, ears, noses, tongues, hands, and feet differ from one another, yet they all are a part of the same body; although this planet has many different nations, races, and geographical regions, yet all of these must rely on the earth for their survival; and although living beings differ in terms of being male or female, young or old, strong or weak, and wise or ignorant, and yet together they form a living entity through the combination of causes and conditions. Even though the forms of phenomena differ in myriad ways, yet they all share the same, pure Buddha nature.

"Coexistence" means compassion and harmony. All sentient beings in the Dharma realm rely upon one another, forming a living oneness upon which all depend for survival. One story from the Buddhist sutras tells about how a blind person, a lame person, and a mute person managed to safely escape from a burning house by helping each other. Besides the talented performances of the leading actors, a brilliant play also requires the seamless cooperation of the supporting roles. Similarly, a peaceful society can only be established through the contribution of every trade and profession and the positive efforts of each individual. Only through compassion can we accept the other, and only through harmony can we survive and coexist together.

As we all know, "oneness" is the contemplation of equality, while "coexistence" is the contemplation of compassion. The essence of Buddhism lies in spirit of equality. From the outset, the Buddha founded the community of practitioners in order to eliminate the inequalities of India's caste system by advocating equality as embodied in these statements: "When all the rivers flow into the ocean, they will only have one taste, the taste of saltiness;" and "when members of the four castes join the monastic order, they all become part of the Buddha's family." The moment the Buddha attained enlightenment beneath the bodhi tree, he made a declaration as incontrovertible and unshakable as diamond:

"All beings of this world possess the excellent quality of the Tathagata's wisdom." This declaration underscores the spirit of oneness and equality in the undifferentiated unity of mind, Buddha, and sentient beings, promoting the ideas of "the equality between Buddha and sentient beings," "the equality between the enlightened and the unenlightened," "the equality between principle and phenomena," and "the equality between self and other." The founder of our faith was truly an advocate and propagator of the contemplation of "oneness and equality."

## I. Equality Encompasses the Combination of Causes and Conditions

We can find in the Buddhist sutras much evidence that "the becoming of one Buddha is facilitated by thousands of other Buddhas." A particularly powerful example of "oneness and equality" appears in the *Lotus Sutra*, in which Sadaparibhuta ("never disparaging") Bodhisattva always embraces the compassionate mind of "oneness and equality" by paying homage to all living beings: "I dare not have contempt for you, as you will all succeed in becoming Buddhas!" Upon his birth in Lumbini Garden, the Buddha pointed one finger to the sky and another to the earth saying, "In the heaven above and the earth below, I am the only Honored One." What this means is that all sentient beings from all Dharma realms of the ten directions are the most supreme and equal without differences; while in the ocean of *prajña*-wisdom, the Buddha nature of all sentient beings is pure and undefiled.

Taking another look at our society, we can see that many types of differences exist: the gap between the rich and poor, the limitations on the exercise of power, the conditions of one's station in life, the level of education, and the differences between the wise and ignorant, the virtuous and immoral. Therefore, I hope that all members of the Buddha's Light International Association (BLIA) will uphold the wisdom of "equality," and embrace the fearless spirit that the Buddha showed in overturning the caste system. We should all endeavor to make the

BLIA:

1. An association that advocates compassion and tolerance.

2. An association that promotes equality among all living beings.

3. An association that values family life.

4. An association that emphasizes social welfare.

## II. Impartial Coexistence and Coprosperity

We say that coexistence is the contemplation of compassion because Buddhism has always advocated "unconditioned loving-kindness and the empathetic compassion of oneness." Compassion means an impartial and loving concern for others, and it means tolerance without conditions. Compassion is not the same as how superiors and inferiors treat each other at work, nor is it the give and take of everyday life, and it certainly is not compatible with the distinctions between rich and poor in society. Instead, compassion means harmony and respect among all living beings.

Therefore, compassion means respecting life; and compassion means coexistence and coprosperity.

Compassion is a fundamental concept in Buddhism, and thus many Buddhist sutras emphasize the importance of compassion. For instance, the *Lotus Sutra* states: "I vow to employ great compassion to open up the door to the sweet dew of the Dharma, and to turn the Dharma wheel of supreme truth;" and "to deliver all beings from their suffering by the power of great compassion." The *Treatise on the Perfection of Great Wisdom* states, "Compassion is the foundation of the Buddhist path." The *Flower Adornment Sutra* states, "All the Buddhas are in essence the great compassionate mind." The *Sutra of the Bodhisattva Bright Net states*, "Great Compassion is the foundation of merits for all the buddhas and bodhisattvas." The *Treatise on the Great Man* states, "All virtuous teachings arise from the compassionate mind." The *Enumerative Discourses of the Buddha* explains: "All buddhas, the World-Honored Ones, have perfected their great compassion, and it is through the strength of their great compassion that they are able to bring boundless benefit to sentient beings." Loving-kindness generates happiness, and compassion relieves suffering; while anything done without an understanding of compassion creates harm.

In this world, though we see wars destroying countries, race hatred causing genocide, and sectarianism dividing religions, and yet we all are inhabitants of this same planet, so we should abandon our own selfishness and prejudices in order to help each other. Next, we should respect the right of every living being to exist, by promoting equality for all through the idea of "oneness," and by propagating the spirit of kindness, compassion, joy, and equanimity through the idea of "coexistence." In doing so, this would enable the earth to become a humanistic pure land of peace and happiness.

In Confucianism, the spirit of "coexistence" within the world of universal brotherhood is expressed by "taking care of one's elders, as well as the elders of others; and by looking after one's own children, as well as the children of others." The altruistic aspiration of "oneness" is aroused in Confucianism "when others are drowning, it seems oneself is drowning; and when others are starving, it seems that oneself is starving," and by the statement that "all within the four seas are brothers." When tolerance is great and compassion fearless, it is like the openness of the oceans encouraging the fish to swim about, and the vastness of the sky allowing the birds to fly. This is how the ocean and the sky perfect their great spaciousness; how the great void accommodates its stars; and how the universe displays its diverse phenomena. This is how the universe can manifest its boundlessness; how the benevolent kings permit all voices to be heard; and how the wise do not reject refined discourse nor opposing arguments. This was how the sages of old were able to spread the benevolence and wisdom; how the Buddha was able to expound the shared truth of the five vehicles; and how the noble teachings were propagated by the Eight Schools together. Indeed, this is how Buddhism is able to manifest its vast sense of tolerance.

From a biological standpoint, we are also able to observe the phenomena of "oneness and coexistence" among all beings. There are three kinds of coexistence in biology: "synoeciosis," the partial benefit of coexistence as between whales and barnacles; "parasitism," the parasitic coexistence as between humans and intestinal worms; and "mutualism," the mutually beneficial coexistence as between water buffalos and tickbirds. Animals and plants enjoy reciprocal benefits and take care of their individual needs by alternately inhaling oxygen and exhaling carbon dioxide. In the food chain, herbivorous animals treat the green grass that covers the land as their food, while carnivorous animals live on herbivorous animals. Bacteria break down and convert the dead carnivorous animals into nutrients, which then accumulate in the ground to nourish the plants and trees in return. This interlinking of the food chain in a continuous cycle of birth and death, demonstrates the causal principle inherent in "oneness and coexistence." In order to preserve their lives, even pelicans help each other in catching fish, beavers cooperate with one another to build dams, and dolphins live in schools. Likewise, human beings rely upon the various trades and professions in society to provide the daily necessities of life. Phenomena do not appear in isolation; they arise only in the context of their settings, thus everything comes into being once the causes and conditions are ripe. Animals and plants coexist together only by being in accord with the principle of "oneness and coexistence;" human beings can dwell together in peace only by being in accord with the principle of "oneness and coexistence;" and our world can maintain its ecological balance and generate immeasurable vitality only by being in accord with the principle of "oneness and coexistence."

## III. The Natural Balance of Mutual Benefit

Humanity in the past lived in an age dominated by the power of spirits, believing that their fate for good or bad was determined by these unseen and mysterious gods. Later on, humans founded kingdoms in which monarchs controlled the people's entire lives, and humanity lived under the shadow of sovereign power. But gradually, as people developed their own wisdom, humanity broke away from the yoke of sovereign power, and advanced into the era of people's rights, so that individuals could make their own decisions. Although the common people in this era of people's rights can live a more dignified life, after all, it is still quite human centric, something that cannot be extended universally to all living beings as a whole. Therefore, now is the time to go further by transforming this era of people's rights into one upholding the right to life through "oneness and coexistence." We must respect all living things, whether sentient or non-sentient, and promote the spirit of "unconditioned loving-kindness and the empathetic compassion of oneness."

It is owing to the lack of "oneness and equality" that social unrest arises continuously nowadays, and it is due to the lack of understanding about "coexistence and compassion" that our present, natural environment suffers so much distress. We should strive to fulfill the ideals of "oneness and coexistence" by promoting the "Seven Admonitions Campaign for a New Life:" to admonish against smoking and drugs, to admonish against irresponsible sex, to admonish against violence, to admonish against theft and stealing, to admonish against gambling, to admonish against the misuse of alcohol, and to admonish against abusive language. In this way, we can purify our minds and improve society. In an effort to save our planet, let us also actively engage in global environmental conservation, working to eliminate the excessive felling of trees, the excessive cultivation of farmland, the indiscriminate killing of wildlife, the uncontrolled construction of buildings, and the senseless way in which things are discarded and thrown away.

"Oneness and coexistence" are universal truths, and yet there are still many people today who go against these by only being interested in matters that concern themselves. This results in the recurring natural disasters and human-caused calamities. Therefore, let us start right here and now, by working hand-in-hand to promote the ideals of "oneness and coexistence;" and let each one of us practice compassion, equality, harmony, and tolerance in our everyday lives. If we can do this, I know it will not be long before we will all be sharing a peaceful and prosperous pure land here on earth.

# Respect and Tolerance

*Monks have always protected the surrounding environment and natural resources. Based on the spirit of compassion, Buddhism promotes vegetarianism to provide safety for all living beings. As Buddhists, we should put forth our best effort to protect all life. Truth is magnanimity. It can encompass all.*

BLIA 4th General Conference
Sydney, Australia
October 14-17, 1995
Edited by Robert H. Smitheram, Ph.D.

Freedom, democracy, and science have now become the hallmarks of our modern century. However, misguided freedom has supplied an excuse for encroaching upon others; false democracy has become a weapon for trampling the weak; and unethical science has become a tool for destroying one's neighbors. In the past, freedom, democracy, and science have been necessities for favorable progress, but now they are the source of so many problems. In these turbulent times, we call upon "respect and tolerance" as a way for people of the world to cultivate increased mutual respect for and understanding of one another. The Buddhist scriptures state: "Buddhist teachings are sought through respectfulness." Buddhism is so meticulous when it comes to the practice of "respectfulness," which is why Buddhists have the distinction in world religious history of never engaging in bloody warfare in the name of religion. So now the question is: How do we actualize respectfulness in our daily life?

## I. Respect the Freedom of Others

During America's revolution for independence, Patrick Henry once uttered these words: "Give me liberty or give me death," while throughout history, the number of individuals willing to sacrifice all in the struggle for freedom are too many to enumerate. Clearly, this shows how priceless freedom is. However, misconceptions about freedom in modern democratic societies have lead to abuse, creating great misfortune and confusion. Regrettable indeed, for the true meaning of freedom is actually a freedom that respects the freedom of others. Among all the various teachings and religious principles, the Five Precepts of Buddhism are best able to embody this spirit of freedom to its fullest extent: no killing is the freedom to respect the lives of others; no stealing is the freedom to respect the property of others; no sexual misconduct is the freedom to respect the integrity of self and others; no lying is the freedom to respect the reputation of others; and no intoxicating substances is the freedom to remain clear-headed so that we will not act rashly. Upholding the Five Precepts means that we know how to honor all the freedoms of others. Consider those convicts held in the penitentiaries, which one among them was not incarcerated for having broken the Five Precepts?

For an individual to keep the Five Precepts is enough to perfect their moral character; a family keeping the Five Precepts will ensure kind parents and obedient children; a community keeping the Five Precepts will ensure a peaceful and prosperous society; a nation keeping the Five Precepts will ensure its wealth and happiness; and a world keeping the Five Precepts will bring forth a Pure Land. Therefore, all members of the Buddha's Light International Association (BLIA) must actively promote the Five Precepts: not only abstain from killing, but also cherish all sentient life; not only abstain form stealing, but also be generous and helpful; not only abstain from sexual misconduct, but also to support the happy homelife of oneself and others; not only abstain from lying, but also comfort all beings with kind words of encouragement; and not only abstain from intoxicating substances, but also develop wisdom so that others can be guided in a good direction with correct knowledge and understanding.

## II. Respect the Value of Life

There are countless Buddhist poems that extol the preciousness of life, and two such examples are as follows:

*Who says the life of animals counts for naught;*
*We all are similar in flesh, bone, and skin.*
*So strike not that bird on the end of the branch;*
*For its chicks in the nest are awaiting their mother's return.*

*My flesh is the flesh of sentient beings;*
*Though the names differ, the essence does not.*
*We all belong to the same family;*
*We merely vary in bodily form.*
*I left others to suffer in pain,*
*For it is their sweet flesh that I desire;*
*No need to wait upon the Lord of Death's judgment;*
*I know myself what such deeds will cost.*

Life is priceless, for no amount of money can buy back a precious life. Therefore, we should respect the value of life, in that not only should we not capriciously harm the life of any living being, but we should also cherish our own life. We should set for ourselves the goal of being a lamp that gives off the warming rays of life, illuminating and comforting those around us; we should vow to be a great tree that projects the cooling purity of life, bringing shelter and protection to living beings; we should swear to act as a bridge that extends the supporting power of life, guiding everyone to the other shore of happiness. We should even gladly serve as a simple raindrop that releases the gentleness of life, nurturing the body and mind of sentient beings.

## III. Respect the Possessions of Others

Each one of us possesses our own wealth and property, as well as our own feelings; and when we lose the things we once possessed, we feel sadness and pain. Therefore, not only should we refrain from building our happiness upon the pain of others by taking what they possessed, it would be far better if we could substitute the concept of "sharing" for that of "possessing." For example, we may not have a big mansion, but we can still enjoy the flowers and trees along the roadside; we may not be millionaires, but if our hearts are pure, the moon and stars are our unlimited treasures.

"Flowing water speaks the words of the Dharma; the mountain scene is none other than the body of the Dharma." This was how the great teachers and great worthies of the past were able to see the form of the formless nature and hear the sound of the soundless world, thereby possessing this infinite universe. Not only had they no desire either for worldly ownership of material things or for the satisfaction of the senses, but they were also able to employ their supreme compassion by undertaking various building projects for the benefit of others. In order to free others from pain and make them happy, they went out of their way to build roads, bridges, irrigation systems, and hospitals. The *Treatise on the Perfection of Great Wisdom* states: "Treat the wives of others as your mother, and consider the wealth of others as fire, for everyone belongs to our family. This is what it means to have a just and fair view." As members of the BLIA, we should model ourselves on this spirit of egalitarian respect of the ancient worthies. We should create more benefit for others, enabling everyone to share a happy life together.

## IV. Respect the Life Force of the Earth

The government and people of Australia have been unified in the implementation of environmental policy, this is why the land there remains so lush and green that even the birds and animals seem part of the human family, and the fish swimming in the sea happily draw near in friendship. This portrait of rich and vibrant life is truly such a wonderful thing, and coincidentally, this also happens to reflect the ecological consciousness that Buddhism has always advocated.

The *Amitabha Sutra* describes the Pure Land of Ultimate Bliss with its bejeweled trees, where water fowl speak the Dharma. In the *Jataka Tales* of the Buddha's past lives, there are stories of how as a bodhisattva, he would dare not raise his voice while preaching so as not to scare other beings, or how he would walk softly so as not to trample the ground; neither would he at any time carelessly throw things away to pollute the land and streams. The ancient practice centers of Buddhism were mainly situated in the wilderness around famous mountains and broad lakes, and the monks living there not only worked together to beautify their surroundings, but they also placed considerable emphasis on protecting mountain forests and river lands. The *Sutra of the Descent to Lanka* states that those who kill living beings for food destroy the seed of compassion. The Buddhist promotion of vegetarianism as well as its practice of setting captive animals free is mostly based upon the spirit of compassion. All of which goes to show that Buddhism directs its purest intentions and employs the most thorough methods as ways of cherishing the life of living beings.

Buddhism believes in the "dependent origination of all phenomena," in that everything in the Dharma world from the smallest mustard seed to the whole universe itself is a part of an interactive relationship. The best way to protect the survival of all living things is for everyone to hold a respectful heart and allow the life force of the earth to continue uninterrupted.

Certainly, "respect" can improve the present environment and bring about a greater social happiness, while "tolerance" is all the more able to develop harmonious human relations and broadly benefit all living beings. For more than a thousand years, Buddhism has spread around the world, assimilating into the local culture to become its own unique form of Buddhism and conferring its benefits upon society. The reason it has been able to do so is because the truth of the Buddhist teachings is unobstructed tolerance, which is why Buddhism has been able to sustain itself in all directions over these many centuries. So how should we spread the Buddhist teachings of tolerance in order to promote harmony in the world?

## I. Be Tolerant of Diversity

Differences in social background, local customs, languages, and modes of thinking, will naturally generate differences of opinion among people. The *Diamond Sutra* says that in order for bodhisattvas to subdue the mind and deliver all beings from their suffering, they must first rid themselves of the Four Marks of Existence: that the self exists, that this self differs from all others, that life is limited to its components, and that life is limited to the physical form. Simply put, we must use our open-minded spirit of altruism to be tolerant of diversity, otherwise, if we cannot liberate ourselves, how can we speak so extravagantly of benefiting others?

Buddhism is the most tolerant of religions in the world. Upon becoming enlightened, the Buddha promoted the idea that "when members of the four castes join the monastic order, they all become part of the Buddha's family." From nobles to commoners, even heretics to prostitutes, in fact, anyone who was willing to commit to the path would be tolerantly accepted by the Buddha as part of the monastic order. This was why the Dharma spread so quickly throughout the whole of India. The students of the Buddha who attained enlightenment amounted to more than twenty-five hundred in number, ten of whom became the Ten Principle Disciples, each with his own specialty. After his conversion to Buddhism, King Asoka immediately abandoned his evil ways of killing and plundering, halted the collection of taxes, and invited talented individuals from all directions. He also treated all religions with respect. Not only did he win the praise of his subjects, but his nation also became prosperous and strong. Buddhism in the Tang dynasty (618-907) witnessed the flourishing of the Eight Schools as each vied with the others to higher levels of development, ushering a glorious age of splendor for Chinese Buddhism. Later on, Buddhism spread to the countries of Southeast Asia where it enriched the local cultures there.

Even today Buddhism remains fresh and strong after all this times, as its influence spreads ever farther. Clearly, the tolerance of diversity does not lead to divisions, for it actually increases vitality and fosters growth, like a great tree blossoming with a profusion of flowers.

## II. Be Tolerant of Wounded Dignity

Prior to undergoing surgery one year, I told my doctor about how as a monk, I have no fear of death, and yet I was just afraid I would not be able to bear the pain of the illness, thereby ruining the dignified image I normally maintain. Dr. Chen replied, "For us doctors, a healthy person has the image of good health, but the sick have the dignity of being ill. To suffer the pain of illness is not something shameful, so even though they cry out in pain, the sick should still be treated with respect." Such a wonderful thing to say! Doctors who care for the patients like a bodhisattva are just like the Medicine Buddha, for not only do they treat the many mysterious maladies of the body, but they also comfort the fear living beings have for pain.

This is what is meant by the expression, "in every family an Amitabha Buddha and in every household an Avalokitesvara:" Amitabha Buddha tolerates the profound ignorance of all beings, and even allows them to take rebirth in the Pure Land of Ultimate Bliss along with all their negative karma. Avalokitesvara Bodhisattva rejects not the defiled turbulence of this world, but instead pilots her boat of compassion to save those from suffering by following their call. It is because of their compassionate tolerance that images of these bodhisattvas have been given a place of honor in the homes of so many Buddhist followers. We can hold on to all living beings as a whole, only so long as we can be tolerant of all their strengths and shortcomings, their wounds and frustrations.

## III. Be Tolerant of the Injuries from Enemies

The *Sutra on the Eight Realizations of Great Beings* states: "The generosity of the bodhisattva is such that friend and foe are considered equally. Old misdeeds are not brought to mind and evil doers are not hated." The highest teaching of the Buddha is that we are all equal. Upon attaining enlightenment under the bodhi tree while gazing on the bright stars of the night, the Buddha exclaimed: "Oh how wonderful! All beings of this world possess the excellent quality of the Tathagata's wisdom." The *Lotus Sutra* describes how Sadaparibhuta ("never disparaging") Bodhisattva honored and praised all beings by saying, "I dare not have contempt for you, as you will all succeed in becoming Buddhas!" Some heard this and became angry, so they hit him with sticks and stones, but Sadaparibhuta Bodhisattva treated them with respect as before; and even upon seeing the arrogant and prideful from afar, he would still greet them politely. Beings who dwell in the Pure Land of Vairocana do not quarrel over self and other, right or wrong; they treat each other with tolerance and respect because they are able to employ infinite compassion and the inexhaustible power of their vow. The reason for this is that they have realized these ideals: the equality between buddhas and sentient beings, the non-duality of self and other, the oneness of friend and foe, and the harmony between self and things. This is how the Pure Land of Vairocana, so bright, so perfect, and so infinite, could be formed.

Our Saha world is a "half-and-half" world: half are buddhas and half are unawakened; half are male and half are female; half are good and half are bad; and half are wise and half are ignorant. Living in such a half-and-half world, we cannot just take the half that benefits us and reject the other half that conflicts with us. We can realize the fullness of existence only through complete tolerance that is accepting of everything. Pouring in hot water cannot cool the boiling tempest; and so hatred will never eliminate hatred. When faced with "that half" that presents life's misfortunes, we can only employ our compassionate mind of unconditioned oneness and use our egalitarian mind of non-duality between self and other, so as to be tolerant of the other side. This is the only way resolve violent conflict and put an end to resentment; and this is the only way to obtain more loving respect and a wonderful life.

## IV. Be Tolerant of Careless Mistakes

"People are not saints, for who among us is without fault? But knowing one's faults and making a change is the greatest good of all." No one likes to make mistakes, and making mistakes does not always lead to something bad, for if one can endeavor to improve, then mistakes often serve as the foundation for success. "Be strict with ourselves, and yet go easy on others." This means that we should diligently correct our own faults, yet tolerate patiently the mistakes of others. We should give others an opportunity to make improvement, guiding them with kindness and wisdom, so that they too can develop the correct understanding. In confronting the mistakes of others, we should try to exchange places with them. We should substitute tolerance for resentment, understanding for disgust, encouragement for scorn, care for censure, concern for neglect, and unity for division. If we can do that, society will surely make better progress, and our lives will surely be much happier.

Our degree of achievement is proportional to our capacity for tolerance. The ability to show tolerance towards one's family makes one a suitable householder; the ability to show tolerance towards one's community makes one a suitable community leader; and the ability to show tolerance towards one's country makes one a suitable head of state. If one can transcend all relativity and show tolerance towards the whole Dharma realm, then one can appear wherever a need is present, and can become a Dharma realm king living a free and easy life. There is a couplet that puts it this way: "The denseness of the bamboo does not hinder the water flowing through; the height of the mountain cannot block the clouds floating by." If we have the capacity for tolerance, then, just like the flowing water and the floating clouds, we can pass through all manner of obstacles to meander as we please through the vast, open world.

As society advances technologically with ever increasing interaction, the importance of "respect and tolerance" is particularly clear. We should respect the freedom of others by upholding the Five Precepts, instead of grabbing and robbing. We should respect the value of life by being generous and charitable, instead of doing injury and harm to life. We should respect the possessions of others by sharing benefits together, instead of acting selfishly for one's own benefit. We should respect the life force of the earth through environmental protections, instead of setting out to exploit and plunder. Furthermore, we should be tolerant of diversity, by employing the generosity of no separation between self and other. We should be tolerant of wounded dignity, by employing the compassionate mind that transcends the duality of the sacred and secular. We should be tolerant of the injuries from enemies, by employing the wisdom of the equality between friend and foe. We should be tolerant of careless mistakes, by recognizing that ordinary and realized beings are the same. If we can hold a respectful attitude as we work and interact with others, and if we can maintain a tolerant capacity as we serve and help all beings, it will only be a matter of time before this world will become a true pure land.

# Equality and Peace

*The great ocean is able to contain all the streams
in the world, and because of this, the ocean is large.
Space is able to contain all the things in the universe,
and because of this, it is limitless.*

BLIA 5th General Conference
Paris, France
August 3-7, 1996

Edited by Robert H. Smitheram, Ph.D.

Lasting peace has been the dream of civilizations throughout human history. In this violent and troubled century that has produced so much war and fear, the dream of forging a lasting peace in the world has grown even more urgent. Our tragedy has been that those of us who are alive today continue to "use war to end war." War does not end war; it only brings more violence and pain into the world!

There are many problems in the world today: the strong exploit the weak, the wealthy prosper while the poor suffer, the world's races and religions often conflict with each other, and throughout most of the world, men and women are treated unequally. These conditions only lead to strife. That is why we say, "Discord arises out of unfair treatment." When people are not treated equally, there will always be complaints and conflict between them. That is why we have chosen "Equality and Peace" as our theme because it is crucial for today's world. I hope that everyone will take the twin ideals of equality and peace to heart, and through our concerted efforts, I am certain that we can succeed in helping all people of the world understand and appreciate the importance of these profound ideals.

Let us begin by talking about equality. From ancient times, people have pondered the meaning and importance of equality, but when it comes to actually implementing this ideal in the real world, their efforts have often failed. There are several Buddhist principles that can help us better understand the deep meaning of equality and how to practice it in daily life. Buddhists often say: "all sentient beings and buddhas are equal," "essence and form are equal," "self and other are equal," "phenomena and principle are equal," and "being and non-being are equal." These basic principles of Buddhism help to elucidate the following four points:

## I. Equality Requires Mutual Respect between Self and Other

The Confucian philosopher Mencius has said, "He who loves others will be loved by them;

and he who respects others will be respected by them." Equality among people can never be attained through the use of force. When there is full, mutual respect among people, then we will be able to create a world in which equality prevails. Like the former division between East and West Germany, and the current division between North and South Korea, as well as the conflict in the Balkans; as long as weapons and anger are employed to solve these problems, peace can never be attained. In 1989, with the respect and tolerance of West Germany held towards East Germany, the Berlin Wall crumbled, and with that, the invisible walls within people's hearts also gave way. With this wall destroyed, the Germans discovered a level of equality and mutual respect that helped them create together a happy future. If only the peoples of the Korean Peninsula, the Taiwan Strait, and of Israel and the Arab Middle East could rise to that level of mutual respect and selflessness, then how could peace not be far behind?

A fundamental Buddhist principle is that

we all should respect and treat one another equally. Buddhists are enjoined to respect all nations of the world, races, social classes, genders, and ages among people. Two thousand five hundred years ago in India, the Buddha said, "All rivers lose their separate names when they flow into the sea; when members of the four castes join the monastic order, they all become part of the Buddha's family." It was because of Buddhism's egalitarian quality of "mutual respect between self and other" and its advocacy of the "oneness between self and things," that monastics and devotees during and after the time of the Buddha were able to unite and carry the teachings of the Buddha to every corner of India. From India, Buddhism has spread easily and quickly throughout the world. Because Buddhists believe in the fundamental equality of all cultures, they are able to respect and adapt readily to the ways of other people. In all of human history, no bloody wars were ever fought during Buddhism's transmission to other countries. Clearly, the mutual respect between self and other is the cornerstone of equality and mutual benefit, as well as the best prescription for peace and progress. People often say, "Perfect equality does not exist in this world." It is true that equality within all worldly concerns is difficult to establish, yet we can start by implanting the ideal of equality within our hearts. For example, a mother teaches her child how to eat by opening her own mouth first and acting as a model for her child. In this way, the milk of human love flows easily between them. A father pretends to be a horse for his children to ride. When they ride on him and play with him, a caring bond of affection forms solidly between them. How can there be any absolute standard for what is great or insignificant, superior or inferior? We can coexist peacefully and share happiness together only when we can eliminate prejudice and treat each other with respect, in the sense of equality between self and other, and the mutual acceptance of each other.

After the Buddha became enlightened, his first words were, "All sentient beings have Buddha nature!" Sentient beings have different forms, different abilities, and different conditions owing to the effects of karma, but beneath these outer differences, the essential nature of all sentient beings is the same. This situation is reminiscent of a story from the Buddhist sutras—an elephant, a horse, and a rabbit are crossing a river: for the rabbit the river is very deep, for the horse it is somewhat deep, and for the elephant it is not deep at all. The conditions for each of these animals are different, and yet the river remains the same. It is the same with the three birds mentioned in the Buddhist sutras—an eagle, a pigeon, and a sparrow: the eagle flies very high, the pigeon not so high, and the sparrow not very high at all. The conditions among them are not the same, and yet the sky itself never changes because of them. We should look upon the suffering of others with the greatest concern and compassion, and embrace the ideals of equality and mutual respect whenever we encounter differences. With this kind of thinking, we will surely succeed in bringing a lasting peace into this world.

## II. Equality Means Understanding the Other's Viewpoint

How are we to establish an enduring concept of equality among people? The Buddha answered this question by telling us to treat others as we would have them treat us, and to love others as much as we love ourselves. The Buddha himself treated others the same as he treated his own son, Rahula. How are we to increase our compassion and care for others? According to the Buddhist sutras, we need to put ourselves in the other's position and ask ourselves the following: if they were in our situation or if we were in theirs, what action should be taken? By doing this, we then can treat others with equality. If all of us were to treat one another with equality, then this world would surely move closer to a lasting peace.

Suppose we see someone with a physical disability and assume an attitude of superiority, how can we achieve respect through equality? We must instead imagine that we are the one with the disability, then we could begin to cultivate the compassion needed to overcome any sense of difference between us. When we are able to see social problems as part of ourselves, naturally we will not abandon or ignore them. Instead, we will be able to treat all problems with compassion and equality. When we are truly able to consider the conditions of others as our own and see that all of us are truly equal, then a lasting peace will slowly but surely find its way into this world.

Devadatta tried to harm the Buddha many times, but the Buddha never considered his attacks to be calamities; instead, the Buddha used them as opportunities to inspire Devadatta to reach higher levels of consciousness. Angulimalya wanted to kill the Buddha, but the Buddha treated him with great compassion and kindness. In the end, Angulimalya was won over to the path of virtue. In the *Lotus Sutra* there is the parable of the burning house, in which a blind man and a lame man were able to save themselves from the flames with each doing what he could to help. In the same house, however, there was also a snake that was physically healthy. But since the tail was proud and would not cooperate with its head, the snake ended up perishing in the fire.

Living beings are different from oneself in external form, and yet the essential nature of all living beings is the same. Though our shapes and sizes may vary, if we place ourselves in the other's position and benefit them accordingly, then we can succeed in promoting equality and in helping others as we help ourselves. All of this can happen with just a turn of thought, and then equality and respect are made manifest. Surely then, wars will end and peace will follow!

## III. Equality Arises Out of a Myriad Causes and Conditions

All the phenomena of the universe are merely temporary manifestations produced through a combination of causes and conditions, for without these causes and conditions, nothing would exist. For example, a person becomes a person because of the actions and the consciousness of the parents. Once the person is born, he or she depends on learned people for education, farmers to grow food for sustenance, workers to make everyday goods, and business people to sell the goods. A flower requires sunlight, air, water, and earth in order to grow, mature, and blossom. A building requires metal, wood, cement, bricks, and engineers for it to be completed. A business enterprise requires capital, market survey, quality improvement, and advertising promotion before the final product can be sold in stores. Everything within the sphere of our daily existence arises from causes and conditions: our parents raise us because they feel their connection to us; our teachers teach us because they understand our need for education; the things we use in our daily lives are produced because of a social need. There is not a single person who can live without the dependence upon causes and conditions.

We are all mutually interdependent because all things in the universe come into being only through their interconnectedness, and they continue to exist solely through their interconnectedness. The Buddhist concept of cause and effect and mutual interconnectedness constitute the truth that explains humanity's place in this universe. For example, when we speak of time, we must conceptualize a past and a present before we can think of a future; when we think of space, we must conceptualize a north, south, east and west before we can think of a center; when we speak of human life, we must understand that our own existence depends on the existence of other beings, for without them we could not exist. Which came first, the chicken or the egg? Is it possible for the fruit on the tree to have nothing to do with the seed on the ground? The Buddha has said, "When there is this, then there is that; when this arises, then that arises; when there is no this, then there is no that; when this is extinguished, then that is extinguished."

The entire system of the phenomena arising out of the myriad causes and conditions is nothing but cause engendering result, phenomenon forming from principle, being depending on emptiness, appearance arising out of conditions, the many being produced by the one, and a human being becoming a Buddha. This means that we all are dependent on one another for our birth and for our continued existence: *in you there is me, and in me there is you.* What arises and passes into extinction is all dependent on causes and condition, for all things in their essence are equally interdependent. If we can comprehend the conditional interdependence of all things, then we will be able to understand the equality which underlies all apparent differences and the unity among all contradictions, all of which leads back to the true, original form behind all things.

All things in the world have differences in form, appearance, energy, and function. But if we delve deeply into their fundamental nature, we will see that they are all truly equal. In comprehending causality by recognizing that there is no existence of self or other without causes and conditions, then we will understand the importance of always planting the seeds for good causes and creating conditions for positive future. When we create good causes and conditions everywhere, then nothing is beyond our power, and we constantly benefit from the good effects we have generated.

Do not think there is anything anywhere that has no connection to you. A blade of grass, a tree, a person, and even a drop of water in the ocean are connected to you. All of them are truly blessings in our lives. Everything is important, and we should be grateful for everything, for it is incumbent upon us to repay the world for all the beauty and wonder it offers us. If we can find within us a deep sense of equality with all things in this world, and create broad connections for a positive future, then can peace in this world really be so far away?

## IV. True Equality Means No Difference between the One and the Many

Most people desire abundance and dislike scarcity, which leads them to be constantly comparing themselves with others and making plans for the acquisition of wealth and power.

Being carried deeper and deeper into delusion by their desires, they create bad karma and much misery for themselves. With so many people like this, disorder and confusion in the world will continue.

On the other hand, when we look from the Buddhist perspective, we soon realize that the one is many, and the many are one. With no difference between the one and the many, the basic nature of everything is entirely complete and fulfilled. All things are created in the same way, and all things partake of the same underlying reality. For example, when a leader from a small country like Luxembourg or Singapore visits a large country like France or the United States, that person is treated with the same respect that a leader from a large country would be accorded. When nations want to get along with one another, it does not matter whether a nation be large or small, or whether it has a large population or not. The value of all nations is the same within a confederation of allies. This is the true meaning of equality, in which there is no difference between the one and the many.

The country of Brazil in South America possesses a huge reserve of natural forest resources that profoundly affects the climate and health of our entire planet. This is why the rain forests of Brazil have largely been protected through the efforts of the United Nations and other organizations. And although these forests merely occupy a certain portion of Brazil, they really affect the ecological existence for all of humanity. News reports often tell of large political demonstrations involving people in the hundreds of thousands. Sometimes these demonstrations can become quite heated and emotional, but with the single word of a respected leader, they usually dissipate almost immediately. In contrast, a cruel dictator with thousands of troops on his side can be overthrown if the will of the people is strong. This shows how there is no difference in the relationship between the one and the many.

The "four little dragons" (Taiwan, Korea, Hong Kong, and Singapore) of Asia are examples of nations with comparatively small populations and little land. But despite these limitations, they have stepped fully onto the world stage and received recognition and respect from much larger nations. A seed of the banyan tree may lie on the ground, but when properly watered and nourished it will produce thousands of valuable fruits.

Daoism says, "One gives birth to two; two give birth to three; and three give birth to all things." One word, a single event, a single person, a single book, or even a single thought are capable of changing the course of a person's entire life. This is because "one" is equipped with many contributing factors, and "one" may also be the cause of many consequences. That is why we cannot simply ignore a small fire, because it may quickly rage out of control. Nor can we serenely ignore the needs and hopes of minority groups, for this can lead to unimaginable racial problems. Never disregard a prince because he is young and small, for one day he may grow up and have power over you. These are all examples which illustrate how the many arise out of the one, there being no difference between the one and the many. Real equality must be based on the larger respecting the smaller, the many respecting the few, the strong respecting the weak, and the rich respecting the poor. Of course, a sense of equality towards all things can become a natural habit for us, and under such a concept of equality, the world will certainly have peace.

So far, I have described "equality and mutual respect," which represent the only way to reach peace. Now, I want to address "peace and coprosperity," without which no discussion of equality and mutual respect is possible.

When talking about world peace in the past, some believed in using the balance of power among nations, while others advocated the use of weapons and intimidation to prevent war. This kind of thinking will never lead to a lasting peace in the world. Only mutual respect and coprosperity among all nations of the world can ever lead to a full and lasting peace. King Dighiti released King Brahmadatta from prison many times, but in the end he gave up his throne so as to avoid war. The Buddha himself once sat in the hot sun to block the way of King Virudhaka's troops, thereby encouraging them to stop their preparations for war. The Buddha also taught minister Varsakara that those who practice aggression will always fail in the end.

Owing to great ideological differences, our world today is scarred by the unequal distribution of wealth, separatist movements, terrorism, and vendettas born in times long passed. Iraq invaded Kuwait and caused so much destruction and suffering. There was fighting in Bosnia, Sri Lanka, and the former states of the Soviet Union. How much hatred and anger, and how many deaths have these wars generated? In Africa there is terrible strife; a militarized line runs through the heart of Korea; and an evil cloud hangs over the Taiwan Strait. All of this casts the whole world with its billions of people into the mire of fear, pain, and suffering. Should we ignore these dangers? Should we close our eyes and shut away our consciences? How can we endure without goodness but only evil? How can we bear there being no peace but only hatred? This is why we must try and apply "equality and mutual respect" as a way of appealing to the people of this world to live together in peace.

Equality and peace are two sides of the same profound truth. True equality is not based simply on appearances or words, nor can it be achieved solely by such measures as the threat of mutually assured destruction, arms control, or a ban on nuclear weapons. We must also emphasize the purification of our hearts and minds, the commonality of our thinking, and the reassessment of our ideas. As to how can we establish peace in this world, I would like to put forward four ideas:

## I. The Application of Compassion can Promote Peace

Compassion as advocated in Buddhism entails both "loving-kindness" and "compassion." Loving-kindness means giving happiness to others, and compassion means relieving others from their suffering. By means of her compassion, Avalokitesvara Bodhisattva is able to enter the hearts of all who believe in her, and occupy a place of honor in their homes. Of course if we want her to, she will also enter every nation in this world. Even if we are not capable of bestowing wealth and glory on others, we must still make a vow to eliminate their suffering.

Though King Asoka conquered the many small states in India, he still could not quell the anger and resentment his war campaigns had provoked. It was only after he applied the transformative power of compassion that he was able to win the people over. Only the power of compassion can overcome cruelty and violence. In order to protect the native peoples of Mexico in the sixteenth century, the Spaniard B. de Las Casas persuaded Charles V to stop his plans for invasion. In this world, only a victory through the Dharma is a perfect victory. The greatest force in the world is not guns and bullets, but rather the power of compassion and patience, for only such power can achieve true victory.

In bringing aid and relief to living beings, we must not only apply the compassion on oneness, we must also utilize unconditioned compassion to far a greater degree, as way of broadly saving living beings from suffering and pain. We must not only refrain from committing negative acts, but we must also positively look for opportunities to do good deeds. We must not simply talk about compassion for a short time, instead we must be earnest and steadfast in our acts of compassion; we must not practice compassion in hopes of gaining some reward, but rather do so with no expectation of return. Only compassion and equality can lead to peace and prosperity.

## II. The Elimination of Selfish Attachment can Promote Peace

The Chinese character for "I" or "self" contains an element that means "spear," the connotation being that the self is the greatest factor in creating disputes and conflict. In English, the word for "I" is a single capital letter, indicating just how conceited and arrogant the self can become. The truth is that because we have such a strong sense of self, we always think in terms of our wealth, our opinion, our profit, and our social standing. From this we generate untold suffering and negative karma. When we are locked into our sense of self, we see the whole world through a kind of prejudice.

In China, there were the Warring States (403-222 BCE); America had its Civil War; South Africa its racial conflicts; and Europe its religious wars. All of these were caused fundamentally by this strong "attachment to self." Lao Zi has said, "The greatest trouble for us human beings is that we have a body," while the Buddha has emphasized, "Ignorance and suffering all are due to the self." If two people live together and both have a strong attachment to self, they will not be peaceful for long. If each member of a family always expects everything to go his or her own way, that family will experience many problems and conflict. If nations and societies all act in the same way, there will never be any peace.

During the Period of Warring States in China, Queen Zhao questioned a minister from the state of Qi. First she asked him about the common people; then she asked him about the collection of taxes, and lastly, she asked him about the king. The minister of Qi was not pleased with the order of her concerns, but the Queen was not so concerned about herself or the King of Qi, for she was more concerned about the common people and their welfare because she was not attached to the sense of self. This is the only way the harmony of a nation by the people, of the people, and for the people can come about. It is the "I" that is attached to self, but this self can grow beyond the little self to a larger sense of self, and from the selfish self to a selfless sense of self.

Towards the end of World War II, President Roosevelt asked Venerable Master Tai Xu, "How can we attain world peace?" Master Tai Xu answered: "Through compassion and selflessness!" So if we want peace, we must follow the path of purity by eradicating the attachment to self in our hearts first. If the selfish sense of the self in all its aspects is not eliminated, then truly all that remains is an empty illusion! But when the attachment to self is eradicated, selfish desires will no longer exist, and when a sense of selflessness pervades the world, how can war possibly occur?

## III. Open-mindedness can Promote Peace

Open-mindedness enables us to become tolerant, and through tolerance, we will succeed in being in harmony with others and thereby achieve peace. As a piece of land is broad and open, so we can construct great buildings; as the ocean is broad and deep, so beneath its surface it holds an immense variety of life. The ability to show tolerance towards one's family makes one a suitable householder; the ability to show tolerance towards one's country makes one a suitable head of state; and the ability to show tolerance to the great absolute, makes one a suitable Dharma king! The world we live in is only as big as our hearts. Some people say that wars start over bread, and others say that they start over land. The truth is that bread and land are just manifestations of our inner selves.

If we can purify our hearts and rid ourselves of selfishness, then we can enjoy the endless expanse of the absolute.

The great ocean is able to contain all the streams in the world, which is why it can be so large and vast; space is able to contain all the things in the universe, which is why it can be so limitless. Because we can show tolerance to all things that come in through our senses, we are able to employ them. Because we can show tolerance to our parents and relatives, we can have a family. If we can succeed in showing tolerance to all the races and religions in the world, then we will naturally be able to live together in peace.

Our world today is full of conflict and deception because the people's capacity to tolerate normal human differences has been shackled by a desire for wealth and fame that has unsettled the heart and upset the country. We need to take a broader view of time and a wider view of space. We need to use these to enlarge our hearts and show tolerance towards diversity, by considering others as we would ourselves. We can only create broad connections for a positive future by benefiting others; and we can only promote peace through open-mindedness when we offer support everywhere.

## IV. Coprosperity can Promote Peace

Modern sciences have brought us many advances and benefits, but they also have tempted us with greed and competition due to an emphasis on utilitarianism. People use all kinds of tricks and ploys to get ahead, but they only end up bringing suffering onto themselves and chaos into society. We have polluted the world with waste and garbage, squandered our resources, and destroyed too many forms of life. This wastefulness and thoughtlessness have already created a kind of dialectical tension between humans and the rest of the material world. All things in this world are intimately interconnected, so now is the time to promote ecological coexistence and coprosperity.

We should be very grateful that this world has so many races and nations. These differences help teach us to accept one another and form harmonious friendships. There are many religions in the world, including Christianity, Islam, Buddhism, and Daoism, among others. These various religions provide a home for the human spirit and a resting-place for all types of beliefs. Each part of the world has different resources, different plants, and different animals. Different foods are served in different countries, so there are flavors and tastes to suit everyone. This world provides us with all that we need in such abundance and immense variety. So why not work together to establish the notion of mutual prosperity as a collective creation?

Red flowers are beautiful, but the green leaves do enhance their beauty. Our facial features may be attractive, but we need to have healthy bodies to enhance our overall appearance. A grand structure is more impressive when mountains and streams surround it. Now we need to apply equality and coprosperity with a compassionate mind, and employ oneness and coexistence so as to eliminate the attachment to self. In doing so, peace will surely come.

If we cannot subdue one's own Three Poisons (greed, hatred, and delusion), we will be unable to possess the capacity of the Four Immeasurable States of Mind (loving-kindness, compassion, joy, and equanimity). Mencius spoke about how it is better to enjoy music with others than listening to music by oneself. Individual happiness is limited, but if we can learn to expand our happiness to include the rest of the world, then we can really enjoy peace and happiness together. As founder, twenty-five hundred years ago the Buddha put forward his "Six Points of Reverend Harmony Sangha," which represents a forerunner of this coprosperity idea. They are as follows:

1. The harmony of view as a shared understanding: This means establishing a common viewpoint in thought that constitutes its unification.

2. The harmony of the precepts as a shared practice: Everyone is equal under the rule of law that constitutes equality under a legal system.

3. The harmony of pooling all resources: The equitable distribution of economic resources that constitutes parity in economic terms.

4. The harmony of purpose as a shared joy: In spiritual terms, this means sharing the same goal and ideals that constitutes the development of purpose.

5. The harmony of speech without reproach: This means a harmony in terms of language without reproach that constitutes the warm sincerity of language.

6. The harmony of life in communal quarters: This means conduct without violating others that constitutes the loving attitude of being together.

Many civilized nations in the world today are actively implementing very productive policies, such as the social security system, aid to third world countries, technology transfer, religious dialogue, technology integration, and environmental protection. These countries have gone on to create various organizations, including the European Union, the European Economic Community, the North-American Free Trade Agreement, Asia-Pacific Economic

Cooperation, and the World Trade Association. Such organizations are promoting economic cooperation and developing political consensus. Private businesses as well have begun to realize the importance of social ethics, changing their old focus on pure profit by perfecting their services and developing new inventions, which have improved the welfare of all the people.

In the long history of humanity, these efforts only represent a small step out of our narrow circles of self-interest. Nonetheless, we must persist in our efforts with determination by promoting the power of compassion and open-mindedness through education. Culturally, we must promote the virtues of mutual respect and the consideration of others' point of view; and socially, we should practice the truth of "the myriad causes and conditions" as well as "the one and the many without differences." In dealing with others we should eliminate the attachment to self and work together hand in hand, hoping that through the shared prosperity of time and space, we may achieve coprosperity in the world. In this way, the establishment of an egalitarian society and the attainment of world peace are only a matter of time!

# Wholeness and Freeness

*A fist that clenches candy tightly can never be pulled through a narrow jar opening; a foot that is tightly retracted can never step forward. It is only when we can let matters go that we can truly pick them up. To achieve liberation and freeness, we have to learn to let go of everything, open our minds, expand our horizon, and see the big picture.*

BLIA 6th General Conference
Hong Kong
November 29-December 2, 1997
Edited by Robert H. Smitheram, Ph.D.

Wholeness means being most natural and perfect. Wholeness is a much longed for and admired condition. In Chinese, such common phrases as "the beauty of a flower and the completeness of the moon;" "a large family with lots of children;" "a person fully blessed with happiness, wealth, and longevity;" and "a jade without flaws;" are all expressions that praise this state of wholeness. However, in daily life there are many moments when life is not "whole," when joy turns into sorrow as loved ones must part, when our emotions and feelings becomes a mixture of love and hatred, as well as gratitude and suspicion. Just as the sun must go through its course of rising and setting and the moon must go through its cycles of waxing and waning, we too must go through times when life leaves us with many regrets.

When it comes to "freeness," such images of birds flying freely and fish swimming playfully come to mind. From the past to the present, people have always sung praises to "freeness." Just imagine how attractive is the liberation from sufferings and afflictions; and how attractive is the freeness from worries and anxieties! However, we see the decline of peace and order in today's society, the discord within families, the instability in the political arena, and even the lack of understanding among people. Information from all directions constantly bombards us; contradictory ideas disturb and confuse our minds; and materialistic goods strongly tempt us to possess more. All these make us lose our sense of physical and mental freeness wherever we go.

In Buddhism, there is the realm of Nirvana-without-remainder, where chaos, instability, and disorder are completely eliminated; and where permanence, happiness, true nature, and tranquility are to be found. What a state of purity and wholeness that is! The buddhas and bodhisattvas can travel among the different worlds to help all sentient beings find liberation. How unbound and free they are! How then do we find this "wholeness and freeness" in our everyday lives? I would like to offer eight points for consideration:

# I. The Tolerance of Intention Leads to a Human World of Wholeness and Freeness

In this vast world of ours, we enjoy a great diversity of peoples, lands, activities, and material things. If we are restrictive and discriminative in our views, we will find ourselves at odds with others, encountering obstacles at every turn. In Chinese history, there is a famous historical figure by the name of Xiang Yu (232-202 BCE). Possessing unsurpassed military prowess, he was expected to achieve greatness. However, owing to his jealous nature, he lost the opportunity to gain control over the country. Liu Bang (256-195 BCE), in contrast, had an open mind and was very respectful of the learned; and so he was able to successfully plan and implement his strategies, and eventually rose to power.

During the Period of the Warring States (403-222 BCE), people of the state of Chu were not diligent in farming and had a very poor harvest one year. Being resentful and wanting to cause trouble, they crossed the border into the neighboring state of Liang and destroyed the crops there. But as it turned out, not only were the high officials of Liang not angered, they commanded their people to help the Chu people till and fertilize their land. Thus, a situation with a great potential for conflict was resolved peacefully.

We have the saying: "The great ocean can accept the water from hundreds of rivers, which is why it is so great; the high mountains do not reject even a tiny clod of dirt, which is why they are so high." In Buddhism, the expressions: "The mind encompasses the vast space of the universe" and "one thought containing three thousand chiliocosm," all succinctly illustrate the fine meaning of tolerance. Consider the many and varied forms in this world, such as the red flowers and the green willows, as well as the manifestations of diverse capacities, like the flying birds and leaping fish. It is only through tolerance that we can see the meaning of life and enjoy the happiness life offers; and it is only through tolerance that we come to possess wholeness and freeness in our life.

## II. Contentment in Daily Life Leads to a Human World of Wholeness and Freeness

The greatest problem for our lives is the incessant desire that stems from greed; when we get one of something, we want ten; when we get ten, we want one hundred. What comes of it all: at best, all kinds of suffering that press upon us, exhausting us both mentally and physically; even worse is when people ruin their character, leaving a terrible legacy after death. Why bring such trouble on ourselves!

It is said in the *Sutra of the Buddha's Bequeathed Teaching*s, "The way of contentment is where wealth and stability reside;" and it also states, "A person who is content still enjoys peace and happiness even while sleeping on the ground; a person who is not content still feels dissatisfaction even while living in Heaven;" and "a person who is not content feels poor despite their riches; a person who is content feels rich despite their poverty." Confucius's famous disciple Yan Hui (521-490 BCE) is another example. He lived down a ramshackle lane with a bamboo dish for rice and a gourd for drink, but he "did not allow his joy to be affected by it." In another example, a man named Yen Chu tactfully declined an offer made by King Xuan of the state of Qi to become a high-ranking official, saying, "Eating only when hungry makes my food taste like meat; walking peacefully serves me like a carriage; not committing a crime is my high-ranking nobility. I find my happiness in living a pure and correct life." Later generations praised Yen Chu by saying, "He was able to keep to the truth and return to simplicity; and never in his life did he feel insulted."

The Honorable Mahakasyapa engaged in ascetic practice among graves and slept beneath the trees, and the Buddha even shared his seat with him so as to commend his diligence. The great Buddhist Master Hong Yi (1880-1942) once said, "Even saltiness has its own unique flavor; and even blandness has its own unique taste." It is because these masters and sages of the past cultivated a contentment with few desires, that they were able to transcend the material plane and have compassion for all living beings. Treating nothing as something, they truly knew the boundless Dharma joy. Therefore, contentment is wealth; contentment is possession; contentment is wholeness; and contentment is freeness.

"Nothing" does not mean a lack of something. It is because of "nothing" that we can enjoy the immeasurable and boundless realm of the Dharma, and can identify with the countless and limitless living beings. It is because of "nothing" that we neither shun nor crave the five desires, and neither grow weary of nor are captivated by the world. In order to emancipate all living beings and to benefit societies and nations, the buddhas and bodhisattvas uttered these ultimate words of truth: "One finds lasting happiness within contentment; and one finds peace within patience." Even in a world where imperfection and suffering abound, the buddhas and bodhisattvas can actually find peace, and see every place as a pure land.

I hope that all members of the Buddha's Light International Association (BLIA) can emulate the sages of the past and practice simplicity and contentment as a way to experience wholeness and freeness in the human world. When we can apply the practice of finding lasting happiness within contentment, we can build a life for ourselves that is full of wholeness and freeness.

## III. Equality between Self and Other Leads to a Human World of Wholeness and Freeness

Everything in this world is originally whole and free. However, our ignorance and delusion give rise to perceptions of dualities, such as superior and inferior, coming and going, being and emptiness, arising and ceasing, large and small, internal and external, good and evil, wisdom and ignorance. Such distinctions go on to cause continual fighting among people, deepened antagonism among people, increased animosity among races, and escalated warring tensions among nations.

In recent history, the French Revolution's declaration of freedom, and the American Revolution's promotion of democracy are examples of people fighting for equality, wholeness, and freeness. In Chinese history, one of the main reasons for the revolution led by Dr. Sun Yat-sen in overthrowing the Qing dynasty of the Manchus was to have other nations of the world treat the people of China with fairness and equality. More than twenty-five hundred years ago, Buddhism had already championed the ideals of "all beings already possess the wisdom to realize Buddha nature" and "unconditioned loving kindness and empathetic compassion." In this way, Buddhism has not only advanced the importance of mutual equality, but the teachings have also given us the most complete definition of equality in this universe. Within the monastic community established by the Buddha, its spirit of equality is captured in this declaration: "When all the rivers flow into the ocean, they will only have one taste, the taste of saltiness; when members of the four castes join the monastic order, they all become part of the Buddha's family." Consider how the Avalokitesvara Bodhisattva sails the boat of compassion that brings universal salvation, how Ksitigarbha Bodhisattva brings salvation to those suffering in Hell, and how the Sadaparibhuta ("never disparaging") Bodhisattva always treats all sentient beings with the utmost respect. Consider how the disciples of the Buddhas paid respect to the eight-year-old Naga maiden who came from afar, how Kumarajiva of the Mahayana tradition became a disciple of and a teacher to a Theravada master, and how the pious householder Vimalakirti spoke the Dharma at the local tavern. All these represent the finest demonstrations of the true meaning of equality among people. In fact, treating the rich and the poor equally produces respect for moral character; and treating self and others equally generates harmony between you and me.

I hope that all members of the BLIA will treasure life and imitate the great practitioners of the past: generate the four universal vows of the bodhisattvas, practice the Four Immeasurable States of Mind (loving-kindness, compassion, joy, and equanimity), live a spiritually upright life, give peace and happiness to the living, and provide hope and comfort to the dying. This is how one performs the myriad practices of the Six Perfections and frees oneself from the cycle of rebirth and death. If we can uphold these great vows to bring about such equality, how can life not be whole and free?

## IV. *Prajña*-wisdom for Social Conduct Leads to a Human World of Wholeness and Freeness

We often hear people lamenting, "It is hard enough to know what to do in this world, but even harder to do the right thing." The truth is that this problem arises because we lack *prajña*-wisdom, and so we are not skillful enough in handling matters or dealing with others. What is *prajña*-wisdom? *Prajña*-wisdom is being sensible and acting according to the circumstances; *prajña*-wisdom is being nimble and discerning; *prajña*-wisdom is transforming ordinary consciousness into wisdom; and *prajña*-wisdom is achieving a true understanding of ultimate reality.

When we have *prajña*-wisdom, we are able to know that all beings are fundamentally one entity, and can then generate the aspiration to make the bodhisattva vows, so that by benefiting and helping ourselves and others, we can cultivate the causes and conditions for wholeness and freeness. When we have *prajña*-wisdom, we are able to clearly recognize the nature of emptiness in this universe of phenomena, so that by setting our minds and bodies at ease and remaining steadfast in accordance with conditions, we can achieve the extraordinary power of wholeness and freeness. When we have *prajña*-wisdom, we are able to remove ourselves from deluded confusion and rid ourselves of obsessive discrimination, so that by freeing ourselves from all affliction and ignorance, we can then enter the great path of light that leads to wholeness and freeness. When we have *prajña*-wisdom, we are able to completely eliminate the duality of self and others and unify the contradictions of difference, so that by transcending conflict and discord with others, we can begin a brilliant life of wholeness and freeness.

*Prajña*-wisdom is thus not something we seek from outside ourselves, because *prajña-*

wisdom is actually the natural outflow of wisdom and skillful means that comes from our ultimate true nature; nor is *prajña*-wisdom something faraway from us, because *prajña*-wisdom is to be appreciated right in our daily life with all its activities. In the opening section of the *Diamond Sutra*, we observe how every moment the Buddha emanates the infinite radiance of *prajña*-wisdom through his speech or his silence, his activity or his stillness. When the Buddha put on his robe or held his alms bowl, his hands would emit the radiance of *prajña*-wisdom; when he went on his alms round begging for food, his body would emit the radiance of prajña-wisdom; when he washed his feet, his feet would emit the radiance of *prajña*-wisdom; when he arranged his mat and sat down, his entire body would emit the radiance of *prajña*-wisdom; and when he expounded the Dharma for the benefit all beings, his mouth would emit the radiance of *prajña*-wisdom. All of these are the extraordinary power of *prajña*-wisdom's illuminating radiance. I hope that all of us can cherish this priceless treasure within our hearts and minds and apply *prajña*-wisdom in the ways we conduct ourselves and deal with others, thereby enabling this world to reach the realm of wholeness and freeness.

## V. Peaceful Stability in Society Leads to a Human World of Wholeness and Freeness

In society today, such problems as uncontrolled guns, drug abuse, irresponsible sex, and violent behavior are growing in severity day by day. People live in fear and uncertainty, and cannot find peace and security in their everyday lives, much less possess a life of wholeness and freeness. We see how people harbor resentment nowadays, and even protest on the streets waving placards. I do not believe such behavior can truly solve our problems.

There are many Chinese proverbs that remind us how important stability is to a society, such as: "there are no intact eggs under a toppled nest;" "when the skin is no longer present, can the hair still remain intact?" And "when the lips are gone, the teeth are exposed to the cold." In fact, we are all responsible for the degree of stability or chaos in our society and nation. Each one of us should act like peace officers, so as to uphold justice and honor; each one of us should perform volunteer work, so as to encourage and support one another; each one of us should act like "Good Samaritans," so as to offer our services and motivate others to do good deeds; and each one of us should be good citizens, so as to abide by the laws and shoulder our responsibilities. It is only when society is peaceful and stable that wholeness and freeness can truly be part of our lives. Since May of 1997, the BLIA in Taiwan has organized a series of events in support of the "Compassion and Loving Care Campaign," while on October 5 of that same year, eighty thousand people participated in the pledging ceremony for "People of Compassion and Loving Care." Included among the attendees were people of diverse social backgrounds and representatives from various religious denominations. Together, they all loudly proclaimed: "Purify the mind, re-establish morality, recover the sense of right and wrong, and stabilize society!" As of today, there are two thousand "People of Compassion and Loving Care" teachers who are promoting the ideals of compassion and loving care throughout cities and towns. Their efforts have been well received, for clearly each one of us needs compassion and loving care.

I hope that all of us Fo Guang Buddhists can vow to be at the forefront of the movement for peace and stability in society: to leave our mark on history for the sake of life, to share our kindness and compassion with all living things, to create a Pure Land of wholeness an freeness in this human world, and to build a whole and free society.

## VI. Harmony in the Family Leads to a Human World of Wholeness and Freeness

The family is the refueling station on the journey of life, a safe harbor where we can soothe our wounds, a sanctuary of warmth from loved ones, and a resting spot for the enjoyment of happiness. Harmony in the family is closely connected to the physical and mental growth, and the peace and stability of society and the nation. When we look at our society today, we see there are so many children roaming the streets after school, who are looking for a home outside of their own because their own parents are fighting. Similarly, there are so many adults who spend time downtown drinking, eating, and indulging in amusements after work, because of discord in their families. The hardship and trauma these children and adults have sustained from their families will become social problems that burden the country.

Buddhism places a great deal of emphasis on the happiness of the family. In such Buddhist sutras as the *Sutra for the Well-Born, Sutra on the Teachings to Sudatta's Daugther-in-law*, the *Great Treasury of Sutras*, and the *Great Nirvana Sutra*, not only did the Buddha teach devotees how to practice family ethics, but he also explained how to manage the family finances in an appropriate fashion. In keeping with the times, the relationship between parents and children emphasizes communication and cooperation. Family members nowadays must respect and yield to each other, just like partners dancing the Tango. Family members should know how to appreciate each other's point of view, and also know how to be caring and considerate. Family members should often compliment, encourage, support, and comfort each other; as well as learn to cultivate a sense of humor, and build a warm and pleasant atmosphere. There is the old saying: "The savoriness of the soup comes from the blending of different ingredients; the mutual benefit of a community comes from everyone working together." Only harmony leads to mutual benefit; and only harmony leads to happiness. If everybody can emphasize and pursue harmony in the family more and more, then where in this human world will wholeness and freeness be lacking?

## VII. Health of the Mind and Body Leads to a Human World of Wholeness and Freeness

A healthy body and mind are the most

important prerequisites for wholeness and freeness of the community and the self. Just imagine, if the energy balance of the body is not in harmony, our bodies would not feel well and we would find ourselves sick in bed. Under such circumstances, not only are we unable to pull our own weight, but we would even require the help of others to take care of us. How then could we feel whole and free? When the three poisons of greed, anger, and ignorance burn in our minds, we are creating obstacles for ourselves through negative karma. In this way, not only are we unable to conduct ourselves peacefully, but we will even need the consolation of others. In extreme cases, some people commit all kinds of atrocities, and end up being arrested and imprisoned, bringing humiliation to their families and disruption to society—what wholeness and freeness will there possibly be?

Buddhism teaches us that our thoughts and actions are a continuous whole, and stresses the key importance of a healthy body and mind. The consumption of plain and simple vegetarian meals can nurture our spirit of compassion, bring out the gentler side of our character, strengthen our patience, and build our physical health. Various retreats and cultivation activities can develop discipline in our daily lives and the fine virtues of contemplation and self-reflection. The Buddhist manners of conduct, such as practicing the Five Contemplations During Meals; and the Four Kinds of Comportment of "walking like the wind, standing like a pine tree, sitting like a bell, and sleeping like a bow," also serve the same purpose. In addition, such practices as making pilgrimages, paying homage to the Buddha, studying Chan, sitting in meditation, reciting the Buddha's name, chanting the Buddhist sutras, repenting one's bad behavior, making vows, cherishing blessings, and being appreciative of kindness, can cleanse us of the grime of worldly concerns and greatly advance our efforts towards purifying our hearts and minds.

I hope that all members of the BLIA will have a healthy body and mind. Let all of us progress a step further so that radiance may emanate from our bodies and minds, that we may continuously have the commitment and dedication to serve others, maintain the spirit of giving and self-sacrifice, and join in activities that benefit the public. In this way, we can spread the joy of the Dharma and let all beings experience wholeness and freeness.

## VIII. Self-Liberation Leads to a Human World of Wholeness and Freeness

The Fourth Patriarch of the Chan school, Chan Master Dao Xin, once asked the Third Patriarch, Chan Master Seng Zan, "How do I attain liberation and freeness?" Chan Master Seng Zan simply asked him in return, "Who is binding you?" A reply such as this gets right to the point, clearing away the lingering confusion of centuries, and we cannot help but applaud and exclaim. Indeed, who in this world is most able to tie us down? No one else but ourselves. When wealth becomes our attachment, it then has a lock on our minds and will power; and when power becomes our attachment, it can then shroud our hearts. As in the ancient saying, "Fame shackles and wealth binds;" for truly, there is no telling how many people have toiled so hard after fame and fortune all of their lives, and yet they cannot even catch their breath.

A fist that clenches candy tightly can never be pulled through a narrow jar opening; a foot that is tightly retracted can never step forward. It is only when we can let matters go that we can truly pick them up. To achieve liberation and freeness, we have to learn to let go of everything, open our minds, expand our horizon, and see the big picture. Over the course of history, all buddhas and bodhisattvas have let go of personal benefit for the sake of benefiting all living beings, even at the cost of their own lives. All the heroes of the past and present have given up the ego's safety and security for the sake of securing the welfare of the public at large, disregarding all the dangers they faced. While they relieve the sufferings of others, they also attain freeness and liberation for themselves. The constitutional democracies of Great Britain and the United States have been able to unite their countries to better serve the needs of all. They abandoned narrow perspectives and upheld the rule of law for all, so that they can live in peace. Is this not a perfect example of going from the liberation of oneself to reach the level of wholeness and freeness for all?

The above eight points suggest how we can achieve a life of wholeness and freeness in the human world. The wars and rebellions over the course of history have brought untold miseries, as families were torn apart and individuals were lost. Today, our leaders all maintain an open and broad outlook, actively participating on the international stage, to build nations that are of the people, by the people, and for the people; thereby bringing wholeness and freeness to all people. Let all members of the BLIA wholeheartedly offer incense and pray for peace and unity in the world, for prosperity among all nations, and for security to all people. Let us manifest societies that are whole and free; let us manifest families that are whole and free; and let us manifest a spirit that is whole and free!

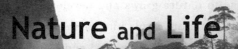

# Nature and Life

*We must learn to revere all of life because all of life is interconnected and all of it depends on all of its parts. All life should be seen as having immense value since each and every instance of life is completely unique.*

BLIA 7th General Conference
Toronto, Canada
October 1-4, 1998
Recorded by Ven. Man Guo
Translated by Tom Graham
Edited by Robert H. Smitheram, Ph.D.

When we speak of "nature," we mean the expression of certain fundamental truths in this world. Nature is a level of truth that is manifested in the world around us, as represented by the cycles of nature: the four seasons, the stages of life from birth to death, the rising and falling of phenomena, the movement of thought from one instant to the next. All of this is natural, and all of this is part of the process of life. What conforms to nature grows and develops; what conforms to nature forms into completion; and what conforms to nature is good and beautiful. When the Buddha became enlightened under the bodhi tree, he saw that the deepest truth in the universe is the "inherent emptiness of all conditioned phenomena," which is, in fact, the "natural principle" of the universe. Nature here thus means the human mind, truth, life, and constant norms of the universe. We can appreciate some of the depth of the Buddha's insight by casting our eyes across the pages of human history. Is there a king, or an emperor, or a regime anywhere in the world that does not conform to the basic pattern of natural principle? Do not nations and eras in their histories rise and fall with the same regularity of all things in nature? And is not the same true for the lives of each and every one of us? When we willingly conform with the imperatives of nature, we experience joy, and when we rebel against them, we experience sorrow. It is good to ask ourselves from time to time, "Am I conforming to the laws of nature in my uses of money? In my uses of language? In my attitudes and emotions? Am I able to conform to nature and not contravene the fundamental principles of everything? The tendency for things to find their natural places cannot and should not be resisted.

We can also see how nature is emphasized by people today in their attitudes toward a nurturing environment, freedom, and democracy. For example, for centuries women in China were forced to bind their feet. With the dawn of the modern era, this practice was stopped and now no one would think of taking it up again, for it was an unnatural thing to do.

During the twentieth century, many English colonies regained their independence, while in the last century American slaves were set free. This change in attitude is the natural evolution of the human race's appreciation of the laws of nature.

There is an old Chinese saying that reveals a deep appreciation for the interconnectedness of the human mind and the natural world. The saying is, "The wise love mountains, while the benevolent love water." The world around us is our origin and our home. All of us are products of nature, and just as our bodies come from the elements of this world, so our conscience also comes from the deep foundation that underlies all things. We must learn to appreciate this profound interconnectedness as we trace a path toward its center, by following our sense both of what is beautiful and what is right.

Buddhism reveres nature by stressing human nature and the human mind above all else. The Land of Pure Crystal Radiance of the East and the World of Ultimate Bliss of the West described in Buddhist sutras are characterized by the beauty of their natural environments, with bejeweled trees, water, and birds that speak the Dharma. The people that live there need only think of what clothing they want or what food they want for it to appear before them. The purpose of these descriptions is to show that there are states of consciousness in which it is possible for human beings to live in perfect accord with nature. The Buddha's Light International Association (BLIA) promotes Humanistic Buddhism as a way of adapting to how the truth of conditioned reality develops, and as a way of emphasizing the manifestation of nature. In the practice of Humanistic Buddhism, it is also our hope that everyone can respect nature. This is important because the only way we are able to achieve spiritual liberation and enjoy freedom in our lives, is by adapting and conforming to nature.

In speaking of "life," we must understand that the definition of life is not simply that one is still breathing, but rather, whether or not the way one "uses" things has value. To live, human beings must use the things of nature, but we only really live insofar as we are contributing to the world. For example, even a piece of paper or a stone can contribute to the world. If someone draws a portrait of a saint on a piece of paper or carves the image of an ancient worthy in stone, those objects will inspire people for years to come, and so in a sense they have a life. In contrast, lofty people with power and money are often seen as contemptible by their fellow human beings. Then, there are others who mange to achieve great longevity without doing anything with their lives. They make no contribution to society whatsoever, and though living, they appear dead, which is why people often call them "walking corpses."

All around us we can see life and the amazing process of life. Birds call, insects sing, waters burble as the sun shines over the resplendent colors of the earth. Life is everywhere and everywhere it is vibrant and active, as the following couplet attests: "Flowing water speaks the words of the Dharma; the mountain scene is none other than the body of the Dharma." If we pay close attention, can we not see that there is nothing in this universe's myriad array of phenomena that does not naturally issue from the very heart of our own being? How sad it is that so many people destroy the causes and conditions that support life, spending their lives encouraging division. This breaches the harmony of life and brings harm to the larger being of the universe, which is quite lamentable.

The Buddha taught that the Dharma realm and the mind are one, that the foundation of the phenomenal universe is the mind. The limitless being of Sakyamuni Buddha is often praised in this way: "His body is the true Dharma, while pure wisdom is his life." And the reason why Amitabha Buddha is known as the Buddha of "infinite light" and "immeasurable life," is because his life completely transcends all limitations of time and space, so that all time and all space become infinite. A mayfly only lives for one day, but after it dies it will be reborn in another form. A human being comes and goes on this earth, but mind and karma will bring rebirth. A seed dropped on the ground may lie dormant for a hundred years; but as soon as conditions are right, it can still grow and blossom. The products of modern technology like test-tube babies and the cloning of sheep have people awestruck over such inventive powers. However, from the Buddhist perspective, the basic cause underpinning such technologies is simply the generation of life through the actions of karma. No matter how much technology advances and changes, it will never invent life, because life is created through the natural formation of causes and conditions.

The *Heart Sutra* says, "Form is empty, and emptiness is form." The flowing movement of our lives through the material world is an example of "form that is empty," while the connectedness of our lives to the vast world around us is an example of "emptiness that is form." This is why when Buddhism speaks of "this world," it means nothing less than the limitless, infinite world of all phenomena in the universe; when it speaks of "living beings," it means nothing less than all living beings in the universe; and when it speaks of "life," it means nothing less than the limitless, infinite life that permeates all things everywhere.

Nowadays, who knows how many beautiful homes have been destroyed in a single day by fighting around the globe. Humanity's unrelenting pillaging of natural resources has sparked the earth's retaliation, while environmental pollution is now destroying our health. Differing views among races, political parties, religions, and regions are generating more conflict everyday, while the surge in international drug cartels, terrorist groups, armed militias, and pornographic rings, are threatening the security of our lives and property. So the theme of "Nature and Life" is a clarion call to awaken humanity, in hopes that everyone will cherish this vibrant life and join in unity with nature. We must transcend our concerns over honor and praise and be fearless in the face of birth, old age, sickness, and death, so that together we can build a pure land. We must champion the profound beauty of nature, declare the greatness of the universe, praise the eternal gentleness of living beings, and honor their eternal existence.

The following four points will further illustrate this theme of "Nature and Life:"

## I. Natural Principle and the Respect for Life

Twenty-five hundred years ago while sitting under the bodhi tree, the Buddha attained enlightenment into the natural principle, which he called "dependent origination." "Dependent origination" conforms to the requirements of truth, in that truth is something universal, inevitable, equal, and eternal. From the changing fortunes of an individual and the succession of seasons on the small scale, to the rise and fall of nations and the creation and destruction of worlds on the large scale, all phenomena in nature operate under the natural principle of "dependent origination." In particular, the relationship between our lives and the natural principle of dependent origination is especially close, because life just does not come out of nowhere, rather, life comes about through the karmic power we have generated ourselves. Life is not the result of just a single cause either, it is produced by the continuous cycle of cause and effect through the past, present, and future known as "The Twelve Links of Dependent Origination:" ignorance, activity, consciousness, name and form, the six sense organs, contact, feeling, craving, grasping, becoming, birth, and aging and death.

"When we are prepared, there are no disasters," that is, if we understand the natural principle of dependent origination, then we will be prepared for whatever may happen to us and we will not be afraid. For example, if we diligently till the land and plant seeds in the spring, then by autumn we will reap a great harvest; so naturally we will not fear the arrival of winter. If we equip ourselves with lights during the day, then we will naturally not fear the arrival of darkness at night. In like manner, no one need to fear old age for if we use our youth and middle age to work hard, then we will be satisfied with our lives when we grow old. And neither is death something to be feared, for if we have lived well and contributed to society, our next rebirth will be a good one.

Douglas MacArthur once said, "Old soldiers never die." What he meant is that their spirit is eternally bound to the soul of the nation. Wen Tianxiang, a famous patriot of the Sung dynasty, has said, "No one in this life has ever escaped death; but one's loyal spirit can be entrusted to posterity." An important part of both of these statements is the message that no one needs to become famous or make immense contributions to live a dignified life. It seems that people in the past were greatly concerned about living with dignity, for they exerted all their efforts in striving for freedom and equality; they worked hard to bring about democracy and universal fraternity, even to the point of willingly spilling their blood and sacrificing their lives. People nowadays are more concerned about dying with dignity, and hope that they can die a happy and peaceful death, even to the point of protesting in the streets with their "death with dignity" slogans.

In Buddhism, we focus instead on the

natural principle of dependent origination, and the concepts of the "freedom of karmic power," the "equality of living beings," "compassion through oneness," and the "continuity of life and death" that are derived from this principle. This mode of thinking is the only way to integrate life with death, so that we can truly develop the dignity of life to its naturally greatest extent. Therefore, we must rid ourselves of the sadness of fatalism and face hardship with courage, so that we can create our own future. We must disabuse ourselves of misguided notions that negate causality, for even a field filled with thorns can be planted with the seeds of future joys, creating for the universe an on-going sense of life. We must discard the false idea that the tools of production determine everything, so that we can create enterprises through a cooperative process that benefit living beings. We must correct the corrupt practices of the leaders of commerce, so that we create beneficial merit in gratitude for our blessings. Let us bequeath morality to this human world; let us hand down wisdom to society; let us confer compassion upon our families, and leave our mark upon history. In this way, we will be living according to the natural principle, and enjoying as well a dignified life!

## II. Natural Life and Living Nature

All living things are closely interconnected with nature, for life is a part of nature—something we should all properly cherish. Unfortunately, having considered itself the "wisest of all beings" for so long, humanity has often ignored the existence of other life, slaughtering the innocent to satisfy a momentary desire. Let me ask: when you lament the soldiers in the world who die in battle, have you ever given a thought to pitiful cries that emanate from the slaughterhouse? When you sigh in sadness over the incessant news of social disasters, have you ever heard the angry accusations of sentient being now lying butchered and cooked on you plate?

The *Dharmapada Sutra* states, "All beings are afraid of dying, and all fear the pain of the lash; forgive others as you would yourself; and refrain from killing and refrain from using the lash. If you always bring peace to all beings without doing any injury, then you will be free from harm in this life and always safe and secure in the next one." The Buddha states in the *Diamond Sutra*: "I will save sentient beings by leading them all to the Nirvana-without-remainder." A positive admonition against killing should both protect and guide, enabling everyone to obtain salvation. Therefore, we should all guard against committing even the slightest pain through harsh words and angry looks; and we should always offer even the smallest joy for the welfare of others with smiling words of praise.

Some people still cling to the mistaken belief that they have the power to control their own lives. But according to the truth of "dependent origination," life is produced from the father's sperm and the mother's egg, and it is maintained by the various professions in society that supply life's daily necessities. Thus, it is clear that there can be no real "self." And since life is the possession of nature with its world of myriad phenomena, so any killing of self or other is a contrary act that goes against nature. Speaking more in broader terms, even a stone or a blade of grass has been formed through the power of all beings in the universe. To violate even the smallest part by reducing its life-span is still an act of killing living beings. For example, vast swaths of forest were cut down for the Yangtze River's Three Gorges Dam, which will make future flooding much worse; while the land in Taiwan has been carved up for buildings, ruining the lower strata of soil. All of this is clear evidence of how, according to the principle of dependent origination, nature retaliates when its mountains and rivers have been damaged. Such current events call to mind the conduct of the Buddha's earlier life as a bodhisattva, who would walk softly so as not to trample the ground; or the Monk Biendanshan, who would simply gather fallen nuts for food, because he did not want to harm the plants and trees. Their examples of compassion are so precious to us! Remember how Amitabha

Buddha's Pure Land is described as having "water and birds that speak the Dharma," and how "when Daosheng teaches even the stones bow in affirmation." All of this underscores the fundamental truth spoken by the Buddha: "Sentient and non-sentient beings alike perfect the ultimate wisdom."

We must learn to revere all of life, because all of life is naturally interconnected and each depends on all the others. All life should be seen as having immense value, since each and every instance of life is formed from natural causes and conditions working over eons of time. Therefore, our lives should proceed in conformance to nature, and adapt to conditions as they arise in accordance to our spiritual capacities. In this way, we will find peace wherever we go and enjoy freedom to our hearts' content, as we merge our small self into the great transformations of the universe. Thus, we will surely be able to employ the light and heat of life, and experience "the oneness of self and matter" in life and nature.

## III.  Nature's Harmony and Life's Eternity

Nature means a natural harmony, and that which opposes natural harmony creates discord. The ancients put it this way: "To struggle by opposing the natural flow brings an illness to the mind." When greed, anger, ignorance, pride, doubt, and jealousy disrupt the mind, one will experience suffering and pain that may lead one down the wrong path to one's everlasting regret. The same goes for how we handle things in life: one-sided romances go against nature, so there will be no "happily ever after;" wealth achieved by ill-gotten means goes against nature, for it will surely be lost in the end; fame attained through shocking comments goes against nature, in the end it will turn into contempt; and a high status that merely serves one's own enjoyment goes against nature, for it will bring forth censure.

What accords with nature is successful, while too much or too little will bring problems in the end. For example, lying down too long, standing up too long, working without rest too long, keeping still without movement too long, and so on, will all disrupt the physiological harmony of the four limbs; then, one starts to get sick, which ruins the function of the body, and leads an untimely death. Likewise, our treatment of the natural world around us will always cause problems when we are excessive in our desires or lax in our vigilance. Over the last few centuries, humankind has learned to manufacture and consume too many material goods, far exceeding the capacity of micro-organisms to recycle it all. This has destroyed the operations of nature, leading to the present series of ecological problems. All of this just goes to show, that once the laws of nature are ignored, the negative consequences are sure to follow.

Nature is like a "circle," for good causes bring good results and negative causes inflict negative results. Cause and effect follow each other without beginning or end. Our very lives themselves are the temporary manifestations of a process of cause and effect that has been going on for eons. Already, each one of us has lived and died a thousand million times. Certainly, death is the beginning of a new life, while each life is a preparation for a death yet to come. Thus, death is never an absolute end to anything and life is never an absolute condition that persists without change. Life is like the fire that consumes one log after another, while death is like changing our clothes. We may look different, but deep down we are the same. Great Buddhist masters of the past all understood completely the continuity between life and death. Bodhidharma (d. 535) faced death with perfect insouciance, while the Living Buddha of Jin Mountain (1852-1935) calmly passed away while taking a shower without protest or complaint. They kept in harmony with Nature, living and dying in complete freedom.

Life is a product of causes and conditions, while death comes with their dispersal. When viewed from the highest level of truth, then there is neither life nor is there death. This is why great Buddhist masters did not seek to escape death, but only sought to perceive self-nature by illuminating the mind. Upon the attainment of enlightenment, all relative distinctions are eliminated, and then an instant is eternity and suffering is enlightened wisdom. They did not seek happiness for themselves, but only wished that living beings could be free from suffering. In their eyes, the bitter sea of birth and death is but a wisp of cloud up in the sky, hardly anything worth mentioning.

The *Book of Changes* states, "The heavens move with constant regularity; the sage improves himself without ceasing." The way of nature lies in eternal diligence and in benefiting self and other. Therefore, we must emulate the fine virtue of heaven, the earth, the sun, and the moon in nurturing all things, so that with the compassion of oneness serving as our material for dealing with the world, we will build a house of sanctuary for living beings in difficulty. We must learn from the marathon spirit of the past sages, so that with limitless life as our brave advance, we can act as sweet dew that cools living beings suffering from the heat of this turbid world.

# IV. Natural Life and the Buddhist Way

If "nature" were to be explained in one word, that would be "Way" (Dao); if "life" were to be explained in one word, that would be "strength." And what is the Way? Master Dazhu Hui Hai (ca. 8th-9th C) has said, "When you are hungry, eat. When you are tired, sleep;" and Master Yaoshan Wei Yen (751-834) has said, "The clouds are in the sky while water is in the bottle." The Way of living is simply to live in accordance with nature. Even the Buddha spoke of five types of "unnatural" people: those who do not smile when they should smile; those who do not feel joy when they should feel joy; those who do not feel compassion when they should feel compassion; those who are not repulsed by things that should repulse them; and those who hear of good things but do not feel glad. The conduct of such people is out of alignment with nature.

What is "strength"? The five powers of faith, diligence, mindfulness, concentration, and wisdom are "strength;" and the Four

Immeasurable States of Mind of loving-kindness, compassion, joy, and equanimity are "strength." To give compassion, joy, and light to people, so that each lamp lights up another in a constant succession is "strength." Thus, if the "Way" of Nature could be combined with the "strength" of life, then this would become the overflowing energy of righteousness in the universe, as well as the Dharma Realm of Ultimate Truth.

If we want to live a true life, then we must live in accordance with the principle of nature. We must honor the rights and feelings of our spouses, children, neighbors, and coworkers. If we want to begin a new business enterprise, we must respect the marketplace and take into consideration all of the many factors that will bring success. If we want to improve the governance of our societies, then we must pay close attention to the needs of the people as we strive to set an example that is worthy of their natural and heartfelt respect. In particular as Buddhists, we must strive to set examples that inspire and comfort our fellow beings. Our words must be truthful and our motives must be pure, for this is the only way that we can be of lasting value to others. If our way of being can be in accord with the "Way" and be combined with "strength," then we will have gotten the Buddhist way of living a natural life just about right.

No one knows how many great masters have become enlightened over the centuries. But after attaining enlightenment, the mountain was still a mountain, and a river was still a river; it is just that the mountains, rivers, and earth itself have merged into oneness with the self, to be used as one pleases. This is what is meant by the couplet: "The greenness of bamboo are nothing but *prajña*-wisdom; the profusion of yellow flowers all represent the profound truth." The Way is one's own sense being, something not sought outside of oneself. And so the external chiliocosm with its living beings of the past, present, and future, is actually a part of one's own mind. Therefore, whether you call it nature or life, it is all still the same truth—the Buddhist way, which means the true Buddha nature inherent in all living beings, as well as the universe as a single totality.

Some years have past since the BLIA's founding, and although compared with the vastness of time and space, we are still but a small tree. Over the years we have promoted the ideals of "Joy and Harmony," "Oneness and Coexistence," "Respect and Tolerance," "Equality and Peace," and "Wholeness and Freeness," which stand in accord with the natural principles of truth. This is why we have been able to weather all the difficulties to stand straight and unshakeable. But now, we must continue to carry on the legacy of all the buddhas and follow the instructions taught by generations of masters, in order to press forwards without complaint or regret, opening a path of peace for generations to come. I hope that the effort we put forth with each tiny step, will develop the power of correct knowledge and realization of this vast universe; and I hope that every spurt of growth we make in the future, will extend its influence of beauty and goodness to the limitless sentient beings far and wide.

# One Truth for All

*Universal truth is beyond duality, beyond pleasure and pain, beyond the selfish interests of the individual who sees only himself and no one else.*

BLIA 8th General Conference
Taipei, Taiwan
May 14-20, 2000
Translated by Tom Graham
Edited by Robert H. Smitheram, Ph.D.

It is already the beginning of a new century, one that will undoubtedly be more technologically advanced and more economically prosperous. As we enjoy the benefits of this new age, however, we must wonder how these material achievements are affecting how the people of the world orient their values. The sense of right and wrong for people today has become confused, creating all manner of disorder for the entire world. In order to address this problem, I thought that I would discuss the subject of "One Truth for All," in hopes of inspiring humanity to create a just and fair society, as well as encouraging everyone to have the moral courage of "one truth for all" so that a form of society based upon "one truth for all" can be established. "One truth for all" means "the cardinal issues of right and wrong." As the proverb states, "I love my teacher, but I love the truth more," for it is the truth of "one truth for all." The Buddha has said, "rely on the Dharma rather than on individuals," and so relying upon the Dharma is "one truth for all."

"One truth for all" is the principle and

wisdom by which good and bad, right and wrong, correct and incorrect, and positive and negative are determined, for "one truth for all" is only possible through wisdom. "One truth for all" means something public rather than private, something universal rather than personal, something that pervades the Dharma realm rather than one-sided, something egalitarian for all living beings rather than discriminatory, something inevitable in all matters rather than changing, and something eternal for all times rather than temporary. This is so because "one truth for all" means *prajña*-wisdom, for enlightenment and liberation can only be attained through *prajña*-wisdom. In the beginning, the Buddha abandoned his princely crown to become a monk because he was moved by the suffering, emptiness, and impermanence of life; he saw the inequalities of the caste system and living beings' confused sense of thinking. This is why he broke with his family ties so courageously to engage in spiritual practice as a monk. The truth that the Buddha realized was simply a manifestation of the *prajña*-wisdom that embodies "one truth for all." "One truth for all" is not focused on the individual self, but rather finds its refuge in justice and fairness. "One truth for all" is not directed at a single group or nation, but rather makes its appeal for the peace and happiness of living beings throughout the entire Dharma realm. Therefore, the Buddha declared just when he attained enlightenment: "All sentient beings have Buddha nature, for everyone can attain Buddhahood." Thus, the truths that "ordinary beings are the same as buddhas" and "all living beings are equal," represent "one truth for all" at its highest understanding.

The truth that the Buddha realized is "the inherent emptiness of dependent origination," in the sense that "all phenomena arise through causes and conditions and pass into extinction through causes and conditions." This explains how everything in the universe operates according to causality, and so humans experience the causes and conditions of birth, old age, sickness, and death, while the world is subject to the laws of formation, abiding, destruction, and voidness. When causes and conditions come together, there is formation; and when they disperse, there is destruction, and so this on-going process of formation and destruction enables the world of Nature to have its flowers that blossom and fade; the world to have its cycle of arising, abiding, change, and extinction; and human life to undergo the transformations of "impermanence" through the rise and fall of poverty and wealth. This is not something ordained by the power of spirits, nor anything that can be affected by earthly authority. It is simply "one truth for all."

The Buddhist doctrine of "karmic retribution through causation" means that "one reaps what one sows." This is a "one truth for all" that is extraordinarily fair. For no one, neither a pillar of society nor the peddler in the street, can escape the laws of causality, where "good is rewarded with good, and bad is repaid with bad." "When the prince breaks the law, his crime would be the same as that of a commoner;" if this could truly be achieved, then that would be "one truth for all." In ancient times, kings and aristocrats possessed gold and jewels, which they buried in their tombs with them in the mistaken belief that these things could serve them in their next life. But such ideas contravene "karmic retribution through causation." A better idea is "you can take nothing with you except your karma," for this then fits the standard of "one truth for all."

"One truth for all" is the just and fair form of discipline that binds social order together, and also serves as an exemplary guide for cultivating one's personal morality. Do not imagine others are not aware of the actions of one's body, speech, and mind, or one's thoughts and intentions, because "the heavens know, the earth knows, you know, and I know." Imperceptibly, the standard of "one truth for all" operates invariably.

There are people in the world who focus on what gives them advantage or disadvantage, while others value the sense of right and wrong. Those who focus on advantage and disadvantage care little for right and wrong, while those who value the sense of right and wrong care little for advantage and disadvantage. So many sages over the course of centuries have disregarded considerations of advantage and disadvantage for the sake of promoting the spirit of "one truth for all," even to the point of willingly giving up their lives. The Song dynasty Neo-Confucianist Chang Zai (1020-1077) has said, "Base your mind on heaven and earth; base your life on the needs of the people; continue the teaching legacy of the past sages; and bring peace to all things." This spirit of "one truth for all" is what the Confucian masters have called the life within life. In his chapter on "The Way of Heaven," Zhuang Zi (369-286 BCE) states, "Having made clear the judgment of right and wrong, the determination of rewards and punishments then followed;" and "I was born together with Heaven and Earth, and I am part of the oneness with all things." When Italian astronomer Galileo refused to repudiate the results of his experiments into astronomy and mechanics, he risked death in opposing the spiritual authorities. All of this demonstrates the great wisdom and courage of having "one truth for all."

In a society that respects ethics and morality, people fully value the principle of "one truth for all," and have a true and real sense of "the cardinal issues regarding right and wrong." But when we consider modern society today, we see that there is something of an ambivalence towards the idea of right and wrong; and one could even argue that for most people around us, there is little regard for right and wrong, that such notions are confused or even totally absent. Since humanity today is unwilling to take the universal truth of right and wrong, then the concern is instead how "winners lord it over the losers," creating a situation in which the expedience of force and considerations over money replace the "one truth for all." Everywhere the opportunists seek advantage and the schemers scheme; and the standards of right and wrong are no longer evident; the truth no longer clear. What has happened to that sense of "innate conscience"?

Democracy and freedom have been offered as modern humanity's finest political goals.

But if I use my freedom to obstruct yours, or assert my ideals as a way of forcing your compliance, then "democracy and freedom" is just a euphemism for something else. When a dictator blithely discusses democracy with his people, where is the "one truth for all" then? Calls for referendum often occur in society today, and enacting referendum is very democratic and accords with the spirit of "one truth for all." But does everyone participating in the referendum really understand the "one truth for all?" Do the decision-makers involved in the whole process have a true grasp of this concept? Does a democracy of fifty-one votes to forty-nine really reflect the "one truth for all"? Clearly, "one truth for all" requires great wisdom and courage to take moral responsibility for what is just and fair. One must care about fairness, honesty, altruism, and selflessness. Only this approach represents the "hopes of the people," for only by fulfilling the needs of the people, can there be democracy and freedom that is "one truth for all."

In the history of Buddhism, quite a few worthy masters gladly passed on their teachings and position to students who had no connection whatsoever with their lineage, the only requirement being that the students selected be capable of shouldering such great responsibilities. Such conduct exemplifies what "one truth for all" means. Regrettably, Buddhist disciples of later generations did not have a sufficient appreciation of "one truth for all," and so some began "relying on individuals rather than the Dharma," while others were "relying upon supernatural spirits rather than the Buddha;" still others were "relying on the teacher rather than principle," as well as those who were "relying on the false rather than the truth." This has fostered an inability to understand the intentions of the founding masters, and has thus led to the gradual decline of the Chan School.

The *Diamond Sutra* speaks of such concepts as "generosity without form," "liberation of beings in egolessness," "practice without abiding," and "enlightenment without obtainment," all of which reflect the meaning of "one truth for all." The *Diamond Sutra* also goes on to state, that bodhisattvas must rid themselves of the four views of existence: that the self exists, that this self differs from all others, that life is limited to its components, and that life is limited to the physical form, for in this way everything is unfixed and formless. Thus, someone who is free from the sense of selfhood would necessarily have no selfish attachments; someone who is free from a self that differs from others would necessarily be able to respect equality; someone who is free from a self limited to components would necessarily not discriminate between external forms; and someone who is free from the sense of a physical self would never remain fixed and unchanging. When these four views of existence are eliminated, we have "one truth for all," and all matters can be handled in accordance with Dharma and principle. This means that one's only concern becomes what is right or wrong, good or bad; ignoring all praise or blame, gain or loss: "I would rather fall straight to Hell, than use the Dharma for personal advantage." All of which exemplify the true meaning of "one truth for all."

This ideal of "one truth for all" must

withstand the test of time; it must withstand the scrutiny of conscience, as well as the judgment of history. When the famous general Cao Chao (155-220) captured the emperor and commanded the feudal lords, some honored him as the great hero for a chaotic time, while others condemned him as a traitor for stealing the throne. For individuals like Cao Chao, even history finds it difficult to render a "one truth for all" evaluation of their achievements and failings:

*During the days when the Duke of Zhou was regent over King Cheng; Before he later faithfully stepped down when King Cheng came of age; Or when Wang Meng honored worthies and respected talent; Before he went on to usurp the imperial throne of the Han dynasty; If they had died right then, before all that later history, How would we know who was loyal and who was traitor?*

This indicates that the "one truth for all" is not so easily determined, for without great wisdom, how would "one truth for all" be recognized?

There are those in this human world who enjoy great success without being truly talented, and there are those outstanding talents who just never get their chance. "One truth for all" also has its application in any discussion of causality over the past, present, and future. Nelson Mandela spent thirty years languishing in jail before he became President of South Africa, while Sun Yat-sen tried to overthrow the Qing dynasty (1644-1911) many times before he succeeded at last. Here too, all human activities depend on both causes and conditions, which is why "one truth for all" plays such a key role. Now in today's world of industrial and commercial enterprises, no one can be criticized for making a reasonable profit. But one cannot simply credit one's own contributions for society's development, for one must realize that all success in this world must be assisted by relevant causes and conditions. For example, skyscrapers require many bricks after bricks and tile upon tile, while blooming plants must be nurtured by the natural elements. To all these many causes and conditions, we should know how to feel gratitude for rendering such silent aids. Only then would we have treated the world fairly according to the "one truth for all." Environmental protection with its emphasis on nurturing ecosystems is being promoted around the world today. But only a small minority is deemed worthy of survival, while the majority of plants and animals only seem deserving of death. Such an unfair environmental concept must await further consideration. "One truth for all" must be applied equally around the world, for "one truth for all" is the standard upon which all living beings rely for survival. Most people today think "one truth for all" is like some superhero; yet there are no superheroes at our sides, are there? "Causes and conditions and the resulting karma" is our "one truth for all;" "The force of good and bad karma" is our "one truth for all;" the same goes for "perfect understanding of principles and things" and "judgments come last." Therefore, I hope that from now on, all BLIA members will be able to make "one truth for all" their standard for how they conduct themselves and handle things. With this keen awareness of what "one truth for all" means, let us make this vow together, to join our efforts in creating a harmonious society, one that reflects the fairness and justice of the all-inclusive Dharma realm.

# The Human World and Life

*The practice of Humanistic Buddhism is cultivation in your daily lives. For example, the practice can simply refer to your dedication and compassion or repentance. Practice is where you give rise to compassion, cultivate humble thoughts, and develop the Bodhi mind.*

BLIA 1st Conference for 3rd Board of Directors
April 18-22, 2001
Johannesburg, South Africa
Translated by Ven. Miao Guang & Shirley Hsueh
Edited by Robert H. Smitheram, Ph.D.

Located in the southernmost part of Africa, South Africa is one of the fifty-three countries in Africa. Not only is Africa the most ancient of lands in the world, but it is also where humankind originated. Nevertheless, due to its long history of tribal disputes, volatile politics, polluted environment, and harsh climates, as well as a severe lack of opportunities for education, Africa is known as "the Land of Darkness." The first HIV/AIDS case was diagnosed in Africa thirty years ago, and among the thirty-six millions HIV/AIDS patients around the world today, twenty-five million of them live in South Africa.

The raging spread of HIV/AIDS imposes an enormous threat on the very existence of humankind, suggesting an ironic prediction that since Africa is the place where humankind began, it may also be where humanity is extinguished. To deal with this global threat, the 1999 Global AIDS Conference held in South Africa focused on discussing possible ways to prevent the disease, and concluded that religion can save humanity from such a disaster, and in particular, the precepts of Buddhism are the fundamental ways to end the spread of HIV and AIDS.

This conclusion suggests that the Buddha's teachings or the Dharma is a ray of light for humanity today; the darker a place is, the more is Buddhism needed. For this reason, the Fo Guang Shan Buddhist Order established Africa's first Buddhist temple in 1992, and in 1994, I conducted an ordination ceremony for five young Africans at Nan Hua Temple. This initiated the first group of African Buddhist monastics and made the propagation of Buddhism available in South Africa. Over the years, Fo Guang Shan Nan Hua Temple and the South Africa Chapter of the Buddha's Light International Association (BLIA) have carried out many cultural and educational activities, as well as charitable aid programs in countries such as Swaziland and Tanzania, earning recognition from the government of South Africa. It is within this context, I would like to share the following four suggestions as encouragement and common direction for all members of the BLIA:

## I. Transform the Dharma using Humanistic Qualities

Humanistic Buddhism is a hot topic today, as well as everyone's most discussed subject. The propagation of Humanistic Buddhism has always been the objective for Fo Guang Shan since its establishment in 1967. I have once said that when I founded Fo Guang Shan, I was doing more than just establishing the hardware, there is also our software which is Humanistic Buddhism. Humanistic Buddhism has not only been constantly on my mind, but I implemented it through my actions and demonstrated it through my ideas. However, when I first proposed the idea of propagating Humanistic Buddhism, I was questioned and rejected by other Buddhists over and over again, simply because they felt that it is my personal conception. In fact, the Buddha was born in this human world, attained enlightenment in this human world, and also propagated Buddhism in this human world. The main audience of his discourse were human beings; therefore, Buddhism is an anthropocentric religion; the Buddha is the Buddha of our world; and Buddhism itself intrinsically contains human characteristics. Thus, Humanistic Buddhism was not invented by any single person, not by the Sixth Patriarch of Chan, Hui Neng nor Master Tai Xu, and neither is it my invention. Humanistic Buddhism is what the Buddha had intended to teach from the very beginning: Buddhism has been humanistic all along.

Since Buddhism is naturally humanistic, why do we emphasize the humanization of its teachings now? This is because throughout my years as a Buddhist, I have seen many educated people struggling with how to relate to the Buddha's teachings despite being Buddhists for decades. For example, Buddhism advocates compassion and yet no one is compassionate, or

Buddhism talks about patience, and no one is ever patient. Furthermore, some people tend to emphasize metaphysics, instead of focusing on the actual practice and experience of Buddhism, or they focus solely on paying homage and being a vegetarian, while neglecting to work on improving their personality and morals, or solving their day-to-day problems; thus, they lack a sense of responsibility towards the world. Still others concentrate on self-practice, while never showing any care or concern for society.

In fact, Buddhism has a very close link with our daily lives, and we cannot just regard its teachings as some object of study. Buddhism is a religion to be readily applied to our daily lives. While human beings need a life, and our lives require the guidance of the Buddha's teachings. We need to integrate Buddhist beliefs into our lives through the process of our religious faith. In other words, we need to use the Dharma as our life's guide, and achieve "the Dharma transformed by life, and a life transformed by the Dharma." What we have when we apply Buddhism to our lives and put it into practice, is Humanistic Buddhism.

How do we practice Humanistic Buddhism? When you are grateful and contented with simple meals, you are practicing Humanistic Buddhism; or when your sole concern is looking clean, tidy, and dignified while wearing plain yet refined clothing, you are practicing Humanistic Buddhism. The practice of Humanistic Buddhism is the practice of cultivation in our daily lives. For example, the practice can simply refer to one's dedication, compassion, or repentance. Practice is where you give rise to compassion, cultivate humble thoughts, and develop the aspiration for enlightenment for the sake of others. The practice of Humanistic Buddhism is, therefore, about treating others with compassion, respect, and tolerance. Learning and practicing Humanistic Buddhism is not some slogan, for without applying the Dharma to our words, and deeds in our daily lives, there will be no truth for us to realize.

Hence, with respect to Humanistic Buddhism,

spiritual cultivation is done through establishing good affinities with others, doing good deeds for others, observing the Five Precepts and the Ten Virtuous Acts, and practicing the Six Perfections and Four Embracing Means. Having morality and compassion in your intentions and actions means spiritual cultivation. On the other hand, if you do not perform good actions, nor speak good words or think good thoughts, you are not practicing Buddhism, because you have neglected the Three Good Practices Campaign. Therefore, "to diligently cultivate the precepts, meditation, and wisdom, and to extinguish greed, hatred, and delusion" will purify the karma created by your body, speech, and mind. This is how the way of Humanistic Buddhism is practiced. In fact, Humanistic Buddhism is essential to every aspect of our daily life. Be it eating, sleeping, walking, making friends, or working with others; all are bound up with Buddhism. Buddhism is not just written in the sutras, nor does it only exist inside the meditation hall or made manifest just in the chanting. The Dharma is present in all aspects of our life and they should be practiced as we go through our daily routine.

Where is the Dharma? It is right in this moment. What is this moment? It is our life. In the past, there were people who focused on spiritual cultivation and liberation from the cycle of birth and death only for the sake of themselves, and as a result, Buddhism has been criticized as an escapist religion. Today, the BLIA has brought Buddhism from the forest into the world, entering societies and families. All of these have fulfilled the founding goals of BLIA: "From tradition to modernism, from the mountain forests to contemporary society, from escapism to redemption and liberation, from solitude to the community, from monastics to all followers, from disciples to teachers, from chanting services to religious enterprises, from performing good deeds to propagating the Dharma, and from being scattered to systemization." These goals also enable society to recognize that Buddhism is a religion filled with bliss, happiness, truthfulness, and virtue, all of which constitute the true meaning of Humanistic Buddhism.

From now on, all aspects of generosity and broadening of wisdom; and the practice of Chan and Pure Land, the precepts and patience, as well as showing gratitude and making vows, are embraced in Humanistic Buddhism. Since the propagation of Humanistic Buddhism can be extensive and profound, I hope that all BLIA members will put extra effort into learning and understanding Humanistic Buddhism. Despite all frequent discussions on the *Suramgama Sutra*, the *Flower Adornment Sutra*, the *Lotus Sutra*, and others, it is clear that people lack of focus on Humanistic Buddhism. Nonetheless, the propagation of Humanistic Buddhism does not rely on lecturing or discussing, because it focuses on actual practice. Thus, the "transformation of the Dharma using humanistic qualities" is what everyone enjoys, comprising the spirit of compassion, joy, money, wealth, and even messages of respect and tolerance, as well as harmonious coexistence. These have long been promoted by BLIA members, for not only do these benefit members of BLIA, but also everyone else in the world, thus promoting world peace.

Furthermore, not only should we offer the Dharma to the world, society, and families, but we must also extend it into people's minds. If there is love in people's mind, there will also be the Dharma. On the other hand, if there is hatred in people's mind, then the Dharma disappears. People adore truthfulness, virtue, purity, and beauty; these are the humanistic teachings of Buddhism. Similarly, people abhor evil and arrogance, therefore the Dharma must be rid of these.

In short, we can carry out spiritual cultivation through our every intention and movement in our daily lives. We should advocate the spirit of benefiting both oneself and others, and also realize "a Dharma transformed by life, and a life transformed by the Dharma." Hopefully, everyone can work together to establish a Humanistic Buddhism that is livable and fun, wealthy, abundant, compassionate, ethical, as well as mutually respectful.

## II. Transform Human Life through the Fragrance of Books

On one's journey through life, one should know how to create joy, value the quality of life, and live a meaningful and worthwhile life. Life is not just about what one eats and what one wears; nor should it just be the pursuit of materialism, money, love, or any of the other objects of the Five Desires. There needs to be *prajña*-wisdom, knowledge, and the continuous cultivation of character and inner beauty. We need to uncover our intrinsic mind and Buddha nature, in order to lead an enriching and interesting life.

How do we achieve an enriching and interesting life? First, we must do as much reading as possible as a way of edifying our lives. Reading not only expands our knowledge and wisdom, but also refines our character and moral ethics. Furthermore, it broadens our minds and visions, allowing us to realize the truth of the universe. When an uneducated and a learned person come together, although both have parents, eat, and carry on with their regular lives, their morals and qualities are different. This is why the ancient worthies always encouraged young people to read, because only by reading can one become wiser and more knowledgeable, and only by reading can one's mind, quality, and character be improved, while those who do not read are likely to be shallow, ignorant, vulgar, and impolite. So our aim is to create a world of knowledge, homes filled with fragrances of books, and an edified life. The starting point lies with each individual's efforts to fill their lives with books, in order to encourage everyone around them to read as well. Therefore, the BLIA along with Fo Guang Shan Monastery have jointly established the Humanistic Buddhist Reading Association to promote the habit of reading.

In the recent years, the Council for Cultural

Affairs and the Ministry of Education in Taiwan have also been actively promoting reading clubs. In response to this campaign, BLIA is promoting the "transformation of human life through the fragrance of books," as a way of raising national interest in reading. Hopefully, everyone can keep in mind that "learning has no boundaries," "knowledge is infinite," and be inspired by the idea that "the pursuit of knowledge is endless." If everyone fulfills their life by doing as much reading as possible, it will further enhance harmony in society, and bring peace and happiness to the world.

Speaking of reading clubs, it is all about reading or studying books rather than simply flipping through them. Thus, the approaches adopted require careful considerations. For example, a book can be fully read, selectively read, alternately read, repeatedly read, or read in unison. Books should not be read in silence, they should be read aloud instead, or even recited in a rhythm as if one is singing. When reading a book, one should read with an agile mind and with a flexible approach. Also when reading, one should be diligent in taking notes, while avoiding rigid or monotonous reading methods. Normally, when we finish reading a book we soon forget its contents, but if we take notes and make occasional reference to them later on, all memories about the book will reappear in front of your eyes. As we review and think about the book repeatedly, the knowledge from the book will enter our blood and nourish our body and mind.

We also need to select and read books that are beneficial. Although I have never received a complete and formal education, I was lucky to become the manager of a small library at the Qixia Temple during the Sino-Japanese War. It gave me the opportunity to read voraciously many books and take notes on them as well. Day after day, and year after year, I felt that I have greatly benefited from the practice. I recall not being able to understand much of the Buddhist texts back then, therefore, I read Chinese historical novels such as the Story of

*Yue Fei*, the Story of *Jing Ke*, the *Romance of the Three Kingdoms*, and *The Seven Chivalrous Knights and the Five Patriots*. These historical novels have had a major impact on my life. For instance, by reading the biographies of heroes and brave men, I learned about how they overcame countless obstacles to ultimately achieve success. Unknowingly, they gave me the encouragement to set goals and work hard. Moreover, the examples set by those honorable and chivalrous men also made me realize that I should aim to be a person who possesses a good sense of justice, honor, and decency.

As the extent of my reading repertoire continued to increase, my vocabulary also vastly improved; therefore, I began to share my new-found knowledge with other people. The reason that I am capable of teaching is because I have always been willing to share with others the stories I have seen and heard about. It is also because I met teachers who did not really know how to teach, but they just kept writing things on the blackboard until the bell rang, and then picked up their books and left without a single word. Also my illiterate mother taught me how to read, because when I read to her, I often mispronounced the words because I did not know that many characters, so my mother would correct me as she listened.

Although my environment did not provide much opportunity for study back then, I believed as long as I was keen to study, the situation would change. From historical novels, I began to read the *Biographies of Eminent Monks.* While the Buddhist sutras and commentaries were too hard to understand, the *Biographies of Eminent Monks* contained stories and records of events. I, therefore, read different editions of the biographies many times, and from these stories, I learned to follow the examples of these great monastics as a way of bettering myself. I feel that today's youth have the concept of a role model, so the many good role models can serve as their guide. For example, Confucius, Chuang Zi, and Lao Zi are role models for all of us. Similarly, in the *Anthology of Ancient Texts*, the eight great writers produced such wonderful writings that surely people can learn much from them. Translators of Buddhist teachings like Kumarajiva and Xuan Zang of the Tang dynasty have also set excellent examples for us to follow through the way they strived to overcome difficulties.

Reading requires persistent effort, and should not be treated as a game or a task that one muddles through. Reading is an attentive profession to be done each day. As the saying goes, "Three days without reading makes one's language tasteless." I already developed the habit of reading at a young age, and if I went without reading for three days, even the food would became tasteless to me. Other than working and talking, I would definitely be reading. When I am away from home, the days would be difficult if I do not have a book with me. Therefore, I am grateful to my attendant for always filling my suitcase with books, so that I am able to spend my hours on the plane without ever feeling bored or lonely.

Planning is also essential when it comes to reading. Young people can read as much literature as possible, including Chinese literature, foreign literature, and biographies. For example, I always paid detailed attention to every issue of *Biographical Literature* and the *Chinese and Foreign Journal* published in Taiwan. Once, I was talking to an eighty-year-old journalist about people from the early years of the Republic of China, as well as who was prominent during the Sino-Japanese War (1368-1644), and who was prominent during the Ming and Qing (1644-1911) dynasties. He was really quite impressed with the fact that I had no difficulty answering his questions, and this was because I have read extensively. I consider the biographies of famous people a kind of literature, for they contain historical evidence, as well as records of generous people and their actions. These books are valuable reading and are well worth our careful reflection.

In addition, I read almost all of the *Classics of Chinese Literature*, including *Record of the*

 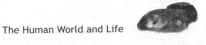

*Journey West*, the *Romance of the Western Chamber*, and the *Water Margin*. However, reading literature is not enough for students as it only adds to the beauty and conception of language. Therefore, for those between the ages of twenty and thirty, history is also an essential reading in addition to literature. For example, I have read all kinds of books on history, including the *Twenty-four Dynastic Histories*. Even though I had limited understanding of history back then, as I recall what I read in these books, I can now slowly gain a clear picture of the complex characters and relationships in history. It becomes all the more wonderful after putting these facts together in order.

From the age of forty to fifty, one should advance from reading history books to works of philosophy. Fundamentally, literature is like a beautiful coat and history is general knowledge, whereas philosophy is the actual essence. This beautiful coat of literature needs to be enriched by the essence of history and philosophy, and even then, it is not sufficient. By the age of fifty and sixty, one must read religious books. When I was young, I could never understand the Buddhist texts that I was reading, nor could I understand what the teachers were trying to teach. However, now I can simply flip through all kinds of books and understand the contents completely without having to read or listen to anyone.

It has been said that "reading is like constructing a pyramid: it must be broad and high." Reading is much more important than eating: while three meals of a day can nurture our physical body, constant reading broadens our wisdom. Reading is similar to running a shop; it needs continuous restocking, or else how can you keep up with your sales? Reading can also be categorized into thorough reading and speed-reading. Some books require detailed concentration, while others can be browsed through briefly. However, the most important of all is extensive reading. I remember asking a monastic the following question over forty years ago, "How do I read the Buddhist Canon?"

He answered, "Read randomly." At that time, I did not quite understand what he meant, but eventually I realized that the so-called "random reading" meant that you read what you can understand. The more books you read, the better you are in linking all your knowledge together and comprehending meaning. Therefore, I hope that all BLIA members can read extensively on literature, history, philosophy, and even the religious books, as well as the technology-related reading material.

If we wish to improve humanity's standard of living, we must encourage everyone to do more reading; read good books, beneficial books, and Buddhist related books. We can only improve our quality and character through reading. Therefore, I wish all BLIA members will not only collect books and keep books on your night stand and desk, but even better is for everyone to have a book in hand. Hopefully, every BLIA member becomes a reader who applies the concepts given in these books to all aspects of their life, creating a life filled with the "fragrance of books." By reading books in this way, we shall be able to improve our quality and character. Therefore, the "transformation of human life through the fragrance of books" is an encouragement for us to put more effort into reading from now on. So, I hope we can all "live with books," and that the world can become a "community filled with the fragrance of books."

## III. Transform the Monastic and Lay Communities with Equality

When I first established the BLIA, I wrote the following verse for its members:

*May palms be joined in every world in kindness, compassion, joy, and giving;*
*May all beings find security in friendship, peace and loving care;*
*May calm and mindful practice seed patience and equanimity deep;*
*May we give rise to spacious hearts and humble thoughts of gratitude.*

The word "equality" here means every aspect of the Dharma. Buddhism advocates equality between the Buddha and sentient beings, between phenomena and principle, between self and others, and between emptiness and existence. The Dharma itself is a rule of equality, and without equality, the Dharma cannot exist. The Dharma represents the teachings about equality, for without equality, there would be no Buddhist teachings. Thus, anything that goes against respect and equality is not of the Buddhist way.

Within the Buddhist community, male and female monastics are treated equally, and monastic and lay disciples are also equal. The Dharma exists where there is equality, respect, and tolerance between people. The Buddha proposed that all sentient beings are equal. Now we advocate "equality among the four groups of the Buddhist followers," "equality between monastic and lay disciples," and "equality between men and women." Those who propose any sort of gender chauvinism have no place in

Buddhism.

"Equality among all sentient beings" is the truth of the Dharma, and it is something that we cannot contravene. Unfortunately, many Buddhist leaders are still reluctant to hand over their authority after holding it for many years. For example, the Director of the Buddhist Association of the Republic of China held his term for many years until his death. Moreover, only male monastics were permitted to occupy the director's chair, therefore, female monastics and lay Buddhists never have the opportunity. This is because male monastics took up the majority of seats in the Buddhist Association of the Republic of China, and once their policies were passed by the majority, they became the rules. Such outmoded, selfish, unfair, and unequal regulations would never be able to exist in the present and future times. Buddhism must modernize, a process that should begin with the modernization of our ideas and regulations. In fact, since every Buddhist sutra and doctrine advocates that all sentient beings are equal, and everyone can be Buddha, why are we misinterpreting the Dharma?

A lay Buddhist who has learned Buddhism for decades, may have enough knowledge, moral stature, and understanding of the Dharma to make him a teacher. However, he will never dare regard himself as a "teacher," preferring to always call himself a "disciple" of the Triple Gem. In order to promote equality between monastic and lay disciples, the BLIA's bylaws state that lay Buddhists can become lay Dharma lecturers and teachers. The only way for Buddhism to spread widely is to give lay Buddhists equal opportunity to take part in propagating the Dharma. Think about it: there are only a few thousand monastics across Taiwan; with such limited resources, and even if we allocated one monastic to each village or town, it would still not be enough. Whereas if we encourage all lay Buddhists in Taiwan or even the billions of lay Buddhists around the world to be teachers and propagate the Dharma around the globe, then it would be possible to achieve the globalization of

Buddhism.

Many years ago, I composed "The Voices of Buddhist Youths Raised in Song:"

*Listen! The truth is calling, shining with glory,*
*The Buddha's children are rejoicing in his light,*
*Their voices resounding through the clouds;*
*The enthusiasm of his children stirs up the renewal of Buddhism,*
*Like a mighty wave that comes sweeping forward!*
*The day of fulfillment is drawing near!*

Even now, I am still deeply touched by this song. As long as we set our hearts on our goal, broaden our vision by looking far into the future, and be tolerant by showing respect and equality towards all sentient beings, that one day will be possible. This closely follows what I have mentioned in my article "On the True Meaning of Buddhist Democracy, Freedom, and Equality" in the third issue of *Universal Gate Buddhist Journal*: "By taking refuge in the Triple

Gem, we are reaching for the Buddha nature shared in common by ordinary persons and the Buddha—this is the spirit of democracy. By taking the Five Precepts, we learn to respect others and refrain from violating their rights— this is the meaning of freedom. To advocate the right to life for all sentient beings is to recognize that all buddhas and sentient beings are the same, for all beings are capable of becoming buddhas—this is the declaration of quality."

The principle of Buddhism is to respect the right of every living being to make their own decisions and the right to life. Therefore, we must relinquish the rigid rules and restrictions that have been placed on lay Buddhists or female monastics for centuries. Not only do such thoughts contradict the Buddhist doctrine, but they are also no longer compatible with the modern trends of democracy and freedom. As the saying goes, "When all the rivers flow into the ocean, they will only have one taste, the taste of saltiness; when members of the four castes join the monastic order, they all become part of the Buddha's family." The water from rivers, streams, and lakes become the same once they all flow into the ocean. Therefore, equality is the key to a peaceful world that we all expect will appear in the future.

"Life education" is a popular subject in today's society. The term "life" here relates to how all forms have a "life," such as a flower, a blade of grass, a grain of sand, a piece of stone, an article of clothing, a table, or a chair. An article of clothing is expected to last for three to five years, but may be ruined in only two to three months if not well cared for, and so its "life" is brought to an end. Not only do human beings and animals have life, plants such as trees, flowers, grass, and even mountains and rivers also have a life of their own. Time itself is life, for life is an accumulation of a series of moments. Therefore, wasting time is no different from killing life, and the same goes to wasting any sort of material goods. In a broader sense, wasting time or material goods can be considered killing. As we live in an era of environmental protection and ecological preservation, only by respecting life and treating every living being equally will we be truly qualified to live in this modern world, while those who neglect the dignity of life do not have the qualifications for being a modern human being.

"Equality and peace" are two sides of the same coin. Today's world is still chaotic simply because inequality still exists. So we experience the strong taking advantage of the weak in politics, the uneven distribution of wealth in economics, religious and racial conflicts, and gender and geographical prejudice. All of these problems that cannot be resolved peacefully are the direct result of the inability of people to coexist with equality. We hope that the world will progress towards a peaceful and harmonious future, and that every nation and race in the world will be treated as equals. Different religions should also see one another as brothers and sisters. The BLIA, in particular, consists of both monastic and lay members.

Anyone who joins this association is like a river or stream that merges into the sea and to become one, and so within the association, there are no considerations regarding who is superior and who is not. In order to actualize the Buddha's concept on equality amongst all living beings, not only are monastics propagating the Dharma, lay followers also have the opportunity to handle a temple's administrative work within the Fo Guang Shan Monastery and the BLIA. Fo Guang Shan and the BLIA are like the two arms of a human being or two wings of a bird; both are of equal importance. Every member of the BLIA must understand the meaning of oneness and coexistence to live peacefully with one another. In this way, we can practice true equality and create a world of equality together.

Thus, members of the BLIA must not hold any kind of discrimination against anything or anyone. Every Fo Guang Shan temple belongs to both its monastic and lay disciples, in which the monastics handle the affairs of Dharma propagation, and the lay disciples assist in the temple's administrative work. Furthermore, while the monastics have responsibility for Dharma propagation, BLIA's lay Dharma lecturers also enjoy opportunities to go on stage and give a Dharma talk. We hope that every BLIA member, whether monastic or lay member, will be able to "transform the monastic and lay communities with equality," so that we can achieve the equality between phenomena and principle, and the equality between being and emptiness, enabling the Dharma to spread far and wide; shining its light everywhere.

## IV. Transform Religious Centers through Localization

In the past, Chinese people always emphasized the spreading of Chinese culture no matter where in the world they resided. Such belief and behavior must be corrected, because every continent in this world enjoys a unique culture of its own. For example, there is the Asian culture in Asia, European culture in Europe, American culture in America, Australian culture in Australia, and African culture in Africa. For this reason, we must respect the local culture, while employing Chinese culture in a sympathetic exchange with the local one, rather than trying to use one's own culture to overwhelm another. I once gave a lecture at Cornell University in the United States. After the lecture, Professor John MacRae said to me, "You are welcome to teach the Dharma here in America. But it seems that you have repeatedly tried to impose your Chinese culture upon ours." When I heard what he said, it became apparent to me that I had been insensitive to the local culture; and I was reminded that the purpose of my visit is to contribute and serve, just as Buddhist practitioners make offerings of flower to the bodhisattvas.

From this example, we can see that although USA or any other country around the world, for that matter, is absorbing other cultures, but they are in reality afraid of being conquered by others. Therefore, the BLIA or as well as a future Buddhism, must promote localization from now on, because Buddhism is not a tool to overwhelm the cultures of other countries. Its goal is to promote unity, coexistence, cooperation, mutual survival, and coprosperity. The BLIA is an organization advancing the principle of Humanistic Buddhism, and wherever we are in this world, we have the duty to develop a localized form of Buddhism in accordance with characteristics of that area.

Localization can be defined as the process of allowing Buddhism to find its roots in the local culture, developing its unique characteristic according to the cultural ideas, geographical environment, as well as customs and habits. This process is the same as when Buddhism was first transmitted from India into China, Indian monks traveled to China for the sole purpose of translating the Buddhist sutras into the Chinese language, while the responsibility of building monasteries and temples rested with the Chinese monastics. That is why Buddhism flourished within Chinese culture. On the other hand, if these Indian monastics like Kasyapamatanga and Dharmaraksa had decided to reside permanently in China and participated in temple construction and Dharma propagation, Buddhism in China would have retained a lot more of its Indian character. The First Patriarch of the Chan School, Master Bodhidharma, appointed his disciple Master Hui Ke as the Second Patriarch, a native Chinese disciple. Master Bodhidharma did so because he wanted to ensure local adaptation. Similarly many years ago, I transferred the abbotship of Fo Guang Shan to Venerable Hsin Ping, because he was a native born Taiwanese. This too is an example of my objective of localization.

Localization definitely represents the future development of Buddhism. Only such a movement will enable Buddhism to expand wider and develop more deeply. I put forward "the transformation of religious centers through local adaptation," mainly because I wanted to enhance the development of Buddhism. It would be such a wonderful situation if Fo Guang Shan's overseas branch temples would have locals serving as abbots or abbesses now, such as an American monastic for Hsi Lai Temple, an Australian monastic for Nan Tien and Chung Tian Temple, and an African monastic for Nan Hua Temple. It is my sincerest wish, in the coming twenty to fifty years, to be able to assist and guide the native monastics to become responsible for the management and administration of these overseas establishments, for this would surely speed up the spread of Buddhism.

Currently, Fo Guang Shan's sixteen Buddhist colleges in South Africa, Australia, India, Malaysia, Hong Kong, Brazil, and other countries are responsible for educating the local youth, as well as preparing personnel to carry out the local adaptation process. Even the Buddhist College at Fo Guang Shan, Taiwan, has students from around the world. It is hoped that in the future, this diversity can be expanded, so that these students will all return to their homeland as BLIA members to establish temples and spread Buddhism, thereby, ensuring that the true lineage of the Dharma will flow throughout all three thousand realms.

Here are the four main points discussed above:

1. Transform the Dharma using humanistic qualities.

2. Transform human life through the fragrance of books.

3. Transform the monastic and lay communities with equality.

4. Transform religious centers through localization.

I hope that in the future, all BLIA members will share a common vision and apply it not only in their lives, but use it as the direction and goal for the joint effort of propagating Humanistic Buddhism.

# To Resolve and To Develop

*May palms be joined in every world in kindness, compassion, joy, and giving;*

*May all beings find security in friendship, peace, and loving care;*

*May calm and mindful practice seed patience and equanimity deep;*

*May we give rise to spacious hearts and humble thoughts of gratitude.*

BLIA 9th General Conference
Tokyo, Japan
April 27-30, 2002
Edited by Robert H. Smitheram, Ph.D.

The United Nations declared 1965 to be the "Year of Development," and clearly, world "development" is a responsibility that should be equally shared by all in this world. We are now in the twenty-first century, a period when technology and communication is advancing at a rapid pace and everyone is concerned with the tasks of developing the world economy. However, the main task for Buddhists in this new millennium will involve the discovery and development of our inherent Buddha nature. The Buddha's Light International Association (BLIA) is a Buddhist organization, and so we must nurture "internal" as well as "external" development. "Internal" development is the active disclosure of our inner nature and mind, whereas "external" development refers to the beneficial advancement of our world.

Take for example the National Aeronautics and Space Administration (NASA) in the United States, which has for a long time been actively involved in the exploration of outer space. Its achievements include lunar landings and the discovery of life-supporting moisture on

Mars, as well as the basic compounds of life in the atmosphere of Jupiter. The Russian Mir Space Station splashed down into the South Pacific Ocean after serving as a space research platform for more than ten years. We have energy experts exploring the deep seas for oil and other resources. Similarly, there are many corporations involved in developing the infrastructure of cities as well as sea and mountain reclamation. Other notable engineering achievements include as well the new airports in Hong Kong, Singapore, and Bangkok.

Beyond this, many educational systems are actively encouraging the development of "gifted" students. We also have literary scholars who are writing exquisite verses and poetry, as well as philosophers who publish their thoughts on the future, including those who actively advocate compassion. All of this is a part of our ongoing effort to help develop and improve the cultural and spiritual existence of humanity. BLIA Members should constantly act in accordance with other members of society to develop themselves. We should have a socially conscious mind, and always be aware of the opportunities to enlighten ourselves as well as others. The "Four Verses of the BLIA" summarize the hopes and aims of all BLIA members:

*May palms be joined in every world in kindness, compassion, joy, and giving;*
*May all beings find security in friendship, peace, and loving care;*
*May calm and mindful practice seed patience and equanimity deep;*
*May we give rise to spacious hearts and humble thoughts of gratitude.*

Through the understanding of these verses, we hope that our members can constantly develop their compassion, generosity, blessings, human relationships, humility, and gratitude. We must rediscover our self-nature, with the ultimate goal being to benefit and liberate both ourselves and others.

Over the many years since the founding of

the BLIA, we have steadfastly been advocating the mutual development of our body and mind, as well as acting in accordance to facts and logic. We should aim not only for financial prosperity in the family, but also for harmonious relationships with others. Our objectives in life should not be restricted to advancement and prosperity, but we should also work towards general welfare of society as a whole. With this theme of "To Resolve and To Develop," it is our hope that in the future, each of us can make the following four resolutions:

1. Resolve to be kind and compassionate, and treat friend and foe alike.

2. Resolve to strengthen our minds by practicing both concentration and wisdom.

3. Resolve to develop the oneness of equality and coexistence.

4. Resolve to achieve the enlightened mind of perfect freedom.

These four resolutions should also be complemented by the following four developments:

1. To develop truth, goodness, and beauty in human nature.

2. To develop the wealth of blessings, wisdom, and virtue in this world.

3. To develop harmony, joy, love, and respect in human relationships.

4. To develop the future oneness between self and the Buddha.

"To resolve" means to build a new sense of self; and "to develop" means to build a new sense of the world. In order to help ourselves, we must enact these resolutions, and in order to help the world, we must fulfill these developments.

## I. To Resolve

Among the many paths in Buddhism, our "resolve" is the singularly most important path, for "to resolve" is the beginning of the cultivation of our minds. Buddhism views the mind as an open field waiting for seeds to be sowed. It emphasizes the importance of a proper cultivation that is required to nurture our path to enlightenment. Therefore, we should resolve to practice the "Four Immeasurable States of

Mind," "Four Universal Vows," "Four Means of Embracing," and "Four Disciplinary Processes," so that we and others can be liberated. Master Shengan once said, "Resolve is the first important step in Buddhism and the ability to maintain this resolve will eventually lead to enlightenment." We as members of the BLIA should undertake these four resolutions:

## 1. Resolve to be Kind and Compassionate, and Treat Friend and Foe Alike

"Kindness leads to joy while compassion leads to the end of suffering." The greatest flaws in our world lie in our discrimination between love and hate, and between intimacy and resentment. However the differences between love and hate, as well as intimacy and resentment are a subjective determination. For example, an open sore will be regarded differently depending on where it is found. If a sore is found on your own body, you would carefully cleanse, treat, and nurse it. Similarly, if our treatment of someone we dislike can be based on love rather than hate, and be based as well upon the recognition of oneness among all beings, it will not be difficult to achieve universal harmony. If we truly believe in "unconditional kindness and universal compassion," it will be easy to accept that all beings are precious and related to one another.

Buddhism encourages us to replace enmity with kindness, and stop conflict with patience. Christianity tells us to "love thy enemy," whereas Confucianism teaches "universal care of the people and the love of benevolence." The Buddha set an example of how it is possible to create conditions for spiritual advancement by showing kindness and compassion to his rival, Devadatta. Unquestionably, kindness and compassion are fundamental to all the teachings of Buddhism, as stated in the *Sutra on Monastics*: "Dharma becomes heresy when it is practiced without kindness and compassion." According to *the Sutra on the Eight Realizations of Great Beings*, "Life and death are like flickering flames, and suffering is endless. Take the Mahayana Vow to offer aid to all things. Vow to take on the illimitable suffering of sentient beings, and lead them all to ultimate bliss." Since the beginning of time, bodhisattvas have resolved to toil and work for the benefit of all living beings, because they recognize the causal link between living beings and enlightenment. Therefore, it stands to reason that kindness and compassion are a direct route to enlightenment.

It is pointless to merely talk about kindness and compassion without actually putting them into practice. In fact, Buddhist sutras contain many examples of how kindness and compassion were practiced. The more notable examples are the vows that were made by various bodhisattvas and patriarchs, including those of Ksitigarbha Bodhisattva, who resolved to liberate all beings from hell before attaining Buddhahood. These saints all resolved to use kindness and compassion to bring liberation to the world.

Kindness and compassion are the purest and highest forms of love. If we can be more considerate and prepared to exchange places with others, kindness and compassion will become a part of one's nature. In this way, we will be able to eradicate greed and craving, hatred and bitterness, pride and arrogance, and fear and apprehension. It was once said, "Personal kindness and compassion bring forth companionship, and communal kindness and compassion result in social unity." In other words, the practice of kindness and compassion by one person will enhance his or her relationship with others. Better still, if kindness and compassion are practiced in society, then we will be rewarded with an environment of harmony and joy.

In his time, the Buddha had brought peace and happiness to all beings through his kindness and compassion. We hope that members of the BLIA can follow his example by taking the first step of treating others as oneself. The *Lotus Sutra* teaches us to regard all beings as part of our own family, irrespective of whether they are our closest intimates or our most implacable enemies. We must show others our love, and ultimately, through our compassion, take all humanity along the great path of light and blessings.

## 2. Resolve to Strengthen our Minds by Practicing both Concentration and Wisdom

To "strengthen" means to improve and to progress. The *Path to Buddhahood* states, "Through the improvement of our livelihood, we can enjoy both material and spiritual joy." In other words, we should not reject and deny the pursuit of personal necessities, affection, and wealth through proper means. However, these are only superficial goals and should be supplemented simultaneously by practicing both concentration and wisdom. We must constantly strive to elevate ourselves through the meditative practices of insight and contemplation, thus complying with one of the guidelines of the BLIA: "We live in the peace and joy of the Dharma. We rid ourselves of suffering and ignorance."

Speaking of "practicing both concentration and wisdom," the *Platform Sutra of the Sixth Patriarch* states, "concentration and wisdom are one and the same." Concentration is our mind's ability to remain composed and undisturbed by external circumstances. Wisdom is the ability to think and act according to the Dharma. A follower once responded to his master's question by suggesting that to solve a problem, one must act with concentration and inspire with wisdom. To be without either concentration or wisdom constitutes a departure from the spiritual path. The *Nirvana Sutra* states, "Too much concentration with little wisdom increases ignorance, while too much wisdom and little concentration leads to erroneous views." The Sixth Patriarch Hui Neng taught: "To constantly maintain a lucid and pure mind will generate wisdom from concentration, and to remain unmoved by external phenomena will generate concentration from wisdom. Since neither concentration nor wisdom is a source of illusory thinking, then the practice of both will lead one to experience our own self-nature." There is no demarcation separating concentration and wisdom. To talk of one is directly related to the other, just like the ocean and the waves, light and a lamp, the two wings of a bird, and the two arms of a human being. There is nothing that is not achievable if we make good use of our concentration and wisdom.

As BLIA members we must therefore resolve to improve our minds by practicing both concentration and wisdom. Buddhism has outlined a number of ways in which we can progressively improve our minds. We can progressively improve ourselves through the ranks of the "Five Mahayana Vehicles" of human beings, deva-gods, sravakas ("voice-hearers"), pratyekabuddhas ("solitary realizers"), and bodhisattvas. Similarly, one can progress along the four levels of Arhatship: the level of entering the stream of Nirvana, the level of one more rebirth, the level of no more rebirth, and the level of full arhatship, and the Fifty-one Stages of the Bodhisattva Development: from the Ten Faiths to the Ten Activities, the Ten Abidances, the Ten Dedications, the Ten Stages, and the awaiting for enlightenment, and onto the final attainment of universal enlightenment. Therefore, do not expect our own enlightenment to come all of a sudden; it will most probably be achieved through a gradual progression.

Today's Buddhist communities are composed mainly of practitioners and their families whose relationships are founded on mutual respect and affection. It would be unreasonable to expect our practitioners to exclude and reject the normal pursuit of jobs, reputation, and the general enjoyment of their lives just because they are Buddhists. This is why the BLIA has always emphasized that the monastic community must cultivate "the mind of renunciation," while the members of the laity need only develop "the mind to progress." However, one can strengthen one's resolve by learning more about detachment, and by enhancing our aspiration for enlightenment through concentration and wisdom. Through a combination of kindness and compassion, we will be able to experience perfect fulfillment and understanding of the Truth.

## 3. Resolve to Develop the Oneness of Equality and Coexistence

Most troubles in the world arise out of making distinctions, whether these are between male and female, rich and poor, knowledgeable and ignorant, and native and foreign. As long as we go on making distinctions, there will be contradiction and dispute. How can true harmony exist in this world if we are constantly faced with dispute and conflict? World peace and happiness can be achieved only through the eradication of the distinction between self and other, and the development of "the oneness of equality and coexistence."

The Dharma proclaims the importance "oneness and equality" and the "identification of self with other." It restrains us from killing as this poem relates:

*My flesh is the flesh of sentient beings;*
*Though the names differ, the essence does not.*
*We all belong to the same family;*
*We merely vary in bodily form.*

In truth, all living beings are no different from the Buddha, possessing the excellent quality of his wisdom. It is only through our making of distinctions that we create all the sufferings in this world.

Our human race may have evolved into different colors, shapes, and sizes. However, irrespective of skin color and the like, essentially we all have similar goals in life. These goals generally include personal safety, harmony, happiness, and a comfortable and easy life. Therefore, we should never base our own needs and happiness on the loss and suffering of others. Likewise, we should not show off our achievements by emphasizing the failures of others. Confucius once said, "Do not do unto others what you would not want done to you." Buddhism always advocates the sharing of Dharma joy with everyone in the world. We must look upon all living beings as our companions, as part of our body and mind, and as an integral part of our lives. It is true that living things may come into existence in many different ways and are of varying forms and appearances. Some may have conscious thoughts while others may appear to possess little or no intelligence. However, each of these living beings does have a consciousness that is no different from our own. Our own self-nature is closely linked even with mountains and streams, trees and flowers, because we will eventually attain Buddhahood. The ultimate truth is that all living beings possess a self-nature that is the same for all.

How humans feel about each other often depends on how closely we are related to each other. Take a look around us and we can find that we are often associated with people of the same country, same political party, same office, same school, same hometown, same surname, and same family. We will invariably find that the relationships between husband and wife, father and son, and brother and sister, are often accompanied by great emotional attachments. In order to establish that sense of oneness in this world, we must recognize that each person is somehow related to and dependent on each other. For example, we will starve unless farmers do the planting and harvesting, and we will get cold if no one works in the mills and clothing factories. Without the contributions and hard work of everyone in the community, our lives will be more difficult and full of hardships. Nowadays, it is inconceivable to think how we could possibly exist without considering the contributions made by each and every person in society. If we can establish a sense of identity between self and all living beings under the principle of oneness and coexistence, we need not worry about a world without true peace.

## 4. Resolve to Achieve the Enlightened Mind of Perfect Freedom

The bodhicitta signifies the determination for self-sacrifice so that all beings may be liberated. This is the vow of a bodhisattva who has resolved to achieve full and complete enlightenment for the benefit of all living beings. In the Mahayana tradition, those following the bodhisattva path will practice in accordance with the precepts for the avoidance of evil, as well as diligently apply the Dharma for the assistance to all beings. Clearly, these practitioners are more than just trying to avoid committing bad karma. In fact, they are acting positively to learn as much as they can about the Buddha's teachings so that they will be well-prepared to enlighten others.

In the *Sutra on the Good Precepts of the Bodhisattvas*, it is said that "the two ways to violate the bodhisattva precepts are (i) the loss of the resolve to achieve enlightenment, and (ii) the accumulation of deluded thoughts." It must be understood that a bodhisattva has vowed to enlighten all beings, and if he loses his resolve to practice accordingly, he is no longer a bodhisattva. There are many examples of past sages and patriarchs who showed how to cultivate the practice. For example, according to the *Jataka Sutra* which records the lives of the Buddha before his enlightenment, he sacrificed his life by giving himself up to a tiger and cut his own flesh to feed an eagle. This was his way of accomplishing his great vow concerning the perfection of generosity. Similarly, in one of his other lives, the Buddha willingly allowed King Kaliraja to cut his body without feeling resentment or hatred, thus accomplishing his great vow on the perfection of patience. There are many examples of the Buddha's disciples and monastics who sacrificed themselves for the benefit of others and for the propagation of the Dharma. Maudgalyayana sacrificed his life for Buddhism; Purna put his life at risk by vowing to teach Buddhism to barbarous people; and, in order to print the Buddhist Tripitaka and the Twelve Canons, the Bhiksuni Fazhen severed one of her arms to raise funds. It is hard to imagine that these great vows can be accomplished without the strength to generate the great aspiration for enlightenment. It is also through these sacrifices made by these saints and sages that we are able to benefit from the teachings of the Buddha today.

It should be strongly emphasized that the resolve to achieve enlightenment should be regarded as a long-term aspiration. Once such a vow has been made, we should apply ourselves diligently in every aspect of our lives, no matter how insignificant. A person aspiring to achieve enlightenment should not abandon even a single living being or disregard the smallest virtuous deed. The aspiration to achieve enlightenment requires us to follow the Buddha path and consider the truth as our companion.

The objectives of the BLIA are to introduce the Dharma to all beings, in particular the Dharma that brings forth happiness and joy. The aim is to encourage continued improvement of our characters so that we may be emancipated from our troubles and sufferings, and also to better our quality of life by releasing us from our ego and material desires. As a result, we will be able to appreciate the joy of fellowship with all other beings.

We all go through the different cycles of rebirth, and it is impossible to control our past and future lives. However, we must all at least try to master our present one. Life is meaningless for an unhappy person, even if he or she possesses good looks, vast knowledge, wealth, and power. That is why Buddhism advocates joy in meditation and happiness in learning the Dharma. We are not truly reaping the benefits of Buddhism if we are not conscious of the delight experienced during this learning process. For without "Dharma joy," we will be adversely affected by the abuse and criticism of others, or distracted by discomfort and hardship when we are reciting the sutras, chanting, or assisting others. Therefore, we can always find joy when giving and practicing the Dharma. On the other hand, if we do not feel at ease or happy in our practice, we may not have the correct resolve for enlightenment. We cannot achieve perfection in our practice if we are unable to feel completely at ease. I hope that BLIA members can follow the example shown by Avalokitesvara Bodhisattva, to be completely at ease wherever he may be. Perfect enlightenment is achievable if we can liberate ourselves through learning and practicing, and while helping others to be aware of the Dharma.

## II. To Develop

Since its founding in Taiwan on the February 1, 1991, and the subsequent inauguration of the World Headquarters in the

United States on May 16 of the following year, the BLIA has constantly developed its objectives and goals. The BLIA's development plan is progressive. It starts off from the personal level that encourages goodness, so that its members can develop and improve by themselves. This is to be followed by the creation of BLIA families, society, and finally a Buddha's Light Pure Land. In order to achieve our final goal of a Buddha's Light Pure Land, it is necessary to promote the training of lay Dharma teachers and lecturers. It is also necessary to broaden the international perspective of our members, so that we are more aware of the importance of efficient development of the world's resources, as well as expanding our own spiritual abilities. I hope that everyone will endeavor to practice in the following four areas:

## 1. To Develop Truth, Goodness, and Beauty in Human Nature

Since its founding, the BLIA has repeatedly emphasized the importance of culture, education, charity, regular chanting services, and particularly the instruction regarding the proper education for practitioners. In different parts of the world, the BLIA has organized various study groups, short-term monastic retreats, seminars, children's camps, youth training classes, orchestras, as well as the BLIA Young Adults Divisions and Adulthood Ceremonies.

The purpose of these cultural, educational, and social service activities is to provide our members with the necessary training to develop a truthful, good, and beautiful character. In this world today, we often find that families lack intimate feelings. Likewise in today's society, one rarely finds the desire to perform kind deeds for others, which results in a failure in communication. What is there to look forward to in this world, when it is full of greed, jealousy, violence, and indecency? We humans have failed to discover the goodness that is inherent to our true nature, and are reluctant to share with others all that is honorable and good.

It is most important that we establish and develop an environment of truth, kindness, and beauty in this world. A Buddhist sutra states, "Universal goodness is like parental love. Beautiful goodness will bring forth physical well-being, mental peace, improved diligence, and better human relationships. They will also eradicate negativity, afflictions, and human faults. That is why we should practice universal goodness." No matter where we are, we should all try to set truth, goodness, and beauty as our ultimate goals. This is achievable if the actions of our body, speech, and mind are carried out in accordance with the Buddha's teachings from this day forward:

a) To be truthful and factual in our speech without being ambiguous or flattering (as is stated in the *Diamond Sutra*).

b) To act with goodness, virtue, benevolence, and kindness for the benefit of all humanity (as is stated in the *Agamas*).

c) To think with wisdom, righteousness, compassion, and great vows to bless all beings.

To speak, act, and think correctly constituted the "Three Good Practices," recognized by the BLIA as the path to acquire truth, goodness, and beauty in our character. However, the result will be significantly magnified if governments and all those concerned with the enhancement of human nature are prepared to adopt this same policy. One way to achieve this is to publicly reward and encourage those who are prepared to practice truth, goodness, and beauty. In this world, we should be able to hear good words being said, to feel the sincerity in people's actions, and to perceive the good intentions in everyone's thoughts. We hope that all BLIA members will lead in this endeavor, by learning how to promote the development of a harmonious world so that we can lead a true, good, and beautiful life.

## 2. To Develop the Wealth of Blessings, Wisdom, and Virtue in this World

In this world, everyone would like to develop his or her own career and fortune. But most of all, we hope that everyone is able to see the importance of developing their spiritual assets in blessings, wisdom, and virtue. There are different kinds of wealth: in the narrow sense, wealth refers to money, buildings, land and stock; but when considered in a broad sense, it refers to health, intelligence, relationships, credibility, and morality. Wealth can also be defined as "priced wealth," such as prestige, reputation, and social and historical achievement; or "priceless wealth," such as integrity, conscience, loyalty, and innate character. Wealth can be tangible or intangible; there is present wealth and future wealth; and there is also personal wealth, communal wealth, material wealth, spiritual wealth, temporary wealth, and permanent wealth.

If we can build our wealth upon a foundation of blessings and wisdom, we will be able to enjoy a most satisfactory life, for blessings and wisdom are the ultimate wealth that any person can possess. A perfect example is personified in the image of the Buddha. Therefore, we call upon everyone to develop a kind of "noble wealth." Examples of noble wealth include: the wealth of *prajña*-wisdom and meditative concentration; the wealth of Dharma joy; and the wealth of humility, gratitude, kindness, and compassion. In other words, they are pure wealth, good wealth, and Dharma wealth.

The Buddhist sutras state: "Worldly treasures have their limitations, whereas Dharma treasures are boundless in their usage. Through virtuous practices we shall inherit these timeless Dharma treasures." True wealth is not represented by your bank account balance or your holdings in buildings, land, gold, and stocks, for all of these can be taken away by others. We should recognize that the only wealth that we can truly claim as our own is our faith, contentment, joy, humility, safety, health, and wisdom. Not only do we enjoy the benefits of these types of wealth in this lifetime; we can also share these types of wealth with others in our future lives.

Clearly, we must place equal importance on the creation and maintenance of personal as well as communal wealth. As a result we will be able to enjoy our personal as well as communal forms of wealth such as sunshine, pure air, and clear water. Through this understanding we will be able to appreciate that the mountains and rivers, parks and roads constitute some of the vast wealth that we have inherited from society and this universe. How then can we consider ourselves as poor and impoverished? Contrary to the general belief that the purpose of life in this world is to suffer and struggle, we are here to enjoy peace and serenity brought about by our blessings and wisdom. However, these benefits are possible only if we apply ourselves to our own development.

## 3. To Develop Harmony, Joy, Love, and Respect in Human Relationships

The world is not the possession of any single individual, for our world is a place where many people live and work together. There are billions of human beings in this world, and the only hope for so many people to coexist harmoniously is by nurturing benevolent relationships and satisfying the needs of one another. That is why we have developed sophisticated infrastructures in cosmopolitan cities, established international banking systems, instituted marital arrangements, and provided communal facilities to satisfy our daily needs for clothing, food, accommodation and transportation. However, these developments have also resulted in the creation of dance halls, gambling dens, and drinking clubs and the formation of gang rivalries, which encourage the pursuit of sensory excitement and pollute our spiritual nature. These distorted developments of our society have created much conflict and strife, which in turn has actually emphasized the need for mutual respect and harmony among all beings. It appears that there is a need to reassess the value of respect, love, and harmony in human relationships.

In the past, major religions and philosophers advocated universal love, benevolence, and morality, the ultimate goal being to establish some form of a proper balance in human relationships regarding harmony, love, and respect. Given all these considerations, however, it appears that this relationship is best achieved through the application of Buddhism, for Buddhism emphasizes the practice of our minds which is the origin of everything that is good and virtuous.

Generally, when we talk about developing the world's resources, we are only referring to material development. Being able to transcend spiritual obstacles requires the development of our inner treasures. In order to purify our minds, the BLIA has been developing a series of activities centered on the "Reclamation of Our Minds" campaign. To encourage harmony within society, the BLIA has promoted in the past the "Seven Admonitions Campaign," while another entitled the "Love and Compassion Campaign" endeavored to rediscover the dignity of human nature. Similarly, the purpose of the "Three Good Practices Campaign" was to ensure appropriate interaction between individual members of the community.

General Conferences of the BLIA have focused on such topical themes as "Joy and Harmony," "Oneness and Coexistence," "Respect and Tolerance," "Equality and Peace," "Wholeness and Freeness," "Nature and Life" and "One Truth for All;" their purpose being the promotion of a harmonious and respectful society. Similarly, we have stressed the need to "maintain respect among our members, and always be prepared to welcome their arrivals and see them off on their departures." We have also emphasized the importance of "daily practices and being respectful at all times." All of which are essential for the enhancement of human relationships.

It is also our wish that our members learn from the Buddha's spirit in how he "demonstrated the teachings, and the benefits and joy of their meaning and practice," so that they may explore and develop their inner potentials. We must learn from the respectful attitude practiced by Sadaparibhuta ("never disparaging") Bodhisattva, who stated that "I dare not have contempt for you, as you will all succeed in becoming Buddhas!" We have to fulfill the great vow taken by Samantabhadra Bodhisattva to rejoice when any being performed a meritorious deed. We must follow the spirit of perseverance exemplified by past saints and sages, who prepared to sacrifice their lives for the Dharma. I hope that all BLIA members can follow and accomplish this noble objective.

## 4. To Develop the Future Oneness between Self and the Buddha

The world is progressing at an ever-increasing pace, and we are all following its future progress with great anticipation. "Futurology" is quite the popular topic nowadays, for everyone is concerned about the future and what it may bring. Young people today are aware of the need for career planning and senior citizens are also actively planning their financial futures. Similarly, no government could do without their five-year or ten-year strategic plans, while long term research is conducted on future world development. Clearly, future development has already become an important task of this age.

In the past, Buddhism always encouraged its followers to practice and prepare themselves for their next lives. In other words, these "next lives" are the future. We have scientists nowadays setting up plans to explore and occupy parts of the outer space. This has already led to people purchasing real estate on the moon, while others are even planning to immigrate to other planets. We humans are progressively expanding our ideas and thinking about the universe.

Since the beginning of time, ordinary humans have always tried to develop heaven as their place of eternal peace. In a similar manner, Buddhists are also actively preparing to ascend to Tusita Heaven to be with Maitreya Bodhisattva, or to the Eastern or Western Pure Lands so that they may live and practice with the Buddhas. With its many centuries of experience with the "future," and through the integration with science and other cultures, Buddhism is well prepared to deal with the development of the future. When Buddhists join their palms or prostrate, they are hoping to make a mind-to-mind connection with the bodhisattvas and buddhas. We should now expand this concept of mental connection by seeing ourselves standing side by side with the bodhisattvas, so that one day we can be joined as one.

Whenever we read about the Eastern and Western Pure Lands or the other Buddha realms, we are told of their harmonious existence. No longer are these merely stories recorded in Buddhist texts, they can as well formulate the ideal development for all of humanity. According to the *Treatise on the Buddha Nature*, "Prajña-wisdom is essential for the development of Buddhahood. Great compassion is a necessity for the enlightenment of all beings. With these two virtues we abide in the place of no abiding, from which there is no regression: enlightenment is quickly attained; the five errors are eliminated; and the five virtues are generated. This is why the Buddha said all beings possess Buddha nature."

"The self and the Buddha being one" is not a distant and unreachable dream. It is in fact an undeniable truth. Therefore, we hope that all members of the BLIA can make better use of their time in this world to offer their kindness, compassion, and wisdom, and to rediscover their own true Buddha nature. As long as we are prepared to embrace this truth, and as long as we are able to always be part of the Buddha fraternity, we indeed have attained the unification of self with the Buddha.

In conclusion, "to resolve and to develop" is the mission each one of us undertakes with respect to our families, societies, countries, the universe, and ourselves. From this day forward, we must not waste this excellent Buddhist expression of "making resolutions;" we must not let it become some empty talk of which old folks are prone to speak. We hope that everyone can truly:

1. Resolve to be kind and compassionate, and treat friend and foe alike.

2. Resolve to strengthen our minds by practicing both concentration and wisdom.

3. Resolve to develop the oneness of equality and coexistence.

4. Resolve to achieve the enlightened mind of perfect freedom.

At the same time we must ensure that "development" does not become the sole monopoly of materialist objectives, and so we hope that everyone will truly be able:

1. To develop truth, goodness, and beauty in human nature.

2. To develop the wealth of blessings, wisdom, and virtue in this world.

3. To develop harmony, joy, love, and respect in human relationships.

4. To develop the future oneness between self and the Buddha.

Everyone must be committed to making their resolutions, for there is no time to lose; and we must act now to develop our goals, so that they can be accomplished sooner.

# Self-awareness and Practicing the Buddha's Way

*To be successful in the Buddhist Practice, we must be able to place equal importance on the understanding and application of the Dharma. To practice without true understanding will lead you along a path of illusions.*

BLIA 10th General Conference
September 1-5, 2004
Kaohsiung, Taiwan
Edited by Robert H. Smitheram, Ph.D.

During the past decades, I have observed the rapid growth of Buddhism in Taiwan and in other parts of the world. Along with the number of practitioners increasing each year, people of diverse social backgrounds have actively participated in the propagation of Buddhism. We should applaud this continual trend, however, over the years, I am also aware that Buddhist practice seems to have stagnated over matters of Buddhist "faith," "worship" and "prayer." Many of our practitioners have failed to see the need to apply the teachings of Buddha to their lives, which appears to be the main cause for the decline of Buddhism in the past. For example, Buddhism teaches us to be compassionate, but how many Buddhists really practice compassion? Buddhism requires us to be generous, yet how many Buddhists are prepared to give joyously? Buddhism advocates *prajña*-wisdom, but how many Buddhists can be regarded as realized persons possessing true wisdom? If practitioners do not observe the Dharma, it is no wonder that the quality of cultivation in the Buddhist fraternity is deteriorating.

In order to advance the quality of Buddhist faith, I have advocated the practice of the "Buddha's Way," and designated 2004 as the "BLIA Year of Practicing the Buddha's Way." I hope that all of us can diligently apply Buddha's teachings to our daily lives. For example, the Buddha taught us to be compassionate, thus we must avoid hurting or killing living beings; the Buddha taught us to possess patience, thus we must refrain from being hateful or angry; and the Buddha taught us to establish good relationships with others, thus we must not be selfish or uncaring.

Only through the persistent adaptation of our lives to our faith and by leading our lives according to the Dharma, can we begin to become self-enlightened and self-aware of how the Buddha led his own life; and only then can we appreciate the true meaning of the Dharma and its benefits to humanity. The topic "Self-awareness and Practicing the Buddha's Way," includes four main topics that I hope you can adopt as goals for your future cultivation:

# I. Sublimation of the Self through Self-awareness

Since birth, we have gone through various stages of receiving instruction and education. Up to a certain age, our parents at home would give us the necessary instructions; and when we become older and go off to school, we are taught by our teachers. Finally, when we start working, we will receive further education through interaction in society. However, I consider that the most important form of education as one that is gained from maintaining a constant self-awareness. Self-awareness is essentially a form of self-education. According to the Buddhist sutras, we must rely on ourselves and the Dharma, but never depend on external influence. Similarly, we should teach ourselves to maintain alertness at all times, so that we can assimilate and derive global understanding of all events around us. This is what I mean by self-education.

One of the key methods in Buddhist

cultivation is based on the proper use of the self-aware mind. When the Buddha began his teachings, his intention was to lead us into a realm of awareness, so that we become awakened to the Buddha's insight and wisdom. Through this awareness, we can strive to become equals to the Buddha. Prince Siddhartha became the Buddha because he had realized the truth of life in the universe (self-awareness). With perfect compassion, he then proceeded to teach all beings about this truth, thus helping others to achieve enlightenment (enlighten others). Therefore, he is truly an enlightened person who possesses the quality of self-awareness, the ability to enlighten others, and complete enlightenment. The Buddha means "enlightened one," because he wanted us to follow his lead. He wanted us to understand that the way to Buddhahood is by awakening to the real purpose of our own existence. A person cannot achieve complete enlightenment unless he or she possesses self-awareness and the capability to enlighten others.

Education through self-awareness is

apparent in Western societies. Under their system, young students are taught to think, identify, and solve problems by themselves. The teachers are there to inspire and guide the students about carrying out research and completing assignments. The teachers would very often encourage their students to conduct their own lessons in class. Contrary to this, the Chinese teaching method continues to rely on an unhealthy, force-fed approach. The teachers would stand in front of a class and teach without allowing the students to speak or interact. The students are contained and restrained, thereby, eroding away their instinct for self-education.

By self-education, I mean the ability to be self-demanding, self-learning, self-enriching, and self-reflecting, without relying on the assistance of others. Successful self-education is dependent on the constant questioning, awareness, motivating, and understanding of the self. We can indeed discover our own self through self-contemplation. There are many ways to educate ourselves in Buddhism. These can be achieved through repentance, admission of wrongdoing, reflection, meditative thinking, and self-contemplation. Sometimes we can learn by listening, thinking, and taking action; while at other times, we can learn by consulting and seeking advice from others; sometimes we can learn through meditative thinking; while at other times, we can learn through spontaneous understanding. And sometimes there will be individuals who are unable to study and learn alone, but if you resolve to provide assistance, you will improve your own skills by teaching others as well.

Self-education is most effective if we rely on ourselves at all times. Let me tell you a story about the Chan School. A long time ago, Master Dao Qian and his good friend Master Zhong Yuan traveled together on foot on a study tour. They had journeyed a long distance and Master Zhong Yuan was finding the trip extremely difficult and tiring, so on many occasions, he complained and demanded to end the journey. Master Dao Qian comforted him and said, "We have decided to take this study tour. It is a shame to abandon our quest now since we have already covered so much ground. Will you continue if I promise to help you with whatever you ask of me? However, there are five tasks that I am unable to do for you." Master Zhong Yuan asked, "What are these five tasks?" Master Dao Qian replied quite naturally, "Putting on clothes, eating meals, urinating, defecating, and walking." In a way, Master Dao Qian was suggesting that each person has to solve their own basic needs, if one is to have any hope of accomplishing something.

We can achieve success only if we rely on our own self-knowledge, self-awareness, and self-enlightenment. There is always a limitation on how much assistance others can provide. Asking others to consume our meals cannot satisfy our hunger. We cannot reach our destination by asking others to walk on our behalf. We cannot transfer our suffering to others if we are sick; and when tired, others resting for us will not rejuvenate our waning strength. Therefore, we have to rely on our own cultivation and practice to achieve liberation and enlightenment. Master Zhao Zhou once said, "Even for such a simple task as going to the toilet, you have to do it on your own. Therefore how can you ask someone else to be responsible for your effort in attaining Buddhahood?" We cannot be successful unless we can establish our expectation and determine the direction of our own cultivation.

The importance of self-awareness can be demonstrated from an extract of the *Record of the Mirror of Orthodoxy*, "Only the person who drinks can tell whether the water is hot or cold. Without regaining their eyesight, the blind cannot truly appreciate the true form of an elephant." More than two and a half thousand years ago, the Buddha attained enlightenment under the bodhi tree. His first few words were, "All sentient beings possess true Buddha nature!" Through his words, we know that all beings possess the potential to become buddhas. Therefore, human beings are equal to the Buddha, but owing to the loss of their awareness, their suffering in the cycle of rebirth is prolonged. Our cultivation will help us to discover and become aware of our true nature once more.

Awareness functions to observe, discover, and reacquire, which is different from invention. Invention involves the creation of a new item or knowledge, while to reacquire or discover is to become aware of an existing matter or phenomenon. For example, the famous British scientist Newton discovered the Earth's gravitational force. This is a function of awareness, for even if Newton's discovery did not happen, gravitational force would still function on this Earth all the same. When the Buddha attained enlightenment, he was only becoming aware of the truth of the law of dependent origination, but he did not create such a law. Therefore, in the *Miscellaneous Discourses of the Buddha*, the Buddha taught that, "whether the Buddha appears in the world or not, the Dharma always remains; the Dharma abides in the Dharma realm, and so the Tathagata realizes this directly and attains complete, perfect enlightenment."

Humankind has been living on Earth for a very long time, but why is it that no one ever discovered the gravitational force before Newton?

I believe that it is because Newton had a unique ability to observe. In Buddhist terms, Newton possessed a very high level of awareness, which is very important to the development of personal wisdom. Buddhism places a strong emphasis on the advancement of individual awareness; because it is only through the progressive elevation of awareness that we can develop and enhance our wisdom, which leads to the understanding and appreciation of nirvana.

To be a pratyekabuddha ("solitary realizers") is one level of the four noble realms within the Ten Dharma Realms. Pratyekabuddhas existed before the birth of the Buddha and attained enlightenment without teachers or the assistance of others, and without knowledge of the Dharma. Through their observation of the Twelve Links of Dependent Origination, they became aware of the meaning of life. Mahakasyapa, one of the Buddha's principle disciples, once said proudly, "Even if I had not encountered Sakyamuni Buddha, I would have still become an enlightened one of solitary realization."

Indeed, Mahakasyapa possessed an extremely high level of awareness. When the Buddha spoke the Dharma on Vulture Peak, he held up a flower without uttering a word. With the exception of Mahakasyapa, not one single person in the audience was able to comprehend the Buddha's meaning. For his part, Mahakasyapa was able to establish a simultaneous bond with the Buddha, and returned a smile from the bottom of his heart. After that, the Buddha passed the essence of the Chan teachings onto Mahakasyapa, and said, "I have this treasury of the eye of the true Dharma, the wondrous mind of nirvana, the true form of reality without characteristics, a profound teaching that is not based upon the written word, but it is a separate transmission beyond the teachings; this I entrust to Mahakasyapa." At that moment, the Chan School of Buddhism was established through this rapport between the teacher and the student. This is another manifestation of self-awareness.

In China, the Chan School always advocates "enlightenment through awareness." All problems are to be solved by personally contemplation without disclosing the answers to others. Once

Master Zhi Xian was stumped by his colleague Master Ling Yu who asked him, "What was your responsibility before you were born?" When he asked for further explanation, Master Ling Yu answered, "This is my understanding and I need say no more. Even if I provide additional clarification, I do not see how that could benefit you." Master Zhi Xian then returned to the monastery, looked into every book in the library, but failed to formulate an appropriate response . At the end of the day, he sighed and said, "You cannot satiate your hunger by reciting the word 'eat,' or by looking at the drawing of a cake." He then burned all his books and vowed, "From now on, I will not waste my time studying and researching on the Buddhist sutras. I will be better off conducting myself as an ordinary monk."

After taking his leave from Master Ling Yu, Master Zhi Xian traveled to a former place of practice of Imperial Master Hui Zhong and continued his practice. One day, while clearing some overgrown shrubs, his scythe hit the rubble on the ground. The reverberating sound suddenly provided him with the elusive answer, and he found himself awakened to the truth. He recited the verse, "The sound of one strike overcomes the barrier of my past knowledge. I shall no longer rely on theoretical forms of cultivation. In an instant, I am awakened to the age-old Truth without being influenced by the surroundings. Realization comes without trace and does not rely on the display of external etiquette. Words uttered by the enlightened ones are those of complete wisdom." Had Master Ling Yu decided to provide further explanation and clarification at the very beginning, Master Zhi Xian would not have been able to attain sudden enlightenment. The Sixth Patriarch of the Chan School said, "Profound insight cannot be taught. It is always close to you and revealed through contemplation." If you do not recognize your own nature, you will not improve yourself no matter how hard you try to learn from others. It goes without saying that "prized treasures are never given; they are found within your mind and are inherent in your original nature."

Throughout our lives, we require parental

caring, instruction from our teachers, support from society, assistance from our mentors, and encouragement from our friends. However, most important of all, we must rely on our own self-awareness. We must not lose our awareness and become totally dependent on others. Let us consider the blood that flows within our body. It provides natural nutrients to ensure health and our well-being. It is far better than any injection of vitamins or supplements that provide limited benefit. When we take refuge in the Triple Gem, we are really taking refuge in the Triple Gem of our own self-nature. We are seeking to discover and understand ourselves. Humanity's true nature is originally pure and unspoiled, but it can lose its purity with a single ignorant thought, thereby, prolonging one's suffering in the bitter sea of rebirth. To rediscover ourselves, we must place our faith and devotion in Buddhism and remove the mask from our own face. We must understand and assess our current disposition with frankness, all of which cannot be attained by relying on others, for we must depend on our own awareness to achieve these goals.

Awareness is the prerequisite wisdom for attaining profound nirvana. Very often we have said that we are resolved to attain enlightenment and to practice the bodhisattva path. But do we truly understand the meaning of becoming a bodhisattva? Chapter Four of the *Treatise on the Perfection of Great Wisdom* states, "One who has self-awareness and enlightens others is a true bodhisattva." If this merit is carried out to its fullness, then we are on the path to Buddhahood. The essential merits required to become a Buddha are derived from practicing self-awareness, enlightening others, and attaining complete enlightenment. In other words, in the process of our cultivation, we shall use our awareness to guide our lives, and rely on this awareness to complete our journey to enlightenment. Based on our aspiration for enlightenment and cultivation of the bodhisattva path, we can travel on the road of awareness and enlightenment.

It is not difficult to develop our awareness if we pay attention, examples of awareness and enlightenment are relatively easy to find. According to Confucius, "Each person should reflect upon themselves three times a day." This is similar to Buddhism's "Hence forth, I repent each and every one of my wrong deeds." These are the implementations of self-awareness. Chan Master Pu Jue of the Sung dynasty once said, "If practitioners divert their criticism of other to themselves, their cultivation will improve immensely. It does not matter if you are happy or angry, peaceful or excited, every moment is the right moment to appraise yourself." Every error committed needs to be identified and put right by the application of a self-aware mind. The scholar Liang Qichao once said, "I shall not be deterred from declaring war on yesterday's 'me'." This is not unlike a famous Confucian saying, "If you can renew yourself from day to day; then let there be a daily renewal." One of the preconditions of Buddhist monastic life is "to diligently cultivate the precepts, concentration, and wisdom; and to extinguish greed, hatred, and delusion." Therefore, we can overcome greed, anger, and delusion, if we are constantly aware of our dedication to the precepts, concentration, and wisdom. Such is the means and ways to improve our lives.

Self-awareness is a path taking us to ultimate liberation. To be able to say, "I know," "I realize," or "I understand" is worth more than a thousand lectures conducted by others. But if we refrain from exercising our awareness and simply relying on others to solve our problems, then, as the *Sutra of the Buddha's Bequeathed Teachings* says, "The fault is not with the guide who shows the right path, if the traveler refuses to walk; the responsibility is not with the physician who prescribes the right medication, if the patient chooses not to take it." Likewise, the *Diamond Sutra* expounds that "all material forms are false delusion;" and "those who seek me with form and sound are perverted in their ways, and cannot perceive the presence of the Tathagata." You will deviate from the Path if you are attached to external influence, for only with proper recognition of your self-awareness, can you reach the Buddha within your mind and discover your own true nature. From this point forward, I hope that all members of the BLIA can employ your awareness to elevate your intrinsic quality. At the same time, you should regularly study the Buddhist sutras and attend Dharma talks, so that by contemplating what you have learned and heard, you will gain wisdom. You should continue to apply yourself diligently to the understanding and application of the Buddha's teachings, as this will advance you to the next level by the practical implementation of your self-awareness, thus assuring your enlightenment.

## II. Develop Buddhism though Localization

In line with the rapid progress made in information communication and modern transportation, the whole world is advancing towards globalization in many areas. We are witnessing the transformation of this world into a "Global Village." It is an indisputable fact that we have in this world many different countries and ethnic races. What strikes fear in these countries and races, is the possibility of being invaded and conquered, resulting ultimately in the loss of their cultures. I was on a world tour teaching the Dharma some time ago, and was invited to give a lecture at Cornell University in the United States. After the lecture, Professor John MacRae said to me, "You are welcome to teach the Dharma here in America. But it seems that you have repeatedly tried to impose Chinese culture upon ours." When I heard what he said, it became apparent to me that I had been insensitive to local culture; and I was reminded that the purpose of my visit is to contribute and serve, just as Buddhist practitioners make offerings of flower to the bodhisattvas. Therefore, we must respect the cultures of other countries and societies; and to accept the unique characteristics of these cultures. We learn from the Buddhist sutras that the Eastern Pure Land has it own characteristics, which are different from the special features of the Western Pure Land. Similarly, there are differences between practicing in secluded monasteries and practicing Humanistic Buddhism in society. To be able to share and coexist irrespective of such differences will ensure a more colorful and attractive world.

When Buddhism was first transmitted from India into China, Indian monks traveled to China for the sole purpose of translating the Buddhist sutras into the Chinese language, while the responsibility of building monasteries and temples rested with the Chinese monastics. That is why Buddhism flourished within Chinese culture. On the other hand, if these Indian monastics like Kasyapamatanga and Dharmaraksa had decided to reside permanently in China, and participated in temple construction and Dharma propagation, Buddhism in China would have retained a lot more of its Indian character. Have you ever wondered why the First Patriarch of the Chan School, Master Bodhidharma, appointed Master Huike as the Second Patriarch, instead of choosing someone of Indian descent? It was because Master Bodhidharma was aware of the importance of ensuring that his teachings would be adapted locally. Similarly many years ago, I transferred the abbotship of Fo Guang Shan to Venerable Hsin Ping, because he was a native born Taiwanese. This too is an example of my objective of localization.

The localization that I am advocating is benevolent, friendly, harmonious, and enhancing, and does not involve rejection or denial. For example, when participating in the Independence Day parades on July 4, I noticed that most Chinese Americans still regarded themselves as Chinese first and American second, despite having lived in the United States for many years. Therefore, I would like to encourage our BLIA members, when taking part in the Independence Day parades, to proclaim publicly that "I am American." Since we have chosen to live in the United States, we should recognize ourselves as part of this new home. It is not right to create for ourselves "a country within a country." It is natural to expect an exchange of cultures, but, if we think carefully, we would not like to find a United States of America or a Japanese Empire embedded in the middle of China. I would suggest that all aspiring immigrants, no matter where you are going, you should be prepared to settle down and embrace wholeheartedly your new country.

You should adapt to the local environment, culture, and way of life. You should never try to purposefully cling to your old background and customs, creating tiny enclaves within another country.

In the past, no matter where they went or what they did; Chinese immigrants always emphasized the notion of "popularizing and preserving the Chinese culture." This is a patently wrong idea, because each place has it own unique culture and history. Europe has its own European culture; America has its own American culture; and Australia has it own Australian culture. So, we must respect these local cultures. It may be acceptable to introduce Chinese and other cultures into another country, but we must never attempt to use our Chinese culture to subjugate or replace another culture. For members who came from different parts of the world, successful propagation of Buddhism is dependent on how well we can adapt our work to local needs and cultures.

In the course of spreading Buddhism that began almost twenty-five hundred years ago, the fundamental nature, principles, rules, and instructions of the Dharma have never changed. However, when Buddhism was transmitted to China, Japan, and Korea, it became Mahayana Buddhism; and when Buddhism was transmitted to Sri Lanka, Burma, and Thailand, it became Theravada Buddhism. Similarly, when it was transmitted to Xinjiang, Tibet, and Mongolia, it became Esoteric Buddhism. Each of these forms of Buddhism has evolved into its current state through the gradual influence of local climate, geographic conditions, customs, and traditions. It is a clear example of conforming to and complying with the local environment. A Catholic priest, Father Ting Song-yun once said to me, "If you had been born in the West, you would probably be ordained as a priest. If I had been raised in the East, I might be a Buddhist monk now." For example, in a country with abundant timber, you will find that the people use a lot of timber furniture. Similarly, in a land with a large supply of quarried stone, you will find the popular use of more stone products. Therefore, these are clear adaptations to the most appropriate conditions and resources, and has nothing to do with being right or wrong.

Our discussion now is about local adaptation to promote Buddhism. Buddhism is not a tool to overcome the cultures of other countries. Its goal is to promote unity, coexistence, cooperation, mutual survival, and coprosperity. The BLIA is an organization advancing the principle of Humanistic Buddhism, and wherever we are in this world, we have the duty to develop Buddhism in that area. However, we must always be aware of the different characteristics of a given place, so that we can realistically adapt ourselves to the local requirements. So long as the principles of the Dharma are not altered, we should emphasize and promote the retention of the local characteristics. Both the United States and China are large countries. We know that the United States has a federal system; it is also governed by fifty-one different state governments; similarly, China has a central government that oversees thirty-six provincial governments, self-administrative zones, special economic zones, and minority ethnic zones. These are all good examples of exercising the principle of localization.

In March of 2004, the BLIA and Buddhist communities in China co-organized the "Chinese Buddhist Musical Concert." The performances were held at the Dr. Sun Yat-sen Memorial Hall in Taiwan, the Kodak Theatre in Los Angeles, and the Queen Elizabeth Theatre in Canada. The programs were performed by over one hundred members of monastic orders from the Mahayana, Esoteric, and Theravada traditions from eight famous temples on both sides of the Taiwan Strait. The performers might have come from different backgrounds, but this only enhanced and emphasized their individuality, while the chanting was both sonorous and wonderful.

The above demonstrates that Buddhism may exist in many forms such as the Northern, Southern, and Esoteric traditions, and it must be recognized that these different forms of Buddhism all possess their own special features and characteristics. It is unnecessary to change these characteristics even though they may differ in language, styles of music, and forms of clothing. To be successful in the international development of Buddhism, we must ensure the rigorous implementation of the principle of localization.

During the BLIA First Meeting of the Third Board of Directors held in Johannesburg, South Africa, in April 2001, I proposed the following "Four Transformations:"

1. Transform the Dharma using humanistic qualities.

2. Transform human life through the fragrance of books.

3. Transform the monastic and lay communities with equality.

4. Transform religious centers through localization.

When I proposed "transform religious centers through localization," I am referring to the hundreds of temples and Buddhist centers founded and operated by Fo Guang Shan and BLIA. Their ownership belongs to the community rather than any individuals. In fact, I ask all BLIA members to make a common vow, aiming to transform all of these establishments by adapting to local culture and conditions over the next twenty to thirty years. At the conference, I had suggested to the audience to visualize what a spectacular achievement for Buddhism it would be, if we are able to install abbots or abbesses of native origin in all of the overseas temples: just imagine having an American monastic for the Hsi Lai Temple, an Australian monastic for the Nan Tien and Chung Tien temples, and an African monastic for the Nan Hua Temple. It is my sincerest wish, in the coming twenty to fifty years, to be able to assist and guide the native monastics to become responsible for the management and administration of these overseas establishments. Nowadays, Fo Guang Shan Buddhist College is regularly receiving many applications from overseas. I hope that BLIA can attract more members of all ethnic backgrounds, so that light of the Buddha and his teachings can be found in every corner of the world. I believe that this is the best way of "practicing the Buddha's Way."

# III. Improved Income from New Buddhist Enterprises

We need either a legitimate job or business to be able to lead a proper life. Our wealth, comfort, and stability are the result of our daily hard work, which also enables us to perform good and benevolent tasks for others. One cannot be expected to carry out significant charitable deeds if oneself is poor and starving.

It is essential to satisfy our daily needs for clothing, food, lodging, and transportation. Even if you are a perfectly enlightened Buddha, your daily livelihood is what keeps you alive in this world. In Buddhist cultivation, it is not necessary to maintain a poverty-stricken and austere lifestyle. In fact, Buddhism encourages its practitioners to be prosperous by being successful business persons or industrious employees. According to the *Sutra of Great Treasures*, "Lay practitioners can amass wealth legitimately, for it does not contravene the Dharma." By being well off and self-sufficient, we will be able to provide for our families, help our relatives and friends in need, and support the propagation of Buddhism. Putting it another way, we must conduct our lives by "right action" and "right livelihood" according to the Eightfold Noble Path. The *Connected Discourses of the Buddha* indicates that Buddhism acknowledges that proper livelihood can be achieved by engaging in any of the various lawful professions, such as farming, herding, trade, or investment.

In Buddhism, "right action" is to conduct oneself in a correct manner; while to have a "right livelihood" is to depend on some appropriate profession, business, or employment for your livelihood. According to the *Commentary on the Stages of Yogacara Practitioners Treatise*, "Right livelihood can be defined as the pursuit of clothing, food, and miscellaneous items by proper means." Buddhism does not discourage the accumulation of wealth by its practitioners. A country grows stronger because its people are sufficiently wealthy. Likewise, the propagation of Buddhism will become more successful if the economic status of its practitioners is thriving and prosperous. Therefore, so long as your actions do not harm other members of society, there is nothing wrong with your involvement in successful economic ventures.

It is regrettable that in the past, a number of patriarchs and sages had demanded their lay followers to live up to the standard of monastic practice. They suggested that "money is a horrible thing, for it is like a poisonous viper." Others suggested that "couples married because they were enemies in their past lives." They would even refer to children as debt collectors from the past. According to them, everything in this world relates to pain and suffering. However, they are not aware that their method of teaching is contrary to human nature; while their method of liberation will never appeal to the spiritual needs of the people. So it is no wonder that people who did not understand Buddhism would run away as fast as they could, if you asked them to become a Buddhist follower.

In fact, most people in the past misconstrued Buddhism's doctrine of emptiness as only emphasizing a spiritual life, dismissing altogether the material one. However, according to the *Amitabha Sutra*, by residing in the Western Pure Land you can have your every wish granted. Its land and buildings are well endowed with gold and other treasured objects. Everywhere you go, you will meet up with bodhisattvas wearing jeweled crowns and well adorned robes; so grand indeed are these majestic worlds. What I do not understand is that, up until now, there are many practitioners who maintain the notion that you have to lead an austere life to become a good Buddhist. With this idea in their minds, they are prepared to be impoverished in this life in exchange for the possibility of leading a better life in the Pure Land after death. This kind of thinking created insurmountable obstacles in the propagation of Buddhism in the past. Many years ago, on my visit to a number of European museums, I remember seeing many Catholic Churches. They are all majestic and glittering buildings, a clear demonstration of the Church's power and wealth in the world. Looking back over the past thirty or forty years in Taiwan, it seems that churches and banks usually occupy the best locations in town, while Buddhist temples could only be found at the end of ramshackle and obscure byways.

In fact, Humanistic Buddhism advocates that we should all have a good living and lead a comfortable life without feeling guilty. Buddhism does not require its practitioners to be poor or refrain from enjoying proper pleasures. It encourages us to earn our living by proper means, and enjoy as much spiritual and physical pleasures as we can. Even though there are limitations to physical wealth and enjoyment, nevertheless, we are in a better position to appreciate the Dharma joy with the help of these limited achievements. Without being hampered by material hardships, we are in a better position to harvest both spiritual and physical wealth in our lifetime. Buddhism was transmitted from India into China, Korea, and Japan many centuries ago. One of the main reasons why it was so widely accepted was because of its strong emphasis on assisting the economic livelihood of its followers. The functions of Buddhist institutions are not limited to propagating the Dharma, they are also used as religious, cultural, artistic, and educational centers. These functions are usually associated with other community functions, such as agricultural production, business economy, and social welfare.

Traditionally, monastic buildings are built to high aesthetic standards of grand and imposing features. The construction of grand halls, pavilions, landscape gardens, and majestic courtyards have earned them a reputation of being the "Buddhist Pure Land." In effect, Pure Land is the description applied to a pure, tranquil, and sublime realm, a world of peace and tranquility. Although Buddhism discourages excessive physical indulgence, it also recognizes the benefit of reasonable and appropriate physical wealth and pleasure. Buddhism may not place an absolute importance on the accumulation of wealth, but we must accept the fact that money is needed for the purchase and installation of adornments in temples. People usually visit and pray in the temples because they are magnificent and grand; and people usually will not pay respect to Buddha images unless they are gracefully decorated. We practitioners have vowed to be reborn in the Western Pure Land, because we are told about its land covered in gold, its jeweled pavilions, and majestic buildings.

Buddhism may consider the ability to lead a plain and simple life very meritorious, however Buddhism needs sufficient infrastructure and facilities to accommodate the public and its followers. The famous Chinese poet Dufu once wrote in *Song on the Grass Hut Blown Down by the Autumn Wind*: "Would that I could obtain a vast mansion of a hundred million rooms, to shelter the poor masses from cold and see their smiling faces." The monastics are required to lead a simple life, owning only the bare essentials in clothing and other personal possessions. On the other hand, lay practitioners should be provided with a fresh approach to their view of life. "Even a clever housewife cannot provide boiled rice from an empty pot;" and "a poor couple finds no pleasure in life." From these old Chinese proverbs, we can appreciate the fact that personal cultivation will not progress smoothly unless you are financially stable. Without money, how will you care for your parents? Without money, how will you provide for your family? And surely without money, you will not be able to support the temple and carry out charitable deeds. Therefore, it is not unreasonable to say that every aspect in our lives evolves around money. A country needs to have an abundant treasury before it can implement its policies and programs. To be able to support its spiritual programs, as well as its medical, charitable, educational, and cultural services, Buddhist establishments require a substantial input of properly acquired wealth. Therefore, Buddhism does not reject money that is obtained through proper means which are needed to purify and benefit the society.

"To resolve" is a frequently used term in Buddhism. A lay practitioner may commit to acquiring fame and fortune in society, as well as starting a family life. This resolve is acceptable by Buddhism, for according to the

*Vimalakirti Sutra*, Vimalakirti observed the Dharma diligently, while at the same time he was a successful businessman involved in trading, farming, and other businesses. Possession of money and wealth did not appear to hamper his devotion. In fact, he made good use of his wealth to deliver others from sufferings. With the help of money, he was able to transform the world into a land of purity. The duality of the Buddhist community ensures the complimentary existence of the monastic and layman communities. Master Vimalakirti had been successful both as a layman and a Buddhist practitioner. Clearly, there is no conflict in making a comfortable living while at the same time, cultivating your faith. It also demonstrates that possession of sufficient financial support is a prerequisite that supports the turning of the Dharma Wheel.

In this modern society, we can observe that financial groups have their group assets; individuals have their personal assets; political parties have their party assets; and religious groups have their own assets. In undertaking any enterprise, we should not regard profit as the only consideration. There is also a need to put in place a robust organizational structure, the skillful use of human resources, and clear managerial and developmental strategies. As Buddhist practitioners, we should regard the propagation of Buddhism as our lifetime objective, so that "Dharma propagation is my family goal and benefiting others is my career." Profit making may not be the primary objective in the teaching activities of monastics. But, this does not mean that we have to reject the significance of profitable Buddhist enterprises, and the contribution they make. We know that Humanistic Buddhism is the "application of spiritual belief in our daily lives." It especially focuses on ensuring the happiness of the practitioners. Therefore, with its active development and implementation of cultural, educational, and charitable activities, Fo Guang Shan is acting in accordance with the principle of "following the Buddha's Way." In the past, Buddhism placed great emphasis on Dharma learning and cultivation, and neglected the necessity of business acumen. However, I consider both matters of equal importance. Whereas the "forest" monastics can continue to improve their practice in seclusion, the "humanistic" monastics can promote and propagate Buddhism through public speeches and publication of books and literature.

Moreover, lay practitioners can assist with the development of BLIA ventures by participating in the running of BLIA teahouses, cultural shops, vegetarian restaurants, tourist agencies, and other consultancies. All of the above establishments allow us to create new and genial relationships with the general public. To help improve the quality of life, we may also become involved in setting up factories, farms, power and utility facilities, department stores, hotels, insurance firms, newspapers, as well as radio and television stations. With the arrival of global information technology, there is also a need to further develop electronic and internet access to Buddhism.

In the past, temples and monasteries provided landscaped areas for visitors' relaxation. We can, perhaps, expand this concept and develop tourist areas promoting Buddhist themes. Nowadays, the "user pay" concept is an accepted fact in society. It is obligatory to pay entry fees when visiting museums and landmark areas. Therefore, it would not be unreasonable to place a realistic upkeep fee for entry into future Buddhist museums, exhibitions, and theme parks. However, visitation to temples for Dharma services and practice must always remain free to all, though naturally, practitioners may of their own accord make appropriate donations to the temples. Currently, there is no clear demarcation between entry fee and donation in China, Korea, and Japan, and I can see that there is an urgent need to review these situations. Today, you are expected to pay when attending Buddhist schools and hospitals. This is no different from the past, when charges were levied on temple owned farm lands and houses. Historically, temples had owned and operated money-lending institutions, setting the precedence for the establishment of banking facilities at the temple for the convenience of practitioners.

In earlier times, when an organized economy was still in its infancy, Buddhist temples would often release funds to help relieve the financial difficulties of their practitioners. There are recorded examples during the various dynasties when the temples provided invaluable assistance to the governments to relieve famines and other disasters. It also recorded throughout the ages that Buddhist temples were involved in activities relating to food production, accommodation, stationary products, education, charities, medications, hospitals, disaster relief, funeral services, bathhouses, and infrastructure construction. All these activities were considered invaluable to the national prosperity and the benefit of its population.

The economy is the life blood of people's livelihood. In India, during the time of Sakyamuni Buddha, the monastic income was derived from a system of alms giving. When Buddhism was transmitted to China, succeeding generations of the Chan School masters promoted farming and forestry production, while more recently, Master Tai Xu advocated combining Chan with manufacturing industries. Nowadays, we are seeing to the funding of organized foundations. What I envisage for the future is a joining of the ancient alms system with farming, industrial, and modern economic enterprises. Such areas of enterprise as orchards and vegetable gardens, timber forests, rental housing and farm land, factory production, Buddhist publishing houses, Buddhist arts and crafts, regular service donations, special and funeral services, café and vegetarian food outlets, social activity promotions, Dharma teaching sponsorship, entry fees to special events or exhibitions, charitable services, meditation and accommodation, cooperative funds, and special support committees, all represent the inevitable trends for modern economic development in Buddhist society.

In summary, Buddhism considers wealth a neutral commodity; it is neither good nor bad. Buddhism does not totally negate the benefit of material wealth. Money may be a poisonous viper, but it can be turned to good use for sustaining the propagation and cultivation of the Dharma. It should be regarded as the basic necessity for the development of Buddhism. Buddhist colleges, meditation and recitation halls, schools, hospitals, radio and television stations, and magazine publishing, all require money for their operations. Therefore, money is not necessarily a poisonous viper, for according to the Buddhist sutras, there are "pure wealth," "good wealth," and "noble wealth." As long as it can be put into proper use to promote the Dharma and benefit other beings, it is more meritorious than trying to practice under the pretense of austerity. Wealth put to a good use is in fact more meaningful and wise. As a result, it is necessary to reevaluate the importance of economic development in Buddhism. As long as the principle of right action and right livelihood is adhered to, I can see no problem in trying to be profitable in our enterprises. I believe that no practitioner should feel ashamed just because one is wealthy; so long as the money is used for personal happiness and for the benefit of the people, society, and nation. On the other hand, poverty will often attract criminal behavior.

From now on, I hope that members of

the BLIA will resolve to engage themselves in new and successful Buddhist ventures to enhance our economic standing. This will foster better opportunities to implement the ideals of Humanistic Buddhism for establishing a stately and dignified Pure Land in this mundane world.

## IV. Dedicate Our Vows in the Practice of the Buddha's Way

Before we start any task, we must set ourselves a goal. Once a goal is set, we will be able to identify a direction in which we can apply our energy and effort. To set a goal is to "make a resolution," or in Buddhist terms, "to resolve and make a vow."

Normally, the level of personal achievement in society is determined by our childhood aspirations. In Buddhism, the level of our cultivation achievable by a practitioner is determined by the intensity of his or her vows. According to all the Buddhist sutras, all the bodhisattvas achieved enlightenment through the power of their vows. The *Larger Sutra on*

*Amitayus* speaks of the forty-eight great vows made by Amitabha Buddha, while the *Sutra on the Merit of the Medicine Buddha's Original Vow* describes the twelve vows undertaken by the Medicine Buddha to relieve beings from their sufferings. There are many other examples, including the eighteen great vows of Manjusri Bodhisattva, the eighteen great vows of Samantabhadra Bodhisattva, the ten great vows of Avalokitesvara Bodhisattva, and Ksitigarbha Bodhisattva who committed himself to this vow: "If the hells are not emptied, then I vow not to become a Buddha." The above are just a few illustrations of the great vows undertaken and carried out by the buddhas and bodhisattvas.

Throughout history, many eminent monks and great worthies have vowed "to ensure that Dharma remains for a long time, and to liberate all beings from sufferings." Master Xuan Zang successfully completed his vow of traveling westward to India and returning with the Buddhist sutras, after vowing, "I would rather die by taking a single step towards the West, than save my life by taking a single step towards the East." Master Jian Zhen delivered the Dharma to Japan, as a result of his vow of "death is of little consequence when compared to this great mission." More recently, Venerable Ci Hang said, "I vow resolutely to learn and follow the most supreme teachings, not for my own enlightenment by becoming a bodhisattva or even a Buddha, but to allow all beings of the Dharma realm to be enlightened with complete wisdom." They are all role models that Buddhist practitioners should follow.

To resolve to carry out a great vow is fundamental to becoming a good Buddhist. Our resolve will strengthen our confidence and determination. It can intensify our aspiration for enlightenment and elevate our faith, as well as enhance our morality and integrity. Therefore, we should resolve to take appropriate vows as part of our daily practice. For example: I vow to care for my parents and to be cordial with my neighbors. I vow to offer my service for the society. I vow to sacrifice myself for the good of the community. I vow to promote world peace so that all people can live in harmony. I vow to serve as a bridge so that people can safely cross the stream. I vow to be a tree offering coolness in the summer heat. I vow to be a drop of water to nourish the parched land. I vow to be the sun and moon shedding light on everyone. I vow to be a breeze giving comfort to all beings. I vow to be kind and considerate, so that each of us can be carefree. I vow to a flower bringing beauty to the world. I vow to be the rivers and the mountains providing landscapes to be admired. I vow to be a cool fresh stream to quench the thirsty travelers.

To make a vow is like winding up a clock or filling a car with fuel, providing the energy needed to move forward. To make a vow is like a ship's compass or a student's daily course of study, providing a goal for our lives. To make a vow is the very first thing we should learn in our Buddhist practice. The *An Inspiration for the Bodhicitta Pledge* states, "The key to entering the Way is having resolve; the essential for cultivation is making vows. With a firm vow, then sentient beings can be saved; with resolve, the path of Buddhahood is attainable."

Chapter Seven of the *Treatise on the Perfection of Great Wisdom* states, "To practice without a vow is an aimless gesture. A vow is your guide to enlightenment. It is similar to an apprentice who must work under the direction of a master goldsmith, before he is able to craft the gold into a particular design;" and "to propagate Buddhism is a solemn duty which cannot be accomplished without proper resolve. It is like an ox pulling a cart, which will not reach its destination without a driver."

In addition, the *Great Collection Sutra* teaches, "Making a vow can destroy all evil hindrances." The *Treatise on Arising the Mind of Enlightenment* states, "Our aspiration for enlightenment must be aroused with the greatest of sincerity. Once our vows are initiated, we must implement them with due care, diligence, and purpose." From the above, it is clear that the path to the Buddha's Way starts with our vows. It is true that our action or "cause" leads to an "effect." However, without a direction or a "vow," all our actions will be without direction or meaning. Therefore, our resolve for our vows supports and motivates all our spiritual cultivation.

To resolve and make a vow is usually associated with Buddhist practices. However, to resolve and make a vow is not a Buddhist monopoly. In fact, everyone in the society needs to establish goals by vows and determination, in order to be able to complete our tasks to the best of our abilities. To resolve and make a vow is a continual source of energy that is found within ourselves. The *An Inspiration for the Bodhicitta Pledge* says, "Diamond's hardness cannot be compared with the strength of our vows. The immensity of the universal is tiny when compared with the consciousness of our own mind." Our achievement is dependent on the vastness within our conscious mind, and our strength is derived from the determination of our commitment. Therefore, the way to Buddhahood will not be denied to us, as long as we can be resolute with our vows.

Just like attending classes, the quality of our vows will improve with time. Initially we start with a vow of small significance, but in time, we will learn to elevate the intensity of our vows. Thus, for example, one can vow to recite many Buddhist sutras, to carry out good deeds for the benefit of all beings, and to make Buddhism known to all beings. One can also resolve to be a supporter of the temple, to be servants to all beings, to be a provider to the family and an outstanding example of the society. To be able "to resolve" and follow the "Buddha's Way," is doing what the Buddha has done; now that is something truly wonderful.

Speaking about the "Buddha's Way," I remember Mr. Tsao Chung-chih, the founder of "Life Line." His wife is a devout Buddhist, who had taken refuge in the Triple Gem at the Pumen Temple some forty years earlier. She was completely captivated by my concept of the Humanistic Pure Land. Since then, she had been constantly persuading her husband to visit temples and listen to sermons and teachings. At the time, Mr. Tsao was not a Buddhist, but followed his wife's wishes out of love for her.

At the end of a particular service, Mrs. Tsao took her husband's hand, walked up to me and said, "Master, will you please enlighten my husband, so that he will believe in Buddhism and be able to pray to the Buddha?" I could see at that moment Mr. Tsao was totally embarrassed. To ease the awkward situation, I said, "It is not necessary for Mr. Tsao to practice the rituals of Buddhism, as long as he is conducting himself in the 'Buddha's Way'." Mr. Tsao was delighted when he heard what I said. Afterwards, he would say to everyone he met that "Master Hsing Yun told me that I do not have to perform the customary Buddhist rituals, as long as I am applying myself to the 'Buddha's Way'."

Ever since that meeting, Mr. Tsao has untiringly participated in many charitable and benevolent social activities. For example, he has founded "Life Line" in Taiwan, which helps the destitute and impoverished to a better life. He has established the Tsao Family Foundation to provide education subsidies to needy students, and to supply wheelchairs to tens of thousands of handicapped persons. Each year he would donate millions of dollars to disaster appeals.

In addition, he is a passionate supporter of Fo Guang Shan and BLIA, providing valuable contributions to the establishment of Dharma centers and religious activities. He has also given generously to the installation of multi-language plaques around sacred sites in India and Sri Lanka that commemorate historic Buddhist events.

Many would congratulate him for his good deeds, but he would invariably reply "To recite Buddhist sutras is good, but not as good as listening to Buddhist teachings. To listen to teachings is good, but not as beneficial as to teach the Dharma. However, the best deed of all is to practice what the Buddha has taught. I am merely conducting myself in the 'Buddha's Way'."

To conduct oneself in the "Buddha's Way" is to follow and practice the teachings of the Buddha. Every day we greet our fellow Buddhists as "practitioners," that means we are practicing the Dharma. A true practitioner is one who not just listens and learns, but puts into action what the Buddha had said and done in his life time. Every Buddhist sutra always starts with the words "Thus have I heard" and ends with "Faithfully received and put into practice." To be able to faithfully receive the Dharma and put it into practice is in reality to actively apply ourselves in accordance with the ways of the Buddha. Therefore, the fundamental objective of a practitioner is to implement the following "Buddha's Way:"

1. To be compassionate and generous is the Buddha's Way.

2. To be charitable and benevolent is the Buddha's Way.

3. To serve the society is the Buddha's Way.

4. To be moral and ethical is the Buddha's Way.

5. To preserve personal integrity is the Buddha's Way.

6. To observe the precepts is the Buddha's Way.

7. To be respectful and tolerant is the Buddha's Way.

8. To carry out good deeds is the Buddha's Way.

9. To be repentant and grateful is the Buddha's Way.

10. To tolerate loss and injustice is the Buddha's Way.

11. To be patient and accepting is the Buddha's Way.

12. To observe the four objects of unfailing faith is the Buddha's Way.

13. To progress with time is the Buddha's Way.

14. To be an integral part of the Dharma Realm is the Buddha's Way.

15. To integrate and coexist with all beings is the Buddha's Way.

16. To apply Buddhism to the world is the Buddha's Way.

The Buddha once said, "There is no distinction to be made between the mind, the Buddha, and all beings." The Buddha is an enlightened being, and all beings are future buddhas waiting to be enlightened. The Buddha has completed his enlightenment with no further need to revisit mundane existence. Conversely, all beings have yet to achieve their enlightenment, and thus remain in the cycle of rebirth. If we do what the Buddha did, we can be assured of being released from sufferings and awakening to the joy of enlightenment.

To be successful with Buddhist practice, we must be able to place equal importance on the understanding and application of the Dharma. To practice without true understanding will lead you along a path of illusion. However, to practice solely based on belief and understanding is also insufficient, because you are biased towards the theoretical aspect of Buddhism and do not reap the full benefit of this great religion. A wise practitioner is able to place equal importance on understanding and the practical application of the doctrine. To understand is to have faith, and to apply is to practice the "Buddha's Way." To understand wisely is to be able to be self-aware, and to apply ourselves to the Buddha's Way is to help others to become awakened. Since we consider ourselves Buddhists and are resolved to cultivate ourselves, we must make sure that we live our lives according to the Dharma. By appropriately praising others, we are following the Buddha's instruction on generosity through kind speech. To be constantly conscious of the unique relationships between self and others, we will become aware of the existence of oneness with all beings. To serve untiringly looks like you are doing it for others, but actually you are helping yourself. Being grateful and respectful to others looks like you are doing it for others, but actually you are the one who is benefited.

Ever since the Ming (1368-1644) and Qing (1644-1911) dynasties, many devoted practitioners had been able to provide comprehensive knowledge and explanation on the Dharma. They were able to talk about the profound mysteries and discuss with great proficiency about spirituality. Unfortunately, not many of these learned persons managed to practically apply their theories to their lives. It is difficult to expect consistency of words and actions, if you have not actually experienced what you have taught. Take, for instance, when you are reciting the

Amitabha Buddha's name, are you able to maintain complete dedication in your recitation? Similarly when you meditate, have you reached the state of *samadhi* concentration? When you are praying, are you aware of the improvement of your personal attributes? During chanting, do you derive great admiration and faith in the Dharma? When faced with obstructions in the course of your various practices, do you have the necessary strength and patience to overcome these obstacles? Therefore, it is more fitting to take a simple step, rather than to talk about running a mile. All of the above illustrate the importance of self-awareness and the "Buddha's Way."

In closing, I would like to emphasize again that self-awareness is a means of self-development, whereas the enlightenment of others is the way of the Buddha. To have self-awareness and the resolve to practice the "Buddha's Way," is proof of our coexistence with the Buddha. If a person possesses Buddha nature, what he sees is the Buddha's world, what he hear is the Buddha's sounds, what he smells is the Buddha's fragrance, what he speaks is Buddha's word, and what he does is the Buddha's deeds. If everyone possesses these profound qualities, then and there, we have the Buddha's world: How can a family not be blessed and happy? How can a society not be safe and secure? How can a nation not be strong and prosperous? Finally, from now on, let each of us make a solemn vow and say to ourselves: "I am a Buddha."

# Change the World and Benefit Humanity

*For Buddhism's sake, I have dedicated my whole life to "changing the world" and "benefiting humanity," because these represent the true meaning of "it's all for Buddhism's sake."*

BLIA 11th General Conference
Taipei, Taiwan
October 4-8, 2006
Translated by Ven. Miao Guang
Revised by Ven. Miao Hsi & the Fo Guang Shan
International Translation Center
Edited by Robert H. Smitheram, Ph.D.

Throughout the past fifteen years, members of the Buddha's Light International Association (BLIA) around the world have been striving to change the world and benefit humanity. Everyone here has tirelessly devoted your efforts to propagating Buddhism, establishing subchapters, organizing a wide range of activities, and has supported and helped promote the events and undertakings of Fo Guang Shan's branch temples. Not only have you dedicated your time and built upon your religious experiences, you have also created a new history for both yourselves and society. As I witness the growth of BLIA and your achievements in the globalization of Buddhism, I offer my most sincere praises and admiration to all. At the same time, I would also like to use this opportunity to propose "Change the World and Benefit Humanity" as a new theme, which also expresses my expectations and wishes for every BLIA member.

Speaking of "changing the world" and "benefiting humanity," I am reminded of a thought that has been in my mind ever since

I became a Buddhist monk at the age of twelve, because "it is for Buddhism's sake," which indeed it has. Despite having grown up inside a monastery living a frugal and simple life, I never for a moment felt mistreated or deprived, because it was all for Buddhism's sake. I became ordained for Buddhism's sake; I remained firm against temptations of rich offerings for conducting chanting services, because I was devoting my life to propagating the Dharma and benefiting sentient beings for Buddhism's sake; I declined positions of abbot and those of authority and fame from a young age, because I had my own way of thinking, and it was "all for Buddhism's sake."

What do I mean when I say, "it is for Buddhism's sake"? I knew that for the sake of Buddhism, I had to study, travel, and learn; I had to be diligent, resolve to make things happen, develop good connections, and establish all kinds of Buddhist undertakings. For this reason, I broke with my usual unwillingness to be trapped by an endless array of chanting services, and actually volunteered to chant for people in the morgue and even agreed to conduct over-night chanting services just to raise funds for the first Buddhist College that I was establishing. I was very clear about what I was doing, because it was all for Buddhism's sake. Even when faced with all kinds of hardships and difficulties in my attempts to establish Fo Guang Shan temples and to promote Buddhist culture, art, charity, and other Dharma propagating events, the thought of giving up never for once crossed my mind, because it was all for the sake of Buddhism. For the same reason, I have continued my hectic schedule of traveling around the world to give Dharma talks, despite being eighty years old now. Everything I have done is for Buddhism's sake.

For Buddhism's sake, I have dedicated my whole life to "changing the world" and "benefiting humanity," because these represent the true meaning of "it's all for Buddhism's sake." Therefore, I propose the following four suggestions based on the topic of "change the world and benefit humanity." May all BLIA members find mutual encouragement and future direction in them:

1. Change the world and benefit humanity by self-awareness and integrity.

2. Change the world and benefit humanity by the motive force of being resolved.

3. Change the world and benefit humanity by participation and involvement.

4. Change the world and benefit humanity by the power of the enlightenment vow.

## I. Change the World and Benefit Humanity by Self-awareness and Integrity

Buddhism is a religion that emphasizes the pursuit of enlightenment. Prince Siddhartha reached Buddhahood not only by becoming enlightened himself, but he also enlightened other beings, and perfected his own practice and wisdom. This is exactly what his teachings embodied, "to enable sentient beings to realize what the Buddha realized, and to attain the enlightenment the Buddha attained," which helped them to appreciate their equality with the Buddha. Therefore, the main purpose of learning Buddhism is to seek wisdom and pursue enlightenment.

Enlightenment consists of two parts, first it is the wisdom that enables one to become awakened to the wondrous truth and nirvana, while the second is to allow true wisdom to arise and convert illusion into truth. Although learning Buddhism requires us to learn from the Buddha, enlightenment itself must be attained by our own effort. By relying on others, our achievements will be very limited; especially when it comes to enlightenment and spiritual practice, for these can only be accomplished by self-awareness. For example, we ourselves must become aware of the worries, sorrows, and distress of life; become aware of the fact that life and death are both impermanent; and become aware of the fact that people change very quickly. We must also become aware that our world is unstable and subject to perilous danger, and as such, it is not the ultimate place for us to settle our body and mind. Only with self-awareness can we find the strength to deal with these worries and illusions, resolve to maintain our integrity, and find peace and stability. Without self-awareness and self-awakening, even the Buddha cannot help us attain enlightenment or attain Buddhahood.

Speaking of "becoming a Buddha," the word "Buddha" as described in *Treatise on Buddhahood*, refers to a state that "under any circumstances or form, is able to enlighten oneself and others. A Buddha is like someone who has awakened from a deep sleep, or a lotus flower that has come into full bloom." While the Buddha is enlightened to the truth of this universe, he is still an enlightened sentient being, and sentient beings are buddhas-to-be. Since a Buddha originates from a human being, every human being has the potential to become a Buddha, because his or her pure nature is no different from that of a Buddha. For this reason, the *Lotus Sutra* explains the greatest regret of all living beings, by using such examples as a beggar who unknowingly carries a priceless pearl in his sleeve, implying the poor man is unaware of the treasure that he owns.

When we resolve to learn about Buddhism, our most important objective is to eliminate our worries and uncover our Buddha Nature, and the way to do so is to observe the precepts, practice meditation, and cultivate our wisdom, in order that we may extinguish the flames of greed, hatred, and ignorance. Once we eliminate the Three Poisons and allow the Three Wisdoms to shine, we will be able to put an end to our beginningless ignorance, and this is what we mean by self-awareness. In other words, it is what the Chan School means by "realizing enlightenment" or "perceiving true nature."

The lineages of Chinese Chan schools have always placed much emphasis on "self-awareness," in that we must do all inquiry and thinking by ourselves, because no one can offer us specific instructions. When the Buddha picked up a flower on Vulture Peak to show the assembly, only Mahakasyapa knew what he meant and smiled back, therefore the Buddha announced, "I have this treasury of the eye of the true dharma, the wondrous mind of nirvana, the true form of reality without characteristics, a profound teaching that is not based upon the written word, but is a separate transmission beyond the teachings; this I entrust to Mahakasyapa." With a flower and two smiles, Chan was transmitted from a master to his disciple the moment an unspoken connection is established between them. This is also what we mean by self-awareness.

Self-awareness is also a way of self-education, and this too is mentioned in the Buddhist sutras, "Rely on yourself, rely on the Dharma, and rely on nothing else." Self-education is the key to our success, as we must clear of our own faults and ignorance; we must educate ourselves and teach ourselves how to rectify our shortcomings. In other words, we must be demanding of ourselves, and attain the ability for self-learning, self-enrichment, and self-reflection. We need to learn to seek the cause in ourselves, and make consistent effort in questioning ourselves: be self-aware, be one with our own initiative, and enlighten ourselves. Through continued self-reflection, we are able to find our true self. Otherwise, it will be as the *Sutra of the Buddha's Final Teachings* indicates, "The fault is not with the guide who shows the right path, if the traveler refuses to walk. The responsibility is not with the physician who prescribes the right medication, if the patient chooses not to take it." If we do not even attempt to enlighten ourselves, not only will the Buddha not be able to help us, but even a world of books on Buddhism will not enable us gain understanding of the profound *prajña*-wisdom. Therefore, we must read extensively and study deeply the Buddhist texts; the process of listening, thinking, and practice will enable us to be self-awakened and self-enlightened.

The *Sutra of Complete Enlightenment* states, "The gold itself does not come into being because it is smelted, but the form of gold is perfected by the smelting, and after such refinement, it will never revert to course ore." The process of learning Buddhism is like excavating a gold mine; although the Buddha nature is an intrinsic part of us, without spiritual cultivation, it is like the gold buried deep within a mine that will never be discovered. The following are some methods of self-assessment that should enable us to know whether we do or do not have self-awareness and integrity:

1. Do I have confidence in taking refuge in the Triple Gem?

2. Am I clear about the concept of the Five Precepts?

3. Do I possess the right understanding of causes, conditions, and effects?

4. Am I sincere in serving and helping others?

5. Am I protecting the Dharma in a proper manner?

6. Am I participating in activities and events with pure motivation?

7. Are my practices of Buddhism improving day by day?

8. Do the principles of the Dharma shape my thoughts and deeds?

If we have positive and confident answers to the above eight questions, then not only do we have self-awareness and firm belief in the Dharma, the teachings of the Buddha, but we also have the ability to maintain our integrity on the path of spiritual cultivation and a mind open to the Four Immeasurable States of Mind (loving-kindness, compassion, sympathetic joy, and equanimity) and the Six Perfections (generosity, morality or upholding the precepts, patience, perseverance, meditative concentration, and *prajña*-wisdom). We may even progress to make a strong resolve and help all sentient beings to become liberated from suffering. Otherwise, our life will have been lived in vain, because we will have never really benefited from being a Buddhist. For this reason, I have proposed self-awareness and integrity as the first point, because without self-awareness, no matter how precious the treasure we are given, how many principles are taught to us, they will all be useless. Only with self-awareness will we see the need to keep improving, maintain our own integrity, and then change the world and benefit humanity.

## II. Change the World and Benefit Humanity by the Motive Force of Being Resolved

Among the thousands of ways to practice Buddhism, to resolve is the most important, just as it is said in *An Inspiration for the Bodhicitta Pledge*, "The key to entering the Way is having resolve; with resolve, the path of Buddhahood is attainable." To resolve is to cultivate our mind and to construct a more complete self. Buddhism uses a field or a ground as a metaphor for the mind, since no seeds can grow in an uncultivated field. Similarly, without first developing the field of the mind, the aspiration for enlightenment cannot be cultivated. Hence, to resolve becomes the first step in practicing Buddhism; for example, to resolve to develop the Four Immeasurable States of Mind and the Four Universal Vows of the Bodhisattva. Only by then will we be equipped with the motive force to put into practice the Four Means of Embracing and the Four Disciplinary Processes, so as to enlighten ourselves and others.

Speaking of resolve, BLIA members have for the past fifteen years resolved to take on the roles of presidents, executive members, Lay Dharma lecturers, elder advisors, and elders; some have resolved to participate in reading clubs, subscribe to Buddhist publications, sponsor the printing of the Buddhist sutras, promote the *Merit Times*, recruit members, donate money, take part in relief programs, support temples, lead pilgrimages, attend Dharma services, distribute food on Dharma Day, propagate the Dharma, and take part in alms processions to raise funds for Buddhist education institutes. We have even reached out to schools and prisons by providing civic education and spiritual counseling and giving Dharma talks. We have proven with our actions that Buddhists in the twenty-first century are on the move. We now know how to make ourselves heard, and have extended our influence outside our families to connect with society and conduct exchanges with the community. Take for example what has occurred over the past fifteen years, the BLIA has organized general conferences, board of directors' meetings, international young executive conferences, men's fellowship conferences, women's fellowship conferences, scout meetings, and so forth. Having encouraged exchanges between East and

West, and the various continents, these events have spread Buddhism far and wide, and have enhanced inter-personal harmony. These can only be accomplished because of the motive force that has been generated from our resolve.

To resolve means to cultivate the field of your mind, which is also the first thing we have to learn as Buddhists. Without cultivating and developing the field of our mind, no matter how good the external conditions we possess, or how much fortune and merit we may have, the sprout of the aspiration for enlightenment will never grow. This is similar to a seed without a good and fertile land, no flower or fruit will ever grow from it. Therefore, if we wish to open up and develop our spiritual wealth or utilize the energy of our minds, we must begin by becoming resolved. In this world, the bigger your resolve is, the greater your success will be, because the power of being resolved is indeed inconceivable. While Confucians urge people to have aspirations, practitioners of Buddhism encourage people to make vows. Aspiration or vow, both of them are in fact being resolved.

Once you resolve to do something, you will have an aspiration; once you resolve to do something, your vow will be accomplished.

The power of resolve can indeed be wondrous. For example, if you resolve to eat, not only will you be full from the food, you will also find it extra tasty; if you resolve to sleep, not only will you get a good night's sleep, it will also be extra peaceful. Once you resolve to do something, the outcome of your endeavors will be very different. Just as the verse says, "The same moon outside the window becomes different when plum blossoms are present." However, it is a pity that most people tend to search from without rather than from within, and end up neglecting the endless treasure hidden inside. While they know the need to cultivate the wastelands and hillsides in the physical world so as to turn them into farmland or construction sites, they have failed to utilize their inexhaustible inner treasures and energy. Therefore, the wise learn to seek from within, so we should turn away from the external and develop our inner treasure and energy instead.

To resolve is like a small investment that brings a ten-thousandfold profit, therefore, Buddhism encourages people to resolve to be compassionate, to resolve to develop the aspiration for enlightenment, and to resolve to improve the mind. Now, how exactly do we become resolved in this way? The following are some suggestions:

1. The resolve that stems from "feeling ashamed over how little one knows:" For example, we need to admit that there are many classic literature that we have not yet read; there is still much concerning science and technology that we do not know; there are still many philosophical theories that we do not comprehend; and there are still many forms of interpersonal interaction that we have yet to master. Thus, we must feel ashamed for our incompleteness. But, when we do feel ashamed for having little talent and insufficient learning, we will be inspired to learn and absorb as much knowledge as possible. We will encourage ourselves to learn how to drive, how to use a computer to manage information, how to

keep the books, or how to sing or play musical instruments, if we have not already known any of the above.

2. The resolve that stems from "feeling ashamed over how limited our abilities are:" For example, I feel ashamed for not being thorough enough in completing a task, for not fulfilling my duty as a teacher, or for not being accomplished enough as a leader. As we feel ashamed over our incompetence, we can resolve to strengthen ourselves in order to become more dependable and responsible.

3. The resolve that stems from "feeling ashamed over how impure our minds are:" For example, we are ashamed that our minds are often filled with greed, hatred, and defilement, that our minds are filled with thoughts that offend others, or that our minds are full of crafty schemes and nefarious plots. As we feel ashamed for the impurity of our minds, we can resolve to improve and purify ourselves.

4. The resolve that stems from "feeling ashamed over how weak our good thoughts are:" For example, we feel ashamed over not

being able to maintain kind thoughts, or for not devoting all of our energy to doing good deeds. For these reasons, we can resolve to do more good deeds, give more generously, and bring more joy to others.

Other than the above, we also need to develop our true mind in the following four ways:

1. Develop a true mind that is as vast as the ocean: Not only is the ocean a palace for aquatic animals, it is also a place filled with inexhaustible treasures. Take a look at oil drillers today. Do they not always dig deep in the ocean for the oil? The ocean's resources are usually what supports and makes a country wealthy; this is why every country protects its territorial waters, because in essence they are protecting their national resources. Our mind is also like the ocean; it is a womb that nurtures the treasures such as compassion and the aspiration for enlightenment that are to be developed.

2. Develop a true mind that is as immense as the space: The universe can be used as a

metaphor for our mind, "the mind is like the universe; its capacity is as immeasurable as all the grains of sand." The universe contains the sun, the moon, and the stars; and within the universe there exist thunder, lightening, rain, and dew. Every phenomenon is embraced within. Therefore, the nations of the world are all interested in exploring the universe, hoping to discover treasures contained therein. Our mind too is like space filled with limitless treasures of joy and contentment. It is only through development that we can discover them.

3. Develop a true mind that is as boundless as the earth: The earth is our mother that nurtures our life. Not only does the human race depend on the sky and the ocean's resources for food, but we also depend on the earth to survive. The earth supports all forms of life that grow on it, while underneath it are the mines of gold, silver, copper, and other kinds of minerals. Our mind too is like the earth, in which our true Buddha nature lies deep within. We must know where to dig and how to develop it, in order to uncover these treasures.

4. Develop a true mind that is as our original nature: Each one of us possesses an intrinsically true nature. Once we uncover our true nature, one that is like the ocean, like the space, and like the earth, we can then take one step further and uncover our original state, returning to our native home to retrieve what has been ours from the very beginning.

In general, anything that enables us to accomplish the ultimate goal of benefiting both oneself and others, as well as enlightening both oneself and others, must never be lost or forgotten by Dharma learners. These include: gratitude, humility, commitment to the path, merit, devout faith, respect, tolerance, and patience, all of which are ways of making one's resolve that no Buddhist can do without.

To resolve means to have goals, in other words, to make vows. To resolve has its motive force, just as any machine is characterized by the strength of its motive energy. We must also ask ourselves what is the strength and capacity of our motive force. Power and motive force come from our resolve; the greater our resolve, the more powerful we will be. Therefore, I hope all BLIA members will strive to resolve, and use the motive force gained from such resolve to change the world and benefit humanity.

## III. Change the World and Benefit Humanity by Participation and Involvement

Every phenomenon in the world depends on a set of causes and conditions for its existence. "Things are formed through the combination of conditions, and things are destroyed when those conditions disperse." Without the necessary causes and conditions, not only would it be difficult to accomplish a goal, the very survival of the individual is also at stake. Therefore, we cannot survive apart from other people, because they are our causes and conditions, as well as the criteria for our survival. This is why Buddhism emphasizes "dependent origination," "collective effort," and "formation though the combination of conditions."

In Buddhism, human beings are referred

to as "sentient beings." In other words, they are beings that come into existence once the necessary conditions come together. In this world, there is no time or place that would enable any individual to exist alone, because beings must depend on each other in order to survive. Only when the conditions concerning us come together, will we be able to live. For this reason, we must allow these conditions to come together, and then share them with others, and allow other people to benefit from them as well. We must never leave the crowd and become selfish practitioners, because Buddhahood can only be attained by interacting with sentient beings, for without them, not only would we be unable to survive, Buddhahood as well would be out of reach.

The word "beings" has such wonderful meanings; for example, "all beings are equal," "treat other beings as you treat yourself," "make other beings the top priority," "the unified will of all beings makes an impregnable stronghold," "the hands of many beings make for easy work," and so on. It is also said in the Buddhist sutras, that every Dharma gathering or undertaking requires the presence of an assembly of beings to happen. Therefore, the only way to succeed is by working side-by-side with other beings. This is the truth no one can deny!

Speaking of the importance of "multitude," if we look at nature's kingdom, we will see that trees grow in "multitudes" to make a forest; while flowers, plants, and animals grow and flourish in "numbers." Therefore, we have such phrases as "birds of a feather flock together." Human beings are no exception. We all come into this world empty-handed, and even though we may have a family, assets, and a career while we are alive, we still have to leave empty-handed in the end. Therefore, the best possessions we can ever own in this life are the Dharma, merits, virtues, fields of merit, and the future. These are the resources that can be sustained over time, representing as well the highest value in life.

In particular, the most valuable things in this world are neither gold nor jade, nor houses nor cars; the most valuable thing is our conditions or affinities with others. We need to have good conditions between ourselves and others in order to have harmony; we need to have good conditions between ourselves and phenomena in order to succeed in what we do. The same is true between people and society, between all phenomenal things, and between "you," "me," and "him" or "her." There has to be the right conditions in order to achieve fulfillment and merit. Thus, there are many good deeds worth doing in this world; for example, giving, abiding by the law, supporting others, and serving others. Amongst all the virtuous practices, there is nothing more important than "giving others some positive conditions."

"Condition" is not a special Buddhist term; rather, it is the truth of the universe and life. "Condition" is a part of every one of us; it is what keeps us moving in life. Take "opportunity" as an example. In simple words, it means the right condition; everything in this world depends on a set of "conditions" to happen. A house lacking something as little as a brick or a tile, is still deemed incomplete. On the journey of life, some people have come across another who offered a hand in times of difficulty, which resulted from good connections having been made in the past. Therefore, developing good connections or affinities today will be helpful to us in future times of need. It can be said that making good connections or affinities is the safest investment one can ever make.

Since human beings depend on causes and conditions to survive in this world, I hope BLIA members will collaborate with the multitude and get involved with different activities, so that we can all develop extensive and positive connections. The more connections we have, the greater our success will be. In particular, we must establish various types of Buddha's Light programs in order to benefit humanity. In the past, people used to think that Buddhist activities were nothing more than chanting Buddhist sutras or holding services for the dead, or that these activities revolved around a lifestyle deep within mountain forests where Buddhists remain self-sufficient by farming. The truth is, Buddhists have for the past thousand years remained connected to society by providing medical treatment, social welfare, educational services, and cultural programs, dedicating themselves to the well-being of society and the benefit of humanity.

For example, the monastic granaries during the Northern Wei dynasty (386-534) assisted the government in ending a famine. The monastic storehouses from the Southern and Northern dynasties (420-589), and the "inexhaustible storehouse" owned by the Three Stages Movement of the Tang dynasty successfully established a series of oil mills, pawnshops, hostels, tea houses, refectories, and grinding mills, so as to make life more convenient and the nation more prosperous. In particular, the development of monastery-based Buddhist activities to help and benefit people was the main reason why Buddhism was able to flourish and prosper during the Sui (581-618) and Tang dynasties (618-907). The grain mills, rice mills, and warehouses set up by Buddhists enabled people to develop their livelihood; the hostels for travelers and stalls for horses and donkeys made traveling convenient for merchants; the tuition-free schools, private academies, Buddhist text repositories, and translation centers for the Buddhist sutras enhanced society's level of culture and education; monastic granaries and storehouse stabilized the nation's finance; while the clinics and pawnshops helped take care of the needy.

On a broader level, all Buddhist temples and monasteries over the ages had engaged in activities to help and benefit living beings. For example, such undertakings included the opening of wastelands for farming; the digging of wells and ditches, and creating of irrigation projects and water conservation programs; the construction of roads, bridges, public toilets, and pavilions which made traveling convenient; the establishment of mills, public bath houses, famine and poverty relief, medical treatment and supplies, care for the young and old, emergency relief, free schooling, and even free burial services. Indeed, one could say, that ever since it came to China, Buddhism has kept up with the changing times and contributed to developments from agriculture to industry, from travel services to hospice care, from pawnshops and oil mills to warehouses and watermills, and from charity to culture and education. Not only has Buddhism contributed to the development and prosperity of the economy, it has also enhanced society's level of education and culture.

Today, as BLIA members whose aim is to realize Humanistic Buddhism, we need to continue to establish all kinds of Buddhist activities under a well-structured plan, in order to benefit society. For example, we can establish Buddhist lending libraries, to provide Buddhists and members of society access to a variety of Buddhist publications and Dharma implements, as well as audio and visual media in order to enhance the propagation of Buddhist culture. We can also establish Fo Guang Yuan art galleries, Buddhist tea houses, translation centers, and medical centers in different places. Even the promotion of reading clubs, Sounds of the Human World Music Competitions, spiritual conservation programs, and environmental protection projects, can enable us to establish a connection between people and Buddhism through the use of language, public talks, music, art, relief programs, and medical treatment, in order to bring benefit and happiness to all.

BLIA members also have the opportunity to enroll at educational institutes established by Fo Guang Shan for all levels of study, or join the Buddhist Studies Institutes to study Buddhist texts and do research, so as to promote the ideals and discourse on Humanistic Buddhism. You can also go to Fo Guang Shan's Meditation Hall or Amitabha Chanting Hall to experience the dual practices of Chan and Pure Land, and actualize the ideal of equal emphasis on Buddhist understanding and practices. You can even join the Fo Guang Shan Order with a salaried job within the organization.

The following are some examples of areas of activity suitable to Buddhists for the reference of BLIA members:

**Culture:** Newspapers, radio stations, television stations, record companies, Buddhist libraries, art galleries, cultural centers, publishing, translation, theaters, concert halls, and conference centers.

**Education:** Schools, kindergartens, tutoring classes, literacy class for foreigners, continuing education institutions, arts and crafts centers, Buddhist seminaries, and community colleges.

**Social Welfare:** Hospitals, rehabilitation centers, dialysis centers, sanatoriums, retirement homes, senior's clubs, childcare centers, and children's homes.

**Service Industry:** Travel agencies, funeral parlors, florists, shipping companies, consulting services, law firms, insurance companies, job centers, and training centers.

**Industry and Business:** Supermarkets, Buddhist department stores, hotels, vegetarian restaurants, product distribution centers, interior design companies, landscaping companies, power and water utility plants, farms, and factories.

Other than the above examples, BLIA members are certainly encouraged to take part in any undertaking or career that helps change the world and benefit humanity; that contributes to the well-being of the country, its people, society, economic prosperity; and that brings happiness to the general public. As long as these conditions are fulfilled, any member can carry out such work according to their own field of expertise, interest, and financial resources. In the future, BLIA members will also need to work towards the integration of tradition with modernity, so as to transform conventional methods into something acceptable to people today. For example, the manner of gatherings, chanting services, and activities need to be reformed. Extra attention needs to be paid to young adults and scouts, so as to attract them to Buddhist activities. This will certainly contribute to Buddhism's role in changing the world and benefiting humanity.

## IV. Change the World and Benefit Humanity by the Power of the Enlightenment Vow

While Buddhism values wisdom, it places special emphasis on compassion, but with its emphasis on compassion, the importance of practice and vows stand out. All buddhas and bodhisattvas have completed the Buddhist path by cultivating compassion and wisdom, by making vows, and cultivating their practice. That is why it has been said before, that to resolve and make a vow constitute the first step in learning Buddhism. Just as said in the *Treatise on the Perfection of Great Wisdom*, "To practice without a vow is an aimless gesture. A vow is your guide to enlightenment." The *Great Collection Sutra* teaches, "Making a vow can destroy all evil hindrances." From this we can see that no one enters the Buddhist path without cultivating the practice and making vows; and though it is true that results achieved do indeed derive from spiritual practice, but without the power of the "vow," the process of spiritual practice itself would not lead to the intended goal. Therefore, it is essential that students of Buddhism develop the aspiration for enlightenment and vow to attain it.

The aspiration for enlightenment means the achievement of enlightenment for oneself and others, that is, the great vow to "seek

Buddhahood above and the liberation of sentient beings below." The main reason that Buddhism declined in the past was because Buddhists did not strive hard enough to cultivate their compassion and wisdom, or make vows and cultivate the practice. Take the Four Universal Vows of the Bodhisattva for example, most people merely recite the vows but do not really discuss their significance; or if they do discuss them, they do not try and practice them; or if they do try, they do not get anywhere. Therefore, if we wish for Buddhism to prosper today, then Buddhist followers must have wisdom and compassion, make vows, and cultivate the practice. For example, Sakyamuni Buddha made the vow as he sat beneath the bodhi tree: "I vow never to rise from my seat unless I achieve Buddhahood." Amitabha Buddha made forty-eight vows to create the Western Pure Land of Ultimate Bliss; the Medicine Buddha made twelve vows to adorn his Eastern Pure Land; while the bodhisattvas Manjusri, Samantabhadra, Avalokitesvara, and Ksitigarbha have also based their practice on compassion and the making of vows. Other examples include Master Xuan Zang who traveled westwards in pursuit of the Buddhist sutras, and Master Jian Zhen who traveled eastwards to Japan to propagate the Dharma. Their spirit and resolve "to change the world and benefit humanity" is something worthy of our emulation. In fact, every practitioner of Mahayana Buddhism is obliged to follow and practice the Four Universal Vows of the Bodhisattva. Therefore, every BLIA member who vows to practice the bodhisattva path needs to cultivate the aspiration for enlightenment and the power of vows, in order to change the world and benefit humanity. This is why if ever Humanistic Buddhism deviates from the aspiration for enlightenment, it would become mere worldly teachings that no longer accords with the Buddha's way.

How exactly do we develop the aspiration for enlightenment and how do we generate power from making of vows? The *Suramgama Sutra* states, "A deviant cause will only result in a tortuous effect." Cultivating resolve and making a vow must accord with the criteria set forth in The *Awakening of Faith in the Mahayana*: grand, correct, perfect and true. "Even if a flaming wheel of iron rotates on the top of my head, I still will not relinquish the aspiration for enlightenment because of the burning pain." By making such a vow, we shall not diverge from the correct path. The following are some examples of vows that BLIA members can make:

1. I vow to be a Buddhist of orthodox faith who shares the Dharma with the world.

2. I vow to spread the orthodox faith of Buddhism throughout the world.

3. I vow to go to remote areas and outlying territories to propagate the Dharma.

4. I vow to go to areas of distress and offer my love and care.

5. I vow to dedicate all my property to a Buddhist organization for its sustained management; I vow to dedicate my legacy to a Buddhist organization for the benefit of all sentient beings.

6. I vow to build a Buddhist family of

correct understanding and correct view, and value the religious heritage within the family.

7. I vow to follow one teacher and one path, and will protect the true Dharma.

8. I vow to write, speak, practice, and spread the Dharma.

Other than the above, modern Buddhists also need to vow to consider the needs of life and help society by providing relief to those who are suffering. Examples of such specific action include:

1. Set up "Dharma hotlines," enabling those in need who have no one to talk to, a chance to open their hearts on the telephone, and even receive guidance and comfort provided from the Buddhist perspective.

2. Set up "relief centers" to guide those lost at life's crossroads back onto the right track.

3. Set up "Dharma counseling centers" to provide answers to those who may have doubts or problems with their life, career, family, and personal relationships.

4. Set up "senior's clubs" to offer the elderly a place to get together, drink tea,

play chess, read, and chant. Through these interactions with others, they will also find peace of mind from the Dharma.

5. Set up "senior's home" through the spirit of "taking care of one's own aged parents and extending that care to all aged seniors. In this way, those elderly who live alone can be free from the suffering of loneliness and helplessness.

6. Set up "open shelters" to provide temporary places to stay for the sick and needy, so they can rest, recuperate, and get back on their feet again.

7. Set up "career centers for women" to offer career advice to women from rural areas seeking jobs in metropolitan districts; and help them find temporary accommodations while they are in-between jobs, so as to protect them from being deceived by unscrupulous persons.

8. Set up "visiting teams" to visit hospitals or homes of the sick under an organized plan to chant for them, give them blessings, and give them books on Buddhism, so that they may find comfort in their hearts.

9. Take part in programs such as Fo Guang Shan Mobile Clinic that delivers medical supplies to remote areas, so that the healthy can provide financial support to the poor who are sick and in need of medical attention.

10. Organize "emergency support groups" to offer immediate relief to those whose homes have been destroyed by natural disasters. This is also what we mean by "relieving those in urgent need is more important than helping those in chronic poverty."

11. Allocate a tenth of your income for donations.

12. Spend a few hours each week on volunteer work for religious or charity purposes.

Being resolved and making vows are not practices exclusive to Buddhists; every member of society has the obligation to do so. Once one has resolved to commit, the accomplishment of a task then becomes possible; once a vow is made, a clear goal will then be in sight. In particular, a chaotic society is the cause of many people's worries and sense of insecurity. Therefore it is vital that every member of society resolves and vows to play their roles well; for example, "as a police officer, I vow to fulfill my duty in eliminating crime, and to fight against the evils of society in order to bring safety and stability to people;" "as a housewife, I vow to be good to my in-laws, to educate my children, to be thoughtful of my husband, and to protect the morals of my family;" "as a student, I vow to excel in both my studies and conduct by studying hard, being good and caring for my parents, respecting my teachers, and getting along with my friends." If everyone in the nation vows to bring happiness, act generously, and share their joy with others, then our society is bound to be full of harmony.

In short, making a vow is like excavating an endless source of energy within our minds, a treasure that can never be exhausted. By constantly making vows and resolutions, we will be able to leave our own mark on history, leave our contributions to the family, leave our compassion to society, and leave our bright hopes to the world.

May all BLIA members, men or women,

young or old, possess the compassion, the wisdom, the vows, and the practice to change the world and benefit humanity, by the power of their aspiration for enlightenment. In so doing, the spread of Buddhism throughout society and into everyone's hearts will surely happen soon.

The establishment of BLIA has not only brought the religious faith of Buddhists to a higher level, it is also a revolutionary movement within the history of Buddhism. Over fifteen years since its dedication to the propagation of Humanistic Buddhism, BLIA members have made tremendous progress in making Buddhism more life-oriented, more modernized, more adapted to local needs, and more international in perspective. I hope in the future, each of our members can follow the Buddhist spirit of compassion and wisdom, maintain your self-awareness and integrity, and fill yourselves with motive force gained from your resolve to support and participate in the propagation of Buddhism. Furthermore, with the aspiration for enlightenment and the great vows as support, may we dedicate our hearts and strength to the propagation of Buddhism, to the purification of the world, and to the happiness and well-being of humanity.

當代人心思潮

*Modern Thoughts, Wise Mentality*

國際佛光會主題演說(1992-2006)

星雲大師 著

國家圖書館出版品預行編目資料

當代人心思潮＝Modern thoughts, wise mentality／
星雲大師著；妙光法師等翻譯.--初版.--臺北市：香海文化,
2006[民95] 面； 公分 --（人間佛教叢書）（人間論叢）
中英對照 ISBN 978-986-7384-54-6(精裝)
1.佛教-語錄
225.4 96000174

人間佛教叢書
人 間 論 叢 ❶ | 當代人心思潮

作者／星雲大師
發行人／慈容法師（吳素真）
主編／蔡孟樺
資料提供／法堂書記室
責任編輯／陳柏蓉
封面設計、美術編輯／陳柏蓉
翻譯／妙光法師、妙西法師、Amy Lam、Jeanne Tsai、Raymond Lee、
　　　Shirley Hsueh、Tom Graham

出版・發行／香海文化事業有限公司
地址／110台北市信義區松隆路327號9樓
電話／(02) 2748-3302
傳真／(02) 2760-5594
郵撥帳號／19110467　香海文化事業有限公司
http://www.gandha.com.tw
http://www.ganha-music.com
e-mail:gandha@ms34.hinet.net

總經銷／時報文化出版企業股份有限公司
地址／235台北縣中和市連城路134巷16號
電話／(02)2306-6842
法律顧問／舒建中、毛英富
登記證／局版北市業字第1107號
定價／NT$280元

ISBN／978-986-7384-54-6
2007年11月初版三刷
版權所有　翻印必究

# 一個主題‧一個理念

一九九二年五月十六日，國際佛光會在美國洛杉磯成立。十四年來，佛光會的會員秉持弘法利生，建設佛光淨土的宗旨，在教育、文化、慈善、修行、服務各方面，都有長足的進展，也獲得各界的肯定。二〇〇三年，更由聯合國正式授證為「非政府組織NGO」諮詢顧問。

創會以來，於國際佛光會每年例行舉辦的會員代表大會上，我都會發表一篇「主題演說」，作為會員的精神指標與未來努力的行事方向。

首先，為了把歡喜佈滿人間，使世界不分種族、國籍，皆能融和一體，和睦相處，我提出〈歡喜與融和〉；為了讓大家明白法界一切眾生，都是互相依附、共存共榮的生命共同體，我提出〈同體與共生〉。

在往來頻繁的現代社會裡，以尊重的態度待人處事，以包容的心胸利益他人，是非常重要的，於是有了〈尊重與包容〉；政治上以強欺弱，經濟上

貧富不均，以及宗教、種族的排擠等，都是因為彼此不能平等共存所致，因此有了〈平等與和平〉。

現實生活中有許多的缺憾，如人間的悲歡離合，生命的苦樂無常，環境的污濁惡化等等，都讓人身心不得自在，我想〈圓滿與自在〉應是世人最嚮往、最欣羨的境界了；自然是世間的本來面目，唯有尊重自然，順從自然，我們的心靈才能解脫，我們的生命才能自由，以〈自然與生命〉為題，是希望喚醒人類的覺醒，珍惜生命，言行事理不違自然的準則。

科技文明豐富了物質生活，但也影響我們的價值觀；現代人常常是非觀念混淆，所以提出〈公是公非〉的主題。「因緣果報」、「無我無私」、「緣起性空」之般若真理，是「公是公非」；「公平正直」、「無我無私」之處事原則，是「公是公非」。人人都有「公是公非」的道德勇氣，才能再造一個公理正義的社會。

發心，是佛門很美好的用語，指的是開發我們內心的寶藏。為免流於空談，我提出要發「慈悲心、增上心、同體心、菩提心」四種心。除了開

發內在的心地，也要開發外在的世界，所以還要有四種發展：「發展人性的真善美好，發展世間的福慧聖財，發展人際的和樂愛敬，發展未來的生佛合一。」發心，是建設自己；發展，是建設世界。〈發心與發展〉是每個人對自己、對家庭、對社會、對國家，甚至對全宇宙人類應有的使命。

為了將佛法真正落實於生活，將佛教根植於人間，在〈人間與生活〉的主題中，我推動「佛教四化」，即「佛法人間化，生活書香化，僧信平等化，寺院本土化」。有感於一般佛教徒的信仰大都停留在信佛、拜佛、求佛的階段，我揭示〈自覺與行佛〉，希望人人自我期許「我是佛」，以自覺心昇華自我，用大願力行佛所行。一個宗教能被接受，能互古長存，是因為它將正法弘化世間，並利益眾人，因此，我以〈化世與益人〉，作為大家弘法的目標。

雖然年年主題不同，但是一個主題，一個理念；這些理念不受限於時空，尤其更符合當代社會人心之需求！

「同體」、「共生」、「自然」，是宇宙萬物，生命生存的現象；「歡喜」、「融和」、「尊重」、「包容」、「平等」、「和平」，是世間人際往來應該遵行的準則；「公是公非」、「發心」、「發展」，是人類社會進步與提昇的條件；當每個人都能「自覺」、「行佛」、「化世」、「益人」，就是自利利他，自他都「圓滿自在」了。

香海文化將我歷年來的「主題演說」編輯成書，名為《當代人心思潮》，為了方便更多讀者的閱讀，也將英文翻譯一併編排。我簡略敘說這些主題的緣起與精神，是為序。

——二○○六年 九月 星雲於佛光山法堂

# 目錄

## 歡喜與融和

現世悲苦的實相　不足以代表佛教
佛教的真相是禪悅與法喜
我們要用入世替代出世　用積極取換消極
用樂觀改變悲觀　用喜世摧毀厭世
用歡喜的奉獻
展現國際佛教的生命力與正覺觀

國際佛光會第一次世界會員代表大會
地點：美國洛杉磯西來寺
時間：1992年5月16日

國際佛光會各國地區會長、各位會員代表、各位貴賓：

今天，欣逢「國際佛光會」第一屆會員代表大會，暨世界總會成立大會，有來自世界五大洲，四十八個國家和地區的精英代表，齊聚於美國洛杉磯西來寺，四千餘人參與此一盛會，初步體現了「佛光普照三千界，法水長流五大洲」的理想。

在現代世界文明互相交流，地球村民往來頻繁之際，佛教也逐漸突破舊有型態，走出山林，進入社會；擴大寺院功能，深入人群服務；步向家庭，助益國家，進而超越國界而延伸全球。為了促進人類融和，發揚慈悲友愛精神，國際佛光會乃應運而生。

依星雲個人的體會，本會是具足：

一、信仰的根性——以虔誠信仰的佛法，建立本會的基礎。

二、普及的特性——以普及人間的服務，作為本會的目標。

三、現代的適性——以適應現代的發展，形成本會的風格。

四、國際的廣性——以擴大國際的交流，開闊本會的胸襟。

所以我們主張，佛光會員要能做到：

一、做個共生的地球人。

二、做個同體的慈悲人。

三、做個明理的智慧人。

四、做個有力的忍耐人。

五、做個布施的結緣人。

六、做個清淨的修道人。

在我們步上世界舞台的時刻，呈現給世人的必須是一個歡喜的團體，融和友愛的組織，所以將此次大會的主題定為「歡喜與融和」。

過去，佛教常常給予人們以消極、悲觀、厭世的錯覺，深山苦修，導致佛教積弱不振。誠然佛陀慈悲教誡世間是苦、空、無常，但他同時也指示

對法樂喜悅的追求。因此現世悲苦的實相，不足以代表佛教，佛教的真象是禪悅與法喜。佛教有慈悲喜捨的內容，有利樂人間的聖道，有極樂淨土、琉璃世界的美妙樂悅。凡是在佛法中有體驗證悟的人，總是歡呼著：「法喜！解脫！禪悅！安樂！」在在表現佛教導人歡喜、令人快樂的實情。我相信國際佛光會的建立，一定能把我們的歡喜展現出來，將我們的法樂散佈出去。

我們要用入世替代出世，用積極取換消極，用樂觀改變悲觀，用喜世摧毀厭世。用歡喜的奉獻，展現國際佛教的生命力與正覺觀。

依據佛經記載，佛陀宣講佛法時，他是「助令歡喜」、「歡喜說法」、「示教利喜」的典範，諸弟子聞法皆「心生歡喜」、「願樂欲聞」，大眾更以「歡喜踴躍」、「歡喜信受」、「歡喜奉行」乃至「歡喜讚歎，作禮而去」表達對佛法的信受。這麼一場歡喜春風，早在佛陀時已散發遍佈。佛教所擁有的法喜禪悅，才是真諦寶藏。

所以國際佛光會全體會員，所許的共同的願望：「我們要把歡喜佈滿人

間！」

因歡喜修道而體悟功德者，也所在多有，如：「我於喜樂念中，欲求五功德果。」（《釋提桓因問經》）。「歡喜恭敬心，能問甚深法。」（《華嚴經》〈入法界品〉）。「諸佛子菩薩，住於極喜地時，極多歡喜，多淨信、多愛樂、多適悅、多忻慶。」（《十地經》）。普賢菩薩就是以「隨喜功德」作為第五項修行指標。（《華嚴經》〈普賢行願品〉）。彌勒菩薩也贊成在快樂修行中獲至菩薩行：「以善巧方便，安樂之道，積集無上正等菩提。」（《彌勒菩薩所問本願經》）。

諸佛菩薩當中，以「歡喜」成就佛道的，有眾所熟悉的笑顏常開的彌勒佛之外，尚有：歡喜王菩薩、歡喜念菩薩、歡喜意菩薩、歡喜力菩薩、歡喜快樂佛、歡喜自在佛、歡喜莊嚴佛、歡喜藏佛、歡喜德佛、歡喜無畏佛、歡喜威德佛等（出自《佛名經》），可見「歡喜人生」的提倡，諸佛菩薩早就以此作為修行入佛的常道。

其實，人類生命輪迴的過程已夠苦了，何忍再加諸憂悲苦惱於世間？我們為了解決苦惱的難題，提出一劑「歡喜」的良藥來醫治。我們要創造一個進取的理念：給人幸福，給人快樂；要讓大家分享歡喜，具足希望。佛陀說「諸行無常」當得會意：「無常很好！」無常就是變化，好的會變成壞的，壞的也會變成好的，因為無常，所以一切在「因、緣、果」的法則下，只要善因善緣，均能否極泰來，時來運轉，生機出現而希望無窮。故吾等國際佛光人由尋求自身輕安法喜，體證超越時空的清淨安樂，更要散播自受用和他受用的禪悅給大眾。將我們身口意的無限歡喜，呈獻於法界之內，普世之前。讓那些已經忘了微笑，許久沒有關懷，愁眉深鎖的朋友獲得一份「歡喜灌頂」。讓我們秉持著：「慈悲喜捨遍法界，惜福結緣利人天；禪淨戒行平等忍，慚愧感恩大願心」的理念，開創佛教歡喜的風氣，促使幸福快樂的人間佛教，源遠流長；讓歡喜的人們永保樂觀，就算娑婆八苦交煎，我們也要做到從心不苦，進而做到身不苦，因為在佛光普照下，我們要讓憂苦的陰影

蕩然無存！

在佛光山上，靈山勝境的山門定為不二門，有一則對聯是：「不二本無門，二不二，具是自家真面目；靈山稱勝境，山非山，無非我人清淨身。」

佛陀的清淨法身與眾生的真實自性，是同源一體，無二無別。在佛性中根本存在融和、平等與圓滿的本性，不需外求。今天國際佛光會草創開始，除歡喜外，必能秉著「融和」之容性，吸收會員，接納會友，擴展會務，發揚會風。

「融和」是一種容人的雅量，一種平等的相待，一種尊重的言行。國際佛光會正需具備一份容納異己的氣量，方能有博大的未來。古諺：「泰山不辭土壤，大海不捐細流。」昔日，齊桓公延用敵師管仲，得以九合諸侯，一匡天下；唐太宗推崇魏徵魯直規諫，顯示寬容大度。同樣地，佛門傳頌：「百川匯歸大海，共一鹹味。」「各族入佛，同為佛子。」昔日，剎帝王孫難陀和阿難尚對首陀羅賤民出身的優波離，拜火教的迦葉，好玄論的迦旃

延，尊奉為師兄，概因「四姓出家，同為釋氏」的平等性，由此可知佛陀早就打破種族交界線、階級差別。佛陀慈悲融和的性格，使佛種得以遍撒各地，佛法得以流傳至今。今日，國際佛光會要屹立於世界，更需要努力接納別人，融和眾生，才能成長茁壯。

星雲一向主張，同中容異，異中求同。在佛教裡，南北傳的佛教要融和，傳統和現代的佛教也要融和；禪淨要融和，顯密也要融和；僧信要融和；世出世法也要融和；融和就是中道，中道才是真正的佛法。今日世界更需要融和，國家與國家要融和，種族與種族要融和，士農工商與士農工商要融和，群我之間更要有群我之間的融和，政黨主義應與政黨主義融和，因為融和才是今後地球人的共生之道！

世人以心地不夠寬大的陋習是：「自己萎弱，厭人健全；自己惡動，怪人活潑；自己飲水，嫉人喝茶；自己呻吟，恨人笑聲。」國際佛光人與此

陋習恰恰相反；佛光人是實行菩薩道的：「人在山林，要心懷社會；立足地球，要放眼宇宙；身居道場，要普利大眾；天堂雖好，要美化人間」。處在融和的修行中，平等尊重，有活潑的人我一如，更有健全的自他兩利。

古來的佛教，一直十分注重融攝反對者的理論，以及吸收異論者合理的思想，更不斷取得其他學派、宗教中適合的善巧與方便，以適存於各地域、各歷史、各文化、各社會與環境之中，以發揮佛教強韌的生命力。佛教對外如此，對內更是以融和來兼容並蓄。二千六百多年來，佛教幾經萬花齊放、百鳥爭鳴，綻放出極其繽紛的光彩。在佛理、教義上有頓漸、迷悟、真妄、空有等不同的學說與議論；在印度宗派上有大眾部、上座部的分岐，在中國有八大宗派的不同，不管什麼殊異的發展，但總是不離佛教的三法印和八正道的軌範。可見佛法中蘊涵極深，包容極廣。國際佛光會所推崇的，正是這類融和的佛法。我們的主張是：

一、以平等、尊重和開放的態度，容納異教和異言、異人和異事，但要

正而不邪。

二、以積極、慎重和穩健的作風，吸收其他的精華、特色與方法，但要與人有益。

三、以佛法、豐富和廣博的內涵，滋養世間和人類，同體和共生，但要氣宇胸襟。

四、以融和、交流和溝通的行動，接受文明和訊息，自覺和覺他，但要正心誠意。

所以國際佛光會全體會員共同的願望是：「我們要以融和與世相處！」

融和的重要，從最近發生的洛杉磯種族暴動事件也反映出來。正因為缺少了融和，缺少了包容，缺少了互相諒解，缺少了互相尊重，才會產生種族隔閡，才會產生種族歧視，最後也才會產生種族暴亂。看看世界種族糾紛不斷，國家暴力糾纏不已，現代的文明已影響了和平與安寧，已敗壞了天地法

則與自然生態，這說明了國際佛光會提倡的「歡喜與融和」，不僅是主觀的願望，也確是客觀的需要。就這一點來說，象徵著歡喜與融和的國際佛光會世界總會，此時此地在洛杉磯正式宣告成立，更具有特殊的時代意義。我們在消除種族彼此歧視中扮演一個角色，我們在發展現代文化思潮中促進人類的和諧，我們在提倡弘法利生佛光普照時，帶給世間的希望，我們在復興佛教宣揚法音時，提醒大眾的良知，這是國際佛光人的光榮，也是國際佛光人的義務！

國際佛光會的任務是一件接一件，國際佛光人的精神是一代傳一代。在此，祈願在三寶加被及佛陀慈光下，我們共以信心、耐心與恒心延續佛法慧命，同用佛心與慈念，化解自己和世人的愚昧！我們領納「融和」的無量，付出「歡喜」的布施，實踐國際佛光人的目的：「提倡人間佛教，建設佛光淨土，淨化世道人心，實現世界和平。」

# 同體與共生

同體是平等觀

眾生相狀　雖千差萬別

清淨佛性　卻平等一如

共生是慈悲觀

慈悲　才能容納對方　融和　才能共生共存

國際佛光會第二次世界會員代表大會

地點：高雄佛光山

時間：1993年10月18日

國際佛光會第三次世界會員代表大會

地點：加拿大溫哥華卑詩大學和平紀念館

時間：1994年9月24日

各位會友、各位嘉賓：

感謝佛陀的慈光加被，讓萬千來自世界五大洲，七十三個主要城市的佛教菁英，齊聚在國際佛光會的發源地──台北。在今天的殊勝日子裡，我們佛光會的全體會員，以無比歡喜的心情，隆重地揭開了國際佛光會第二次會員代表大會的序幕。同時，也以共同的理念，提出了「同體與共生」的大會主題。

## 一、同體共生，圓滿世界

佛陀一生說法四十九年，三百餘會，每一次說法，從不以一地、一國、一時、一眾為當機對象。說到地方，總是三千大千無量華藏世界；說到眾生，就是十方法界等恆河沙數無邊眾生；說到時間，則無非三大阿僧祇劫。

佛教講因緣，認為天下本是一家，所有眾生是因緣和合、一體不二。虛空中的日月星辰不分明暗，互相輝映；大地上的山嶽丘壑不論高低，彼此連綿；宇宙間的奇珍異獸不管異同，相輔相成。因此，這個宇宙本來就是「同體與共生」的圓滿世界！

「同體」，含有平等，包容的意思。譬如人身雖有眼、耳、鼻、舌、手、足等諸根的差異，但是卻同為身體的一部分；地球雖然有各種國家、民族、地域的不同，但是卻是共同仰賴地球而生存；眾生雖然有男女、老少、強弱、智愚的分別，但是卻同為眾緣和合的生命體。相狀雖然千差萬別，但是清靜的佛性是平等一如的。

「共生」，含有慈悲，融和的意思。法界一切眾生是彼此互相依附，賴以生存的生命共同體。佛經有一則譬喻說瞎子、跛子、啞巴，藉著互相提攜幫助，終於安全地逃離火宅。一齣精彩的戲劇，除了有主角的精湛演出之

外，還需要配角的無漏配合。我們生存的社會，也需要士農工商各行各業，貢獻每一個人的力量，才能建立祥和而共有的社會。慈悲，才能容納對方；融和，彼此才能共生共存。

## 二、平等包容，眾緣和合

我們知道，「同體」是平等觀，「共生」是慈悲觀。佛教的特色在於平等的精神，佛陀最初創立僧伽教團，就是要打破印度四姓階級的不平等，而提倡「百川入海，同一鹹味；四姓出家，同為釋氏」的平等觀。佛陀初成道時，在菩提樹下，發出金剛一般顛撲不破的宣言：「大地眾生皆有如來智慧德相」，揭櫫心、佛、眾生三無差別的同體平等精神，提倡「生佛平等」、「聖凡平等」、「理事平等」、「人我平等」的思想，我們的教主其實就是「同體平等」觀的倡導者、推動者。

佛經裡可以看到許許多多「一佛出世，千佛護持」的實例，這些都是「同體平等」的有力憑證。《法華經》中，常不輕菩薩常懷「同體平等」的慈悲心，禮敬一切眾生並且說道：「我不敢輕視汝等，汝等皆當作佛。」佛陀降生藍毘尼園時，一手指天，一手指地說：「天上天下，唯我獨尊。」十法界中的一切眾生都是至尊至貴、平等無差的。；般若性海裡，眾生的佛性都是清淨不染的。

反觀我們的社會，卻存有種種差別對待的現象，譬如貧富的懸殊，權勢的大小，出身的高低，教育的差距，乃至智愚賢肖的不同。因此，我希望佛光會員們能秉持「平等」的智慧，懷抱佛陀打破四姓階級的無畏精神，努力推動：

(一)、國際佛光會是一個主張慈悲包容的社團。

（二）、國際佛光會是一個倡導眾生平等的社團。
（三）、國際佛光會是一個尊重家庭生活的社團。
（四）、國際佛光會是一個重視社會福祉的社團。

## 三、無偏無私，共存共榮

在國際佛光會裡，所有的會員不分國家、不分種族、不分男女、不分貧富，都是平等互尊的，因為我們一切會員是「同體共生」的地球人。

「共生」之所以說為慈悲觀，是因為佛教一向提倡「無緣大慈，同體大悲」，慈悲是無偏私的關愛，慈悲是無對待的包容。慈悲不是工作中的上下階級對待，也不是日常生活裡的有無計較，更不是社會上的貧富差別。慈悲是眾生與眾生之間的融和與尊重。因此，慈悲，就是尊重生命；慈悲，就是

共存共榮。

慈悲，是佛教的根本思想，佛教的眾多經典中強調慈悲的重要性，譬如《法華經》：「願以大慈悲，廣開甘露門，轉無上法輪。」「以大慈悲，度苦惱眾生。」《大智度論》：「慈悲，佛道之根本。」《華嚴經》：「諸佛如來，以大悲心為體故。」《明網菩薩經》：「大悲為一切諸佛菩薩功德之根本。」《大丈夫論》：「一切善法皆以慈悲心為本。」《增壹阿含經》：「諸佛世尊，成大慈悲；以大悲力，弘益眾生。」慈與快樂，悲能拔苦，沒有了慈悲，所行的一切都是魔法。

世界上國家與國家之間雖然有戰亂，種族與種族之間雖然有仇隙，宗教與宗教之間雖然有派系，但是大家共同住在同一個地球之上，應該捐棄我見偏執，彼此守望相助，進而尊重每一個眾生的生存權利，以「同體」來推動眾生平等的思想，以「共生」來發揚慈悲喜捨的精神，讓地球成為和平安樂

的人間淨土。

儒家以「老吾老以及人之老，幼吾幼以及人之幼」來發揚大同世界的「共生」精神，以「人溺己溺，人飢己飢」、「四海之內皆兄弟」來體現民胞物與的「同體」胸懷。有容乃大，慈悲無畏，在這世間裡，海闊縱魚躍，天空任鳥飛，因此海天能成其浩大；太虛納星羅，寰宇佈萬象，因此宇宙能現其無邊；仁王成就百家爭鳴，智者不拒雅言異議，因此古往聖賢能揚其仁智；佛陀演說五乘共法，聖教鼓勵八宗兼弘，因此佛教能顯其寬大雍容。

從生物學的角度，我們也可以看到大地眾生「同體共生」的現象。生物學上有三種的共生：

（一）、鯨魚與藤壺之間的「片利共生」；

（二）、人類與蠕蟲之間的「寄生共生」；

（三）水牛與牛椋鳥之間的「互利共生」。

動植物以不同時間呼吸氧氣與二氧化碳，各取所需，相互受惠。在「食物鏈」裡，草食動物以大地的青草為食物，肉食動物則捕捉草食動物為生，細菌又將死後的肉食動物分解，變成養分，回歸大地，孕育草木，如此環環相扣，生生不息，這就是「同體共生」的因緣法。甚至水鳥的鵜鶘互助捕魚，海狸合力築壩，海豚群居團結，保持生機，人類日常生活所需，也是仰賴社會各行各業供給。法不孤起，仗境方生。因緣具足，一切才能成就。

「同體共生」，動植物才能共同存在；「同體共生」人類才能和平相安，「同體共生」大自然才能保持生態平衡，這世間才有無限的生機。

# 四、互利互生，自然平衡

人類過去生活在神權控制的時代，把自己的命運禍福交給冥冥不可測知的神祇決定；後來人類建立了國家，君主主宰人民的一切，人類活在君權的籠罩之下；漸漸地，民智開啟了，人類掙出君權的桎梏，邁向自己做主人的民權時代。民權時代老百姓雖然活得很尊嚴，但是畢竟以人類為中心，不能全面普及於一切眾生。因此，今日我們要進一步從民權時代擴展至同體共生的生權時代，尊重有情、無情的一切眾生，發揚「無緣大慈，同體大悲」的精神。

今日的社會因為缺少「同體平等」的認知，因此亂象迭起；當前的環境因為沒有「共生慈悲」的觀念，因此遭到破壞。我們要努力實踐同體共生的理念，推動誡煙毒、誡色情、誡暴力、誡偷盜、誡賭博、誡酗酒、誡惡口的新生活七誡運動，淨化社會人心；積極響應世界環保運動，不濫伐、不濫墾、不濫殺、不濫建、不濫丟，來挽救我們的地球。

「同體與共生」是宇宙的真理，然而目前世界卻有許多人倒行逆施，自私自利，以致於天災頻仍，人禍不息。所以，我們現在揭櫫「同體與共生」作為這次大會的主題，不但合乎真理法則，更富有時代意義。讓我們從現在開始，攜手推廣「同體與共生」的理念，將慈悲、平等、融和、包容實踐在日常生活中，相信不久的將來，大家必定能共同擁有一個安和樂利的人間淨土。

# 尊重與包容

「尊重」可以改善現有的環境

　　增添社會福祉

「包容」能夠增進人際的和諧

　　廣利一切眾生

奉持五戒　就是尊重自由

包容接納一切　才能擁有全面

的人生

國際佛光會第四次世界會員代表大會

地點：澳洲雪梨達令港會議中心

時間：1995年10月15日

各位會友，各位嘉賓：

大家都是來自全球各個國家的代表，不知道您們是否發覺：我們的主題——「尊重與包容」，正具體地表現在澳大利亞這塊人間淨土上？多年來，我來往於世界各地雲遊弘法，建寺安僧，深深感到在許多國家當中，澳洲政府對於各類種族最為包容，對於各種文化最為尊重，對於海外移民，也多方協助。所以，我們今天聚集在此，以「尊重與包容」為主題，召開「國際佛光會第四次會員代表大會」可說是最恰當不過了。

今天，自由、民主與科學已然成為世界的潮流，但是在人類的濫用之下，自由成為侵犯他人的藉口，民主也變成犧牲弱小的武器，科學更是被野心家利用作為打倒鄰國的工具。過去這三項被認為是社會進步的要素，如今卻弊端百出，值此世局紛亂之際，我們提出「尊重與包容」來作為大會主題，希望能喚起世人彼此的關懷與共識。

經云：「佛法在恭敬中求。」佛教最講究「尊重」的修持，因此在世界的宗教歷史中，唯有佛教沒有發生過流血戰爭，我們應如何將「尊重」的美德落實於日常生活中呢？

## 一、尊重別人的自由

美國獨立革命時，巴特利克曾經提出「不自由，毋寧死」的口號，翻閱中外歷史，為了爭取自由而拋頭顱、灑熱血的人士更是不勝枚舉，可見自由是多麼的可貴！然而令人諷刺的是，現代的民主社會中，往往有許多人曲解自由，任性非為，造成社會種種亂象，誠為可歎！其實，自由的真諦應該是以尊重他人的自由為自由。在種種學說教理之中，佛教的「五戒」最能將自由的精神表露無遺，因為不殺生，是在尊重別人生命的自

由；不偷盜，是在尊重別人財產的自由；不邪淫，是在尊重別人身體的自由；不妄語，是在尊重別人名譽的自由；不喝酒，就不會胡作妄為，守此五戒，就懂得尊重別人的一切自由。我們看監獄裡那些作奸犯科的人，那一個不是因為違反五戒而身陷囹圄呢？

一個人若能奉持五戒，他的人格道德必定能夠健全起來；一家人若能奉持五戒，這一家必定父慈子孝；一個社會若能奉持五戒，這個社會必定安和樂利；一個國家若能持五戒，這個國家必定富強康樂；整個世界如果能奉持五戒，這個世界就是一片淨土。因此，凡我佛光人應該積極的推行五戒，不但不殺生，而且要愛護一切有情；不但不偷盜而且要進一步喜捨布施；不但不邪淫，而且要維護自他家庭的美滿幸福；不但不妄語，而且要以愛語讚美撫慰所有眾生；不但不喝酒，而且要修習智慧，以正知正見來引導別人向善。

# 二、尊重生命的價值

佛教裡有許多偈語都說明了生命的寶貴，例如「誰道群生性命微，一般骨肉一般皮；勸君莫打枝頭鳥，子在巢中望母歸。」、「我肉眾生肉，名殊體不殊，本同一種性，只為別形軀。苦惱從他受，甘肥任我需，莫叫閻老斷，自忖應如何？」生命是無價的，再多的錢財都無法買回寶貴的生命，所以我們應該尊重生命的價值，不但不要任意傷害一切眾生的生命，更要珍惜自己的生命，自許做一盞明燈，發揮生命的光熱，照亮溫暖周圍的人群；發心做一棵大樹，展現生命的清涼，為眾生作庇蔭；立誓做一道橋樑，鋪排生命的張力，導引大家到安樂的彼岸，乃至於甘願做一滴雨露，釋放生命的柔和，滋潤有情的身心。

## 三、尊重大眾的所有

我們每一個人都擁有自己的財物、感情，一旦失去原本所擁有的東西，就會感到憂悲苦惱，因此，我們不但不應將自己的快樂建築在別人的痛苦上，強佔他人所有，最好還能進一步以「享有」的思想來代替「擁有」的觀念。例如：我們雖然沒有花園洋房，但是如果能夠帶著欣賞的眼光，俯視路邊五彩繽紛的花卉，花草樹木就是我們的良朋好友；我們雖然沒有萬貫家財，但是如果能夠保持善美的心情，仰望夜空晶瑩閃亮的繁星，日月星辰就是上天賜給我們的無盡珍寶。

「溪聲盡是廣長舌，山色無非清淨身」，古來的祖師大德們因為能用心眼洞察自然界無相之相，用心耳聽世界無上聲之聲，所以擁有無邊無盡的三千法界，不但無意向外攀緣有窮有盡的五欲六塵，更能以無上的慈心

當代人心思潮　　36

悲願建設各種利生事業，為眾生拔苦與樂。像守綱日夜辛勤，鋪設道路；維溪不計勞苦，興建水利工程；洪防、道積、智嚴等建造病房，照顧貧病；道詢默默修橋行善，達三百餘座等事蹟，皆為時人所感戴稱道。道安大師在烽火亂世，仍講學不輟，度眾無數；太虛大師雖備受譭謗，卻義無反顧，力圖振興教運，挽救國勢，更足以為後世的楷模。《大智度論》云：「視他婦如母，見他財如火，一切如親親，如是名等見。」佛光人應效法古德平等尊重的精神，為眾生創造更多的福利，使大家共享美滿的生活。

# 四、尊重天地的生機

澳洲朝野人士因為能夠一致實踐環保政策，所以處處顯得翁鬱蒼翠，

景色怡人，不但飛禽走獸和人們親如一家，連水中游魚也樂於與人類親近。在澳洲，不論有情無情，都是一片生機盎然的景象，實在是一件非常可喜的事，凡此均與佛教素來提倡的環保意識不謀而合。

《阿彌陀經》裡，敘述極樂淨土行樹羅網，水鳥說法。《本生經》中，睒子菩薩在說話時不敢大聲，怕驚擾眾生；在走路時不敢用力，怕踩痛大地；無時無刻不敢亂丟東西，怕污染山河，可以說佛教裡的諸佛菩薩就是倡導環保，維護生態的先鋒祖師。古來的佛教道場大多建於名山大澤之中，寺眾不但悉心合力照顧周遭環境的清潔美化，對於山林維護，水土保持也都相當地重視。《楞伽經》云：殺生食肉者斷大悲種。佛教的持齋茹素，乃至護生放生，最主要是基於慈悲的精神，這正說明佛教是以最清淨的心靈，最徹底的方式來愛惜眾生的生命。

佛教主張「萬法緣起」認為法界中小至一芥子微塵，大至整個宇宙，

彼此之間都具有互動的關係，惟有大家抱持一顆尊重心，讓天地生機綿延不斷，才能使一切眾生的生存得到最佳的保障。

「尊重」固然可以改善現有的環境，增添社會福祉，「包容」更能夠增進人際的和諧，廣利一切眾生。千百年來，佛教流傳到世界各地，之所以能和當地文化水乳交融，形成本土化的佛教，造福社會人群，正是因為佛法真理包容無礙，故能涵攝十方，源遠流長。我們應如何發揚佛教「包容」的教義，促進世界的祥和呢？

## 一、包容異己的存在

生活環境、風俗習慣、語言文字、思惟方式的差異，自然會形成大家彼此之間不同的意見。《金剛經》上說：菩薩要降伏其心，度脫眾生，首

需去除我相、人相、眾生相、壽者相，簡而言之，就是要我們以無私的心胸雅量，包容異己的存在，否則度己不成，又如何奢言利濟有情？

佛教是世界上最包容的宗教，佛陀成道後，倡導「四姓出家，同為釋氏」，從王宮貴冑到販夫走卒，從異教外道到淫女賤民，只要肯發心向道，佛陀都包容接引，成為僧團的一份子，所以佛法能迅速地在五印度蓬勃發展，廣被眾生，而佛陀的門下成就道果者就有兩千五百人之多，其中十大弟子更是各有專長。阿育王自從信奉佛教以後，不但一改殺戮侵略的惡習，息鼓收金，羅致十方，並且對於各種宗教都予以禮尊崇，凡此不但贏得人民的愛戴，也使得國家更加富強安樂。佛教在隋唐時代，八宗昌盛，競相發展，使得中國佛教繽紛燦爛，事理輝映，後來流傳到東亞各國，豐富了當地文化內涵，直至今日仍歷久彌新，影響深遠。可見，包容異己不但不會導致派系分歧，還能繁衍生機，形成枝葉榮茂，百花齊放的

盛會。

# 二、包容傷殘的尊嚴

今年四月底我住院開刀時，和醫生談及：出家人並不畏懼生死只是惟恐忍不住病痛，使得平日威儀莊嚴的形象受到損害，陳瑞祥大夫回答說：「在我們醫生眼裡，健康的人有健康者的形象，病患者有病患的尊嚴，病痛並不可恥，所以在生病時哭叫也應該同樣受到尊重。」這句話實在太美好了！菩薩般的醫生行者，不就像藥師如來一樣，不但治療眾生色身上的疑難雜症，也撫慰有情心靈上的恐懼創傷。

南丁格爾因為能包容前線傷患的痛苦哀鳴，使血腥遍布的戰地充滿溫馨的氣氛；地藏菩薩因為能包容地獄眾生的貪瞋愚癡，使得淒苦黑暗的煉

獄產生無限的希望。一顆敬重包容心就像一支萬能的點金棒，將缺陷的世界變得如許善美！

所謂「家家彌陀佛，戶戶觀世音」，阿彌陀佛包涵眾生的罪障深重，容許眾生帶業往生極樂；觀世音菩薩不嫌娑婆濁惡，倒駕慈航，尋聲救苦。由於他們的慈悲包容，所以佛教徒們紛紛將家裡最好的位置讓出來，供奉他們的聖像。因此唯有包容眾生的一切長處、缺點、創傷、挫敗，我們才能擁有全部的眾生。

## 三、包容冤仇的傷害

《八大人覺經》云：「菩薩布施，等念怨親，不念舊惡，不憎惡人。」佛教最高的教義，就是提倡眾生平等。佛陀在菩提樹下夜睹明星，

證悟佛道時，曾發出驚歎的感言：「奇哉！奇哉！大地眾生皆有如來智慧德相！」《法華經》中敘述常不輕菩薩經常向人禮拜讚歎，並且說道：「我不敢輕視汝等，汝等將來皆當作佛。」眾人聞言，有生怒者，以杖石擊之，常不輕菩薩卻恭敬如昔，乃至遠見增上慢人，也依然作禮。華藏世界裡的眾生，因為了悟生佛平等，自他不二，怨親一如，物我和諧的道理，所以不但沒有人我是非的紛爭，而且大家都能以無量的悲心，無盡的願力，互相包容，彼此尊重，因此形成光光相攝、圓融無礙、重重無盡的華藏淨土。

娑婆穢土是個一半一半的世界：佛一半，魔一半；男一半，女一半；善人一半，惡人一半；智者一半，愚者一半……，我們生活在這一半一半的世界，不能只要這一半有利我的天地，拒絕那一半障礙我的世界。

唯有統統包容，接納一切，我們才能擁有全面的人生。揚湯不能止沸，以

恨更不能消恨，面對一半不如意的人事，我們唯有以無緣同體的慈悲心、自他不二的平等心來包容對方，才能化解干戈，消弭怨懟，贏得更多的敬愛，獲得美滿的人生。

# 四、包容無心的錯誤

「人非聖賢，孰能無過，知過能改，善莫大焉。」沒有人喜歡犯錯，而犯錯也並不盡然都是壞事，如果因當事者能力求改正，錯誤往往是成功的奠基石。所謂「嚴以律己，寬以待人」，對於自己的過失，固然要嚴厲苛責，對於他人的錯誤，則應以寬容的耐心，給予改正的機會；以權巧的智慧規勸引導，令生正確的見解。華盛頓勇於承認砍斷櫻桃樹的過失，得到父親的嘉許，使得他一生都以「誠實」作為處世圭臬，造就了日後的豐

功偉業;既聾又盲的海倫凱勒，本來性情乖戾，在老師的循循善誘之下改過遷善，終於成為一位偉大的教育家。對於他人的錯誤，我們若能自他互易，立場調換，以包容代替埋怨，以諒解代替厭惡，以鼓勵代替責備，以慈愛代替呵罵，以關懷代替放縱，以同事代替隔閡，我們的社會必定能夠更加進步，我們的生活必能夠更加美好。

我們的心量能包容多少，就能夠完成多大的事業：如果我們能夠包容一家，就可以做一家之主；能夠包容一市，就可做作一市之長；能夠包容一國，就可以做一國之君；能泯除一切對待，包容整個法界，就可隨緣應現，逍遙自在，成為法界之王。偈云：「竹密不妨流水過，山高豈礙白雲飛。」我們若能具有包容的心胸，就可以像行雲流水一樣，穿越重重的阻難，在悠悠天地間任性遨遊。

在科技進步，來往頻繁的社會裡，「尊重與包容」顯得尤其重要，我

們應該尊重他人的自由，以奉持五戒代替侵佔掠奪；尊重生命的價值，以喜捨布施代替傷生害命；尊重大眾的所有，以共享福利代替自私自利；尊重天地的生機，以環保護生代替破壞殘殺。此外，我們更應用人我無間的雅量，包容異己的存在；用淨穢不二的悲心，包容傷殘的尊嚴；用怨親平等的智慧，包容冤仇的傷害；用凡聖一如的認知，包容無心的錯誤。如果大家都能以尊重的態度敬業樂群，以包容的心胸廣利眾生，將娑婆建為淨土將是指日可待之事。

在此祈求佛光加被，祝福大家吉祥如意，大會圓滿成功！

# 平等與和平

世間萬法一如

同體緣生　相依互存

但憑慈心悲願　與樂拔苦

力行人我平等共尊　促成世界和平共榮

國際佛光會第五次世界會員代表大會

地點：法國巴黎國際會議廳

時間：1996年8月5日

各位嘉賓、各位會友：

歡迎各位來到崇尚自由民主的巴黎，參加佛光普照的盛會。永久的和平是千古以來，人人夢寐以求的美景，尤其處在這個是非顛倒、戰爭迭起的時代裡，人人自危，大家對和平更是渴望不已。然而，「以戰止戰」的和平主義經常被人利用，反使人類的禍害頻傳不已！

今天，舉世紛紜，政治上的以強欺弱，經濟上的貧富不均，宗教、種族的排擠，男女、地域的分歧，這些不能和平解決的問題，莫不是因為彼此不能平等共存所引起，所謂「不平則鳴」。因此我們在「國際佛光會第五次會員代表大會」的此刻，提出「平等共尊，和平共榮」來作為大會主題，正是希望來自世界各地的與會大眾都能將平等的觀念、和平的福音帶回去，喚起地球人的覺醒與共識。

關於平等的主張，自古有之，但終未能究竟切中時弊，解決問題。今

以佛法的「生佛平等」、「性相平等」、「自他平等」、「事理平等」、「空有平等」的原則，謹提出四點意見來說明對平等的看法：

## 一、平等必需要人我共尊

先賢曾說：「敬人者人恆敬之，愛人者人恆愛之」。平等不是用強制的手段逼迫對方就範，而應該顧及對方的尊嚴，唯有人我共尊才能達到彼此平等的境地。像東西德過去的隔離、現在南北韓、巴爾幹的分裂，彼此劍拔弩張，一直無法達成和平相處。但到一九九〇年，西德對東德的尊重包容，柏林圍牆倒塌以後，人民心中那道無形的圍牆隨之冰消瓦解，從此大家在人我平等共尊的理念下，攜手共創美好的未來。南北韓、台海兩岸、以阿之間，如果彼此尊重，人我無間，則和平又那會遙遙無期？

在佛教教義裡，對於不同國家、種族、階級、性別、年齡的人們，也最能賦予尊重，平等對待。二千五百年前的印度，佛陀喊出：「四河入海，無復河名；四姓出家，同為釋氏」的主張。正因為佛教擁有「人我共尊」的平等特性，心物一體的平等主張，因此在僧信兩眾攜手合作之下，佛法得以迅速風行印度，乃至流傳世界，也都能與當地文化相互融和，相互尊重，在歷史上唯有佛教在流傳的過程中未曾發生過戰爭流血的衝突。

可見人我共尊是平等互惠的基石，也是和平進步的良方。

有人說：「世間上沒有完美平等的事情。」誠然，事相上的平等很難達成，但我們可以從心理上建立平等的觀念。例如：母親餵幼兒吃飯時，自己也張開嘴巴，作勢誘導，所以母子之間水乳交融。父親以身當馬，讓小孩騎在上面玩耍，因此父子之間心意相通。世間大小尊卑豈有一定的標準？我們唯有泯除成見，彼此共尊，人我同等，相互接納，才能和平相

當代人心思潮　　50

處，共享安樂。

佛陀當初在證悟真理時，第一句宣言就說：「一切眾生皆有佛性！」眾生由於因果業報的千差萬別，在智愚美醜、貧富貴賤上有所不同，但論及全眾生的本體自性，並無二致。這就好比三獸渡河，足有深淺，但水無深淺；三鳥飛空，跡有遠近，但空無遠近。我們應該以悲憫的胸懷來看待眾生的苦難，以人我共尊的平等角度來包容彼此的差異，這才能促進和平！

## 二、平等要彼此立場互易

佛教裡，佛陀告訴吾人，如何建設平等觀念？必須要視人如己，一切眾生皆如羅睺羅，必定能愛人如己。經典上也一再提醒我們，如何增長慈

悲胸懷？見到別人苦難，要設身處地的為對方設想，假如他是我，或假如我是他，如此立場互易才能建立自他平等的相處。能平等相待，世界怎會不能和平？

我們見到一個身體殘缺的人，有我優你劣的心態，怎能達到平等的尊重？必須要想殘障的是我，立場互易以後，自然心境就會不同。

將社會上的醜陋缺失，看成與自己有關，自然不會排斥，自然會以慈悲胸懷，以平等觀念去對待。所以唯有人我互易，異地互惠的平等方式，才能和平共存。

提婆達多多次害佛，佛不以為迫害，反而認為是逆增上緣，指鬘外道兇殘暴虐，佛陀設身處地的施以慈悲，終能感化。

在《法華經·譬喻品》的火宅喻故事中，瞎子、跛子各有殘缺，卻各展所長互助合作，所以能一起逃出火窟，倖免亡身之難，但同為一蛇之身

當代人心思潮　　52

首尾之間卻由於互有排斥，不能相容，所以同歸於盡。眾生與我名雖有殊

而體不殊，惟有互易立場，彼此成就，才能發揚平等的真諦，自利利他，

這都在我人心念一轉，平等現前，尊嚴必見，有何不能息爭和平！

## 三、平等因為是萬法緣生

宇宙萬有不過是個因緣和合的假相，離開因緣，了無所得。即以我人

為例，人之所以為人是個人業識與父精母血的因緣結合，方能出生，其後

生命的延續生存，更須士農工商各個階層提供種種食物資糧；一朵小花，

也必須要陽光、空氣、水份、土壤等因緣和合而開；一棟房子，也要有鋼

筋、木材、水泥、磚瓦、工程師的構思等有形無形的因緣條件才能建成；

工商企業則要先籌集資本、調查市場、改良品質、研究促銷，生意才能順

利開展。在我們生活境遇中，無處不是因緣：父母生養我們是血親因緣；師長教育我們是學問因緣；農工商賈供養我們生活物品是社會因緣；出門乘坐交通工具是行路因緣；觀賞娛樂節目是視聽因緣……人們若離開因緣，任誰也無法生活下去。

也就是說，宇宙人生的一切都是因緣相互成就，相互存在。佛教的因緣果報，正是說明宇宙人生真理的關係。例如：說到時間，必定是有過去到現在才有未來；說到空間，有了東西南北方向才有中心；說到人間，有了你我他，人才能建立共存的生命。先有雞？還是先有蛋？樹上的果子能與地下的種子沒有關係嗎？所以「此有故彼有，此生故彼生；此無故彼無，此滅故彼滅」，萬法緣生的定律不外乎從因生，事待理成，有依空立，相由緣現，多從一生，佛由人來成。這說明：人我彼此相依，互生互存，你中有我，我中有你，緣生緣滅，彼此互為相等。能明白萬法緣生

相。

的道理，才能從差別中求取平等，才能從矛盾中求取統一，發現一如的真相。

世間諸法雖有相狀力用上的差別，但究其法性，則是一味平等。懂得因緣法，認識自他存在離不開因緣，則處處種好因，時時結好緣，人生必能有好因緣，凡事無往不利。所以即使是一人一物，一草一木，即使天涯海角的點滴事物看似與我無關，卻都是我們生活上的恩惠，重要的助緣，我們也要心懷感激，時思報答。人人能平等對待萬物，廣結善緣，則世界焉有不能和平之理？

## 四、平等真義乃一多不異

一般人喜多厭少，以致比較、計較，起惑造業，這個世間也因而紛擾

不斷。其實在佛教看來，一就是多，多就是一，一多不異，性相圓融。因為萬法一如，同體共生。隨舉一法，都與全體有密不可分的關係。例如：小國盧森堡或新加坡的總統到歐美訪問，大國如美法總統，也一樣要親臨機場迎接，以表尊重。因為不管國家大小，人民多寡，在一個同盟之下，價值是一樣的，此即是一多不異的平等真義。

南美的巴西，擁有一片廣大森林資源，具有調節地球上氣溫的作用，聯合國曾明文規定，要巴西保護這片森林，不得任意砍伐。這雖只是在巴西國內的一個定點，但卻可以影響到整個人類的環保存亡。

我們常看到世界各地有著幾十萬人或幾百萬人的示威遊行，過程都非常激烈，但只要為首的領導人，登高一呼，立即可以解散；一個獨裁暴君，不管人口多少、土地大小、語言種類、經濟懸殊，並不會影響其在

當代人心思潮　　56

國際上的地位，就像亞洲四小龍，就是一例。一棵尼拘陀樹的種子埋在土裡，經過灌溉施肥，可以結出萬千果實；道家也說：「道生一，一生二，二能生三，三生萬物。」一句話、一件事、一個人、一本書，甚至一個念頭，都可以決定一個人或一個國家的命運，因為「一」具有眾多的背景，因為「一」可能是眾多的起因。所以我們不要因星星之火而輕視，因它可以燎原；不因少數民族而輕忽，因可能引起難以想像的族群問題；不因王子幼小而輕視，因他總有統理你的可能。這些都是多從一生，一多不異的例子。

平等要能以大尊重小，以多尊重少，以強尊重弱，以有尊重無，以上尊重下。平等是當然的習慣觀念，世界在平等的觀念之下，必定能獲致和平。

上面論及「平等共尊」，才能導致和平，下面要談到唯有「和平共

榮」，才有平等共尊可言！

過去世界對和平的主張，有的認為以權力來促進平衡，有的主張以武力嚇阻戰爭，這種以力止戰，以戰止戰的方法，永遠不能達到和平，只有共尊共榮才能和平！

諸葛孔明七擒孟獲，不以力威折人；長壽王多次釋放梵豫王，甚至讓位免除戰爭；佛陀曾盤坐炎陽之下擋道，令琉璃王兵馬主動休戰，教示兩舍大臣侵略戰爭者，必然失敗！

今日世界，由於意識型態的對立、經濟資源的搶奪、分離運動、恐怖主義、歷史宿怨、我法執著，造成伊拉克和科威特的對立，讓兩個國家妻離子散，家破人亡，母親喪子淚水流個不停；波士尼亞、斯里蘭卡、蘇俄聯邦間的內戰，製造了多少死亡和仇恨！非洲部落的相殘屠殺、朝鮮半島的大戰邊緣、台灣海峽的險惡風雲，都讓舉世滔滔萬億人，處在恐怖、痛

苦的泥淖之中。

現在我們能夠昧著良心，把眼耳關閉，任世間沒有光明只有黑暗？沒有善美只有罪惡？沒有和平只有仇恨？所以我們不得不以「平等共尊」呼籲世界要和平共存！

平等與和平是一體兩面的真理，真正的平等不是表相上、齊頭式的平等，真正的和平也不是只用嚇阻、限武、禁核等外在措施所能達成，我們還必須注意心靈的淨化，思想的共識，觀念的重新評估，對於如何促進和平？我謹提出四點意見：

# 一、用慈悲能促進和平

佛教所提倡的慈悲，「慈」能與樂，「悲」能拔苦，觀世音菩薩以慈

悲可以走進信徒的心中，走進信者的家庭中，當然也可以走入世界和國家，就算我們無力給榮華富貴，但我們也要發願去解除世間人類的痛苦。

阿育王征服印度諸多小國，怨恨不止，以慈悲教化，民心才肯降順，所以用慈悲的力量才能化解兇暴。中國南北朝時代，石勒、石虎因佛圖澄慈悲的感化，而放棄殺戮；十六世紀，西班牙人拉斯卡沙斯（B. deLas Casas）為捍衛印第安人的權益而仗義直言，終於阻止查理五世（Charles V.）大帝出兵攻打美洲大陸。世間上唯有法的勝利，才是完美的勝利，世間上最強大的力量不是槍炮子彈，而是慈悲忍耐的力量，才是真正的勝利。

我們不但要以同體的慈悲來解救眾生，更要用無緣的慈悲為廣大眾生救苦救難；不僅要消極不做惡事，更要積極的行善；不要一時口號的慈悲，還要力行務實的慈悲；不要以圖利求償而行慈悲，更要以無相無償而行慈悲。唯有慈悲平等，共榮的和平才能到來。

## 二、除我執促進和平

華文的「我」，旁邊是個「戈」，暗喻「我」是引起糾紛的最大因素；英文的「我」是個大寫字母，可以見得「我」是多麼的自尊自大！的確，人類往往因為執著於「我」的看法、「我」的財富、「我」的利益、「我」的名位……而煩惱叢生，有了我執，見解就會偏了。

中國歷史上春秋戰國、南北朝時代的五胡十六國；美國的南北戰爭、南非的種族械鬥、歐洲的新舊宗教戰爭，都是為了「我執」而引起的，所以老子說：「吾所以有大患者，為吾有身」，佛教也強調：「無明煩惱皆為我。」兩個人在一起，各有我執就不能和平；一個家庭若各有我執，如選舉時每個份子所支持的對象不同，就會造成家庭糾紛；社會國家若有太強的理念我執，就會無法和平。

戰國時，趙太后問齊使，先問人民、後問賦稅、再問君王，齊使不悅，而趙太后能以民為重的「民本」作風，能不執著自我，才能民治、民有、民享的天下為公！執我非無我，而是從小我到大我，從私我到公我！

第二次世界大戰末期，美國總統羅斯福問太虛大師：「如何才能和平？」大師回道：「慈悲無我！」所以想要求得和平，正本清源之道，首先要消除心中的我執，四相不除，空華亂墜！我執既去，私欲不存，世間無我，戰爭何起？

## 三、從寬容促進和平

寬，則能容；容，則能和；和，則能平。土地寬大，容積率建高建大，；大海寬廣，水底的世界多彩多姿。一個人若心能包容一個家，就能成

為一家之長；包容一個國，就能成為一國之王；能心包太虛，就能成為法界之王！心量有多大，擁有的世界也就有多大！

世間上的戰爭有的人說是為了麵包，有的人說是為了土地。其實真正的麵包和土地，指的是內心的世界，能夠征服內心自我一念，才能擁有無限的空間。

大海能容納百川，大海才能廣大；虛空能容納萬物，虛空才能無邊。

人能包容眼耳鼻舌身等，才能為己所用；包容世界種族、宗教、國家，自然就能和平共處。

今日世界所以你爭我奪，爾虞我詐，正是由於人類的度量被名韁利鎖繫縛，以致人心不平、國土不安，所以我們要豎窮三際，橫遍十方的擴大我們的心胸，包容異己，推己及人，兼善天下，才能廣結善緣，涵攝十方，才能從寬容促進和平。

# 四、共榮體促進和平

隨著科技發達，工商進步，功利主義掛帥，許多人為了在競爭的時代裡求取生存，不惜用盡一切機巧，結果不但自他無法受益，甚至擾亂社會祥和。而今日由於人類長久以來濫砍坡地、濫倒垃圾、濫用能源、濫殺生物，造成「地球反撲」的現象，一場物我之間的戰爭已無聲息的展開了！原來世間的一切，都具有相互依存的密切關係，這正是提倡環保共存共榮的時代！

我們可感謝世間在種族上有黃、白、黑、紅多彩多姿的膚色；感謝有百多個國家可以共同往來，建立美好的友誼；感謝世間上有天主、基督、伊斯蘭教、佛教等各種不同的宗教，讓眾多不同信仰的人們，各有其精神的依託。世界各地依其地理環境，都出產不同的金銀銅鐵，都生長不同的花

草植物；依個人喜好有酸甜辛辣之味，依個人習慣有麵飯飲食，天地間都供應著我們所需，我們怎能不共同建立集體創作的共榮觀念？

紅花雖好，綠葉配襯；五官雖美，也要四肢健全；高樓大廈也要山水圍繞。今日要以慈悲心，平等共榮，以除我執，同體共生，那必然能帶來和平。

一個人若不能征服自己的貪瞋愚痴，就不能擁有慈悲喜捨的胸懷！

古人說：「獨樂樂不如眾樂樂。」個人的福樂有限，唯有化私為公，以眾為我，才能共享安樂。二千五百年前，教主佛陀所標舉的「六和僧團」便是這種共榮思想的先驅。所謂的「六和」指的是──

（一）、見和同解：在思想上，建立共識，這就是思想的歸一。

（二）、戒和同遵：在法制上，人人平等，這就是法制的平等。

（三）、利和同均：在經濟上，均衡分配，這就是經濟的均衡。

（四）、意和同悅：在精神上，志同道合，這就是心意的開展。

（五）、口和無諍：在言語上，和諧無諍，這就是語言的親切。

（六）、身和同住：在行為上，利益他人，這就是相處的和樂。

目前文明國家紛紛實行社會安全制度、物質救援第三世界、技術移轉、宗教對話、科技整合、環境保護等措施，並且創設歐洲經濟聯盟、歐洲共同市場、北美自由貿易區、亞太經濟合作、世界貿易協會等多種組織，一面促進經濟合作，一面達成政治共識。而私人企業方面，也逐漸注重社會倫理，改變過去一味牟利的作風，而以服務完善、創造發明來增進全民福祉。

在人類歷史的長河裡，這些改善雖然僅僅踏出自我框框的一小步，但只要大家肯持之有恆，在教育上，注重大悲力、寬容心的培養；在文化

上，推展人我共尊、互易立場的美德，在社會上，發揮萬法緣生、一多不異的真理；在處事上，消除我執，攜手合作，以期從時間的共榮、空間的共榮，達到人間的共榮，那麼，建立平等社會、達到世界和平將是指日可待之事！

最後祈求佛光加被，祝福大家吉祥如意，大會圓滿成功！

# 圓滿與自在

握糖不放的拳頭　無法掙脫瓶口

緊縮不放的腳步　無法向前邁進

唯有個人解脫自在　家庭方能和睦溫馨

進而促成社會的和諧圓滿

國際佛光會第六次世界會員代表大會

地點：香港紅磡體育館

時間：1997年11月29日

各位貴賓、各位來自世界各地的佛光會會友們：

承蒙佛陀的光明和慈悲，讓我們聚集在世界聞名的「東方之珠」——香港，召開國際佛光會第六次世界會員代表大會，實感無比欣喜。

由於港人的勤奮努力，香江經濟繁榮、訊息快速、社會進步、人才輩出，不但居亞洲之首，而且一直是國際金融、航運、旅遊、資訊、貿易、輕工業的中心，也是世界上最開放的自由港口，尤其今年香港的回歸不但使得兩岸三地的華人感到揚眉吐氣，更讓居住在全球的炎黃子孫倍覺歡欣鼓舞，我們在此地舉行九七回歸後首次佛教的盛會，可說是意義非凡。如果港人能夠將「圓滿自在」的真諦灌輸在生活當中，散發到全球各地，相信香港的未來及世界的前途都會更加幸福美好，所以我們今天在此以「圓滿自在」作為大會的主題，可說是最貼切不過了。

「圓滿」，是最自然、最完美的意義；「圓滿」，是人們最嚮往、最

欣羨的境界，像花好月圓、子孫滿堂、福祿壽全、白璧無瑕等等都是用來頌揚圓滿的辭句。但是在現實生活中，往往有許多不圓滿的時候，像人間的悲歡離合、生命的苦樂無常、感情的愛恨恩怨等等，都有如日之升沉起落、月之陰晴圓缺，總為吾人帶來諸多遺憾。

說到「自在」，像鳥雀飛空、游魚戲水，古往今來皆被人們所禮讚謳歌。無苦無惱的解脫，無憂無慮的自在，多麼令人神往！但當今的社會，治安益形惡化、家庭成員不睦、政經局面動盪、人際缺乏共識、資訊紛至沓來、異說擾亂人心、物慾強烈誘惑……，更讓人感到身不自在，心不自在，處處都不自在。

在佛教裡，無餘涅槃滅除動亂、常樂我淨的境界是何等的清淨圓滿！諸佛菩薩遊諸國土、度脫眾生的情景是何等的自由自在！我們應如何在生活中體證人間的圓滿自在呢？

當代人心思潮　　70

考：

兹先從心意的包容說到人間的圓滿自在，略提出八點意見，供大家參

# 一、從心意的包容到人間的圓滿自在

世界之大，人、地、事、物各有不同，如果胸懷褊狹，排斥異己，自然就會左右碰壁，諸事不順。像中國的歷史名人項羽，武功蓋世，本有勝算之望，但因疑嫉成性，反而錯失天下；而劉邦因氣度恢宏，禮賢下仕，故能運籌帷幄，決勝千里。戰國時代，楚人懶於耕種，收成不佳，憤而挑釁，越界破壞梁國的作物，梁大夫卻不以為忤，反命百姓為楚國土施肥，結果化干戈為玉帛。佛陀在世時，十大弟子各有特長；佛陀滅度後，部派學說百家爭鳴。及至佛教東傳，中國八宗兼弘，開出異花奇葩；禪門

一花五葉，子孫綿延不盡。俗謂：「大海能納百川，故能成其大；高山不辭細壤，故能成其高。」佛教裡「心包太虛」、「一念三千」的主張更言簡義賅地說明了包容的精義。在這個世間上，花紅柳綠，型態互異；鳶飛魚躍，各顯神通，惟有包容，才能贏得有情有義的人生，惟有包容；才能享受有喜有樂的人生；惟有包容，才能擁有圓滿自在的人生。

## 二、從生活的知足到人間的圓滿自在

人生最大的毛病便是貪慾不息，得一望十，得十望百，結果上焉者眾苦煎迫，身心交瘁；下焉者人格墮落，遺臭萬年，真是何苦來哉！《遺教經》云：「知足之法，即是富樂安穩之處。」又說：「知足之人，雖臥地上，猶為安樂；不知足者，雖處天堂，亦不稱意。」「不知足者，雖富而

貧；知足之人，雖貧而富。」像顏回居陋巷，簞食瓢飲，卻不改其樂；顏觸以婉言拒絕齊宣王賜予的高官厚祿，「晚食以當肉，安步以當車，無罪以當貴，清淨貞正以自虞。」後人稱讚他：「歸真反璞，終身不辱。」弘一大師「鹹有鹹的味道，淡有淡的味道」，古聖先賢因為具有少欲知足的修養，所以能超然物外，悲天憫人，以無為有，法喜無限。因此知足是富貴，知足是擁有，知足是圓滿，知足是自在。無，不是沒有；無，才能享有無量無邊的法界，擁有無數無量的眾生；無，才能對五欲不拒不貪，對世間不厭不求。甚至諸佛菩薩為了度脫有情，福利社稷，發出「知足常樂，能忍自安」的至理名言，在任何五濁十惡的環境中，都能安之若素，視為淨土。在此希望所有的佛光會員們都能效法前賢，以清貧知足的修為來體驗世間的圓滿自在；由知足常樂的行證來建設圓滿自在的生活。

# 三、從人我的平等到人間的圓滿自在

世間一切本是圓滿，本來自在，但因一念無明，顛倒妄想，產生上下、來去、有無、生滅、大小、內外、善惡、智愚等對待的觀念，以致於自他之間紛爭不斷，彼此之間對立加深，群我的衝突頻仍，事理的矛盾不已，種族之間仇恨增加，國際之間戰亂擴大。近代法國革命提倡自由，美國獨立主張民主，凡此無非是為了爭取人我的平等，人我的圓滿自在；孫中山先生發動革命，推翻滿清，所提出的口號，也是希望世界各國以平等之心待我之民族。其實，佛教在二千五百多年前，早已有「情與無情，同圓種智」、「無緣大慈，同體大悲」的主張，凡此不但開啟自他平等的濫觴，更是宇宙中最徹底的平等主義，像佛陀組織教團，「江湖溪澗，流入大海，同一鹹味，四姓出家，同為釋氏」的平等宣言，觀世音倒駕慈航，

地藏王地獄救苦，常不輕禮敬一切眾生，睒子菩薩愛惜山河大地，乃至聲聞羅漢遙拜八歲龍女，鳩摩羅什與盤頭達多大小乘互相為師，維摩居士酒肆說法，挑水和尚與乞丐為伍等等，都為平等的真義寫下最佳的註解。其實貴賤平等就是人格的尊重，自他平等就是你的融和，希望本會的會友們都能珍惜生命，效法前賢，發四弘誓願，行慈悲喜捨，過正道生活，給生者安樂，予死者希望，此即所謂的六度萬行，了生脫死，苟能有如此平等大願，人生又何能不圓滿自在呢？

## 四、從處世的般若到人間的圓滿自在

常聽人慨嘆「在這個世間上，做事難，做人更難。」其實這是因為我們沒有般若慧心，待人接物不夠圓融所致。什麼是般若呢？明理隨緣是般若，靈巧通達是般若，轉識成智是般若，證悟真如是般若。有了般若，我

們就能認識到眾生本是一體，從而發心立願，利己利人，達己達人，培養圓滿自在的因緣；有了般若，我們就能認清森羅萬象皆為空性，從而安住身心，隨緣不變，不變隨緣，得到圓滿自在的妙用；有了般若，我們就能夠遠離顛倒夢想，捨去妄念分別，從煩惱無明中跳脫出來，走向圓滿自在的光明大道；有了般若，我們就能夠泯除人我對待，統一差別矛盾，從人我是非中超越出來，開創圓滿自在的燦爛人生。所以，般若不必外覓，因為般若就是從我們真如自性中流露出來的智慧方便；般若也不必遠求，因為般若就在我們日常生活的行住坐臥當中體證。在《金剛經》開頭的經文裡，我們可以看到佛陀在語默動靜之中，時時刻刻都散發出無限的般若風光，像著衣持缽即手中放般若光，托缽乞食即身上放般若光，洗淨雙足即腳上放般若光，敷座而坐即通身放般若光，弘法利生即口中放般若光。其他如雲門的「胡餅」、趙州的「喫茶」、大珠的「饑來吃飯睏來眠」，龍

牙的「掃地煎茶及針罷」等等無一不是般若放光的妙用。希望大家都能珍惜自己心中無價的寶藏，將般若運用在做人處事上面，讓世間的一切都能達到圓滿自在的境地。

## 五、從社會的安定到人間的自在

今天的社會，槍枝、毒品、色情、暴力等問題日趨嚴重，人民生活其中，惶恐不安，無法安居樂業，遑論擁有圓滿自在的人生。但看私下抱怨人心不古者有之，走上街頭持牌抗議者有之，我覺得這些都不能真正解決問題，因為社會和個人有密不可分的關係。中國成語中所謂「覆巢之下無完卵」、「皮之不存，毛將焉附？」、「脣亡齒寒」等等都是用來形容社會安定的重要性，所謂「社稷安危，人人有責。」我們應該人人做警察，

## 六、從家庭的和諧到人間的圓滿自在

伸張公理，提倡正義；人人做義工，守望相助；人人做善人，服務奉獻，勸人為善；人人做良民，奉公守法，盡忠職守。惟有社會安定了，大家才能生活得圓滿自在。自今年五月起，國際佛光會中華總會在台灣各地推出一連串的「慈悲愛心列車」運動，十月五日的「慈悲愛心人宣誓典禮」，計有八萬人與會，各階層人士、各宗教團體均前來參加，大家一齊高呼：「心靈淨化、重整道德、找回良知、安定社會！」目前有二千名慈悲愛心人宣導師在街頭巷尾宣說慈悲愛心理念，受到各地民眾的歡迎，可見慈悲愛心人人需要。希望佛光人都能發心立願，作安定社會的先鋒，為生命留下歷史，為大眾留下慈悲，為人間創造圓滿自在的淨土，為人間建設圓滿自在的社會。

家庭是人生旅途的加油站，是止痛療傷的避風港，是親情溫暖的安樂窩，也是怡情悅性的休息處。家庭的和諧對於個人身心的成長、社會國家的安定，都有連帶的關係。我們看當今的社會有多少兒童因為父母不和，放學之後，寧願流連街頭，吃喝玩樂。這些人在家庭中所受到的挫折、創傷，都將成為社會的問題，國家的包袱。

佛教對家庭的幸福十分重視，佛陀在《善生經》、《玉耶女經》、《大寶積經》、《涅槃經》等經典中，不但教導在家信眾如何實踐家庭倫理，還說明家庭經濟如何運用得當。隨著時代的進步，父母子女之間講究溝通、協調，現代的家庭成員必須要懂得互跳探戈，彼此禮敬讓步；要知道交換立場，彼此體貼關懷；要常常讚美鼓勵，彼此扶持慰勉；要學習幽默風趣，營造溫馨氣氛。古德云：「和羹之美，在於合異；上下之益，在

能相濟。」和諧才能互利，和諧才能歡喜，大家若能注重家庭的和諧，並推廣運用，則人間何處不圓滿？人間何處不自在？

## 七、從身心的健康到人間的圓滿自在

身心健康是群己圓滿自在最重要的條件。試想：身體四大不調，則百骸不暢，臥病在床，不但自己無法奉獻所長，還需要別人照顧，焉能圓滿自在？心中三毒熾盛，則障門大開，起惑造業，不但自己不能安心做事，還需要別人安慰，更有甚者坐奸犯科，鋃鐺入獄，使得親人蒙羞，社會蒙難，更何來圓滿自在之有？佛教講究內外一如，對於身心健康最為重視，像清淡的素食能培養慈悲的精神、柔和的性情、堅強的耐力、健康的體能，各種齋戒活動能培養規律有序的坐息生活、內觀自省的善良美德，其

他如食存五觀、立如松、行如風、坐如鐘、臥如弓等佛門行儀，朝山禮佛、參禪打坐、念佛經行、懺悔發願、惜福感恩等修持方法，對於滌除塵慮、淨化人生都有著莫大的助益。希望凡我佛光會員從身心健康，進一步做到身心放光，時時抱持發心服務、犧牲奉獻的精神，參與公益活動，讓大眾都能廣被法喜，圓滿自在。

## 八、從自我的解脫到人間的圓滿自在

禪宗四祖道信禪師曾問三祖僧璨禪師：「如何解脫自在？」僧璨反問：「誰縛汝？」此話可謂道破千古疑團，令人拍案叫絕。的確，普天之下最能繫縛我們的，不是他人，而是自己。當我們執著於金錢時，金錢就將我們的心志箝制了；當我們執著於權位時，權位就將我們的胸襟套牢

了，自古以來，所謂的「名枷利鎖」，不知弄得多少人終日營營苟苟，喘不過氣來。

握糖不放的拳頭無法掙脫瓶口，緊縮不放的腳步無法向前邁進，放得下，才能提得起。我們要解脫自在，不但要學習放下一切，更要具有曠達的胸襟視野，要想得開，想得遠，要看得寬，看得大。歷來的諸佛菩薩，那一個不是放下個人的私利，為了一切有情的利益，粉身碎骨在所不惜；古今的英雄豪傑，那一個不是放棄小我的安逸，為了全民大眾的福祉，赴湯蹈火在所不計。他們讓眾生離苦得樂的同時，自己也獲得了自在解脫。英美的民主憲政，將各個聯邦結合起來，圓滿各方的需要，拋棄己見，共守律法，和平相處，這不也是從自我解脫，進而達到眾人圓滿自在的佳例嗎？

以上謹提出八點意見說明我們如何在人間獲得圓滿自在的生活。中國

長久以來的戰亂為多少人帶來流離失所、骨肉分散的悲劇，於今，領導者皆能抱持開闊的態度，在國際間穿梭交流，建設大中華民治、民有、民享的社會，讓人民圓滿自在。凡我佛光會眾，亦應全心全力，馨香祝禱：和平統一，國泰民安，實現圓滿自在的社會，圓滿自在的家庭，圓滿自在的心靈！

## 自然與生命

所謂自然　就是人心

就是真理　就是佛道

就是眾生的真心佛性　就是宇宙的綱常


世間事合乎自然

就有生命　就有成長

就能形成　就有善美

國際佛光會第七次世界會員代表大會

地點：加拿大多倫多佛光山

時間：1998年10月1日

各位貴賓、各位會員們：

大家好！今天大家不遠千里從世界各地前來加拿大，參加國際佛光會第七屆世界會員大會，實在非常難得殊勝。尤其眾所週知，加拿大難得天獨厚，資源豐富，但國民仍能具有不濫開採的共識，因此無論是鄉村、都市都能保持旖旎的風光、新鮮的空氣。此外加國政府在保護生態、社會福利等方面也做得十分成功，凡此均贏得世人的青睞，成為大家嚮往邀遊的國度之一，所以我們今天雲集在此，以「自然與生命」為主題召開世界大會，可說是得其所哉。

「自然」是世間的實況，像春夏秋冬四季的運轉、眾生生老病死的輪迴、心念生住異滅的遷流、物質成住壞空的變化，不都很自然嗎？世間事合乎自然，就有生命；合乎自然，就有成長；合乎自然，就能形成；合乎自然，就有善美。

當初，佛陀在菩提樹下證悟宇宙的真理，即所謂的「緣起性空」，實際上，就是宇宙間「自然」的法則。所謂自然，就是人心，就是真理，就是天命，就是宇宙的綱常。翻開中外史籍，歷代的帝王，順乎天命人心者昌，逆於天命人心者亡，他們的興衰與自然法則關係密切。不但如此，吾人的生活也要合乎自然，才能幸福美滿。大家不妨自問：「在金錢的運用上，我能合乎自然，量入為出嗎？在感情的交流上，我能合乎自然，平衡來往嗎？在語言的溝通上，我能合乎自然，顧念對方的需要？在做事的態度上，我能合乎自然，不違事理的原則嗎？」此外，現代人對保育生態、自由民主等方面也都提倡自然。例如：虎狼獅豹雖凶猛殘暴，但是當牠們被放出牢籠，回歸大自然時，牠們也會向你感謝。民國初年，中國婦女從「纏足」的傳統解放為合乎自然的「天足」，直至今日仍受到大眾的肯定與歡呼。近代，英國殖民地恢復佔領地區的獨立、美國林肯解放黑

奴，都是在尊重自然的發展。而今古人士，對「智者樂山，仁者樂水」的謳歌，更是崇尚自然的最佳證明。凡此說明了這是一個自然的世界，我們所擁有的是一個自然的人生，大家都擁有一顆自然的良心，我們應該作自然的擁有，發揮自然的美善。

佛教一向追求自然，重視人心、人性。像東方琉璃淨土、西方極樂世界，不但寶網行樹、水鳥說法，而且人民思衣得衣，思食得食，主要的目的，不外希望大家都能在自然的生活下安居樂業。國際佛光會倡導人間佛教，順應緣起真理的發展，也是重視自然的表現。本會以人間佛教為依歸，今天特將「自然」標舉出來，作為大會主題之一，也是希望大家都能尊重自然，因為唯有順應自然，我們的心靈才得以解脫，我們的生命才能夠自由。

說到「生命」，生命的定義，不在於一息尚存，而應在於是否具有

「用」的價值。人存在於世間，固然可以說有生命，山河大地等能夠為人所用，對於人間有貢獻，也應視為有生命者。例如：一張紙上面畫了聖賢的畫像，一塊石頭雕成古德的相貌，讓人一見生起仰慕效法之心，這一張紙、這一塊石頭就有了生命。反觀一些人雖坐擁高官厚祿，卻為大家所唾棄，或是一些人儘管年壽甚高，但一生無所事事，對社會毫無貢獻，雖生猶死，所以往往被人稱為「行尸走肉」。

其實，我們所生存的這個自然界裡，鳥叫蟲鳴、飛瀑流泉、萬紫千紅、綠葉婆娑，觸目所及都是欣欣向榮的景象，那一處沒有活潑的生命呢？所謂「溪聲盡是廣長舌，山色無非清淨身」，如果我們用心領悟，宇宙中的森羅萬象，那一樣不是從自己的生命中自然流露出來？可惜世間上有許多人將生命的因緣斬斷，強分你我，讓生命的和諧產生裂痕，讓宇宙大我的生命受到損傷，誠為可悲！

佛陀以法界為心，以心為法界，後人讚美佛陀無限的生命是「正法以為身，淨慧以為命」。阿彌陀佛之所以為佛教徒所喜愛稱念，乃因其生命超越時空的限制，所謂「無量光」、「無量壽」，一切時間、空間皆無量也。

蜉蝣雖朝生夕死，但不能說牠沒有再來的時候；人一期生命結束後，也不能說他不會乘願再來。一粒種籽落在土裡，即使千百年後，當因緣際會，仍可以開花結果。現在科技下的產物如試管嬰兒、複製羊等等，雖然令人嘆為觀止，但是以佛教觀點來看，他們的基因也都是由業力潤生而成，可見科學儘管日新月異，還是無法發明生命，因為生命是因緣和合，自然而有的。

《心經》云：「色即是空，空即是色。」我們的生命可以流注於物質世界裡，此即所謂「空即是色」；無窮的萬物也可以和我們的生命結為一

體，此即所謂「色即是空」。所以佛教講到世界，是無量無邊；講到眾生，也是無量無邊；講到生命，不但無量無邊，而且是無限永恆。

今日，世界各地的戰火不知讓多少美麗的家園毀於一旦，人類對於大自然無止盡的掠奪也引起地球反撲，環境污染正吞噬著人們的健康，其他如種族、政黨、宗教、地域之間的歧見、衝突與日俱增，國際販毒組織、恐怖組織、槍枝集團、色情集團的氾濫，在在威脅著大家生命財產的安全。所以國際佛光會揭櫫「自然與生命」為大會主題，也是想藉此喚起人類的覺醒，希望大家能珍惜躍動的生命，與大自然結合為一體，不憂榮辱毀譽，無畏生老病死，攜手共建淨土，倡導自然的美妙，宣揚宇宙的偉大，歌頌生命體永久的和順，禮讚生命體永恆的存在。

下列我提出對於「自然與生命」的四點淺見，希望大家不吝指教：

# 一、自然的定律與生命的尊嚴

二千六百年前，佛陀在菩提樹下證悟了自然的定律，並且名之為「緣起」。「緣起」符合了真理的普遍性、必然性、平等性、永恆性。大自然的一切現象，小至個人的成敗得失、氣候的寒來暑往，大至國家的盛衰興亡、世界的成住壞空，莫不是在「緣起」法則下進行。其中，尤以吾人的生命和緣起法則的關係最為密切。因為生命不是憑空而來，而是由自己造作的業力而來；不是由單一原因而來，而是由無明、行、識、名色、六入、觸、受、愛、取、有、生、老死等「十二有支」三世因果相續而成。

所謂：「有備無患。」人如果懂得順應自然，就無所畏懼。例如春夏努力耕種，秋天積穀存糧，自然就不怕嚴冬來臨；白天準備照明設備，自然就不怕黑夜來臨。老病並不可懼，可懼的是少壯不努力，等到老病時帶

著空白的一生隨著草木腐朽；死亡也不可悲，可悲的是生前不知奉獻社會，等到臨死才帶著滿腔遺憾，邁向不可知的未來。

麥克阿瑟曾說：「老兵不死。」因為他們的精神與國魂永遠同在。文天祥也說：「人生自古誰無死，留取丹心照汗青。」因此，人，不一定要飛黃騰達、福壽雙全，但要活得有尊嚴。過去的人講究生存的尊嚴，極力爭取自由、平等，大力倡導民主、博愛，甚至為此而不惜拋頭顱、灑熱血；現在的人注重死亡的尊嚴，希望能夠死得安樂、死得自在，乃至為此而走向街頭，奔走呼籲。其實，由緣起法則所延申出來的「業力自由」、「眾生平等」、「同體慈悲」、「生死一如」等觀念，才能統合生存與死亡，真正將我們生命的尊嚴發揮到自然的極致。

所以，我們應拋開宿命論的悲情，即使在困頓厄難時，也要勇往直前，創造自己的未來；我們應拔除撥無因果的邪思，即使面對遍地荊棘，

也要散播歡喜的種子，為宇宙創造繼起的生命；我們應丟棄生產工具決定一切的謬論，在互助合作裡創造利眾的事業；我們應糾正經濟掛帥的歪風，在感恩惜福中創造濟世的功德。讓我們為人間留下道德、為社會留下智慧、為家庭留下慈悲、為自己留下歷史，活出自然的定律，也活出生命的尊嚴來！

## 二、自然的生命與生命的自然

一切生命和自然息息相關，生命都是自然的一部份，我們均應善加珍惜。可惜長久以來，自以為「萬物之靈」的人類往往忘記其他生命的存在，為滿足一時的私欲而濫殺無辜。試問：當你為世間的刀兵劫難而悲憤時，是否想過夜半屠門傳出來哀號的聲音？當你為社會災禍頻傳而嘆息

時，是否聽到碗盤中眾生怨怒的訴說？

《法句經》云：「一切皆懼死，莫不畏杖痛，恕己可為譬，勿殺勿刑杖；能常安群生，不加諸楚毒，現世不逢害，後世常安穩。」《金剛經》也說：「所有一切眾生之類，我皆令入無餘涅槃而滅度之。」積極的戒殺應該是護育化導，讓大家都能得度，所以即使是疾言厲色的傷害，我們均應防止不犯；即使是微笑讚美等小小的隨喜功德，我們也必須不吝布施。

有些人以為自己有權力來決定自己的生死，但從「緣起」真理來看，吾人的生命是由父精母血所和合產生，是因社會士農工商提供日用而繼續存活，所以世間上沒有一個實體的「我」。生命既是天地萬物自然所共有，所以凡自殺、殺他都是逆天行事，違反自然。

再從廣義而言，即使一石一木都是宇宙萬有的力量所成，任意傷害，減少壽命，也是殺生的行為。像長江三峽築壩，到處濫伐樹木，導致江

水氾濫；台灣各種建築濫墾坡地，造成地層坍塌，都是緣起法則受到破壞導致山川大地受到傷害，予以還擊的明證。撫今追昔，睒子菩薩為怕踩痛大地而不敢重步走路，匾擔山和尚為恐傷及草木而揀橡栗為食，他們的慈悲多麼可貴！「極樂淨土，水鳥說法」的經文；「生公說法，頑石點頭」的故事，更說明了佛陀所云「情與無情，同圓種智」的理念，誠乃不虛之言。

生命之所以可敬，是因為生命之間有自然的相通互動，彼此依存；生命之所以寶貴，是因為每一個生命乃累劫以來由於自然的因緣所成。所以我們的生命應該順其自然，依照自己的根性，隨順因緣，隨遇而安，隨心自在，將小我融入大化之中，如此必能發揮生命的光與熱，體現自然與生命的「物我一如」。

# 三、自然的和順與生命的永恆

說到「自然」，自然，則和；如不自然，就會導致紛亂。古德云：「違順相爭，是為心病。」貪欲、瞋恚、愚癡、我慢、疑嫉攪動心湖，人就會煩惱愁腸，乃至誤入歧途，千古遺恨。生活上的應世接物也是如此，感情若是一廂情願，不順自然，就不會天長地久；財富若是巧取豪奪，不順自然，必有敗壞之虞；名聲若是譁眾取寵，不順自然，終將遭人唾棄；地位若是坐享其成，不順自然，便會引起非議。

自然，則順。過與不及，終將帶來弊患。像久臥不起，久立不坐，久勞不息，久靜不動等等，都會引起生理上的四大不調，人就開始患病，乃至身根朽敗，與世長辭。此外，近幾世紀來，人類因生產消費過多的物質，遠超過微生物所能還原的程度，而破壞了自然的運作，導致目前生態

系統問題重重。凡此都證明了一旦忽視自然法則，就會自食惡果。

因此，自然就像一個「圓」，好因帶來善果，壞因遭致惡果，因果相續，無始無終。無量劫以來，生命在自然循環下歷經千生萬死。死固然是生的開端，生也是死的準備，所以生也未嘗生，死也未嘗死。如薪盡火傳，生命之火不曾停熄；如更衣喬遷，生命的主人仍未改變。所以古來的高僧大德大事已明，生死一如。像達摩祖師隻履西歸，龐蘊居士拄鋤立化，飛錫禪師倒立而亡，金山活佛淋浴往生……他們順應自然，來去自在，隨緣應化的手姿多麼的灑脫豁達！

生，是因緣生；死，是因緣滅。從聖義諦來看，無生也無死。因此禪門高僧不求了生脫死，只求明心見性。一日開悟，泯除對待，剎那即永恆，煩惱即菩提。像溈山禪師立願來生作一條老牯牛，趙州禪師發心捨報後到地獄去度眾，他們不為自己求安樂，但願眾生得離苦，生死苦海在他

們的眼中，有如片雲點太虛，微不足道。

《易經》謂：「天行健，君子以自強不息。」自然之道在永恆精進，在自利利他，所以，我們應效法天地日月滋養萬物的美德，以同體的慈悲作應世的資糧，為苦難的眾生作庇護的房舍；我們應學習古聖先賢的「馬拉松」賽跑精神，以無限的生命作奮勇的前進，為熱惱的濁世作清涼的甘露，讓生命在自然的法則下綿延永續，和順永恆。

## 四、自然的生活與生命的佛道

「自然」，若以一字解釋，就是「道」；「生命」，若以一字解釋，就是「力」。如何是「道」？大珠慧海說：「饑來吃飯，睏來眠。」藥山惟儼說：「雲在青天水在瓶。」……可見「道」與自然同在，「道」就是

當代人心思潮　　　　98

自然的生活。也因為如此，連大聖佛陀都責備應笑而不笑、應喜而不喜、應慈而不慈、聞惡而不改、聞善而不樂的人為「五種非人」，因為他們的行為是不合乎自然。如何是「力」？信、進、念、定、慧是「力」，慈、悲、喜、捨是「力」，把慈悲給人、把歡喜給人、把光明給人，能讓燈燈相照，生生不息，就是「力」。所以，自然的「道」與生命的「力」若能結合在一起，就是宇宙間的浩然正氣，就是宇宙間的真如法界。

所以，我們想要過如實的生活，就必須順應自然法則：夫妻之間應互敬互諒，鄰里親友應和睦相處，工作同事應互相提攜，開創事業應將市場調查、資金籌措、人力資源、經營計畫等安排妥當，為政治國應了解民意、重用忠良、察納雅言、勤行善法。尤其身為佛教徒，更應以身作則，培福結緣，修定增慧，負起化導眾生的責任。日用中能如是與「道」相符，與「力」結合，那是自然的生活與生命的佛道，則庶幾無過矣！

自古以來，佛教的祖師大德在生活裡悟道者不知凡幾，洞山良价在瞥見河裡自己的倒影時開悟、香嚴智閑在鋤地耕種時開悟、夢窗國師在靠牆就寢時開悟、虛雲和尚在捧杯喝茶時開悟……他們在悟道之後，山仍是山，水仍是水，只是山河大地與我一體，任我取用。所謂「青青翠竹無非般若，鬱鬱黃花皆是妙諦。」道，就是自家風光，不假外求。外在的大千世界、三世眾生，其實就是內心的大千世界、三世眾生。因此，自然也好，生命也好，其實就是真理，就是佛道，就是眾生本自具有的真心佛性，就是宇宙的全體。

目前，國際佛光會已走入第八個年頭，雖然在亙古的時空裡，我們猶如一株小樹，但由於本會歷年來所提倡的「歡喜與融和」、「同體與共生」、「尊重與包容」、「平等與和平」、「圓滿與自在」等理念，都與自然的真理法則契合，所以能歷經風雨而屹立不搖。爾後，我們要繼續紹

承諸佛如來之遺緒，遵循歷代祖師大德之教誨，無怨無悔地向前邁進，為萬世開啟太平的道路。希望今天我們每一小步的努力，都能在浩瀚的宇宙中發揮正知正覺的力量；希望未來我們每一次的成長，都能為無限的生命留下善美深遠的影響。

最後，祝福大家法喜充滿，慧命長存。

# 公是公非

它是一切對錯善惡的法則與智慧
也是維繫社會秩序的公義紀律
更是修養個人品德的圭臬指南

它不以自我為中心
而以公理正義為依歸
以眾生的幸福安樂為訴求

追求公是公非　要有大智慧、大勇氣
對公理正義要負有道德的責任
要講究公平　正直　無私　無我
就有生命　就有成長　就能形成　就有善美

國際佛光會第八次世界會員代表大會
地點：高雄佛光山
時間：2000年5月16日

副總會長、各位理事、各位貴賓、各位協會會長、各位與會的佛光人代表等，大家吉祥如意！

佛教自東漢明帝永平年間傳來中國，今年屆逢二千年，又適值政府首次明定佛誕節為國定紀念日，在這個佛教徒同感殊榮的歷史時刻裡，今天能有來自世界五大洲的佛教菁英共聚在佛光山參加第八次的國際佛光世界會員代表大會，誠乃「千載一時、一時千載」之盛舉，希望本屆的大會能為佛教再創一個發展的新契機。

已是新的世紀開始，無庸置疑的，將是一個科技更發達、經濟更繁榮的新世紀。然而，科技文明雖然豐富了物質生活，卻也改變了人類的價值取向，現代人的是非觀念混淆，造成整個世界的脫序亂象。因此，本次大會特以「公是公非」為主題，希望藉此呼籲舉世人類能共同再造一個公理正義的人間社會，希望人人都有「公是公非」的道德勇氣，人人都能樹立

「公是公非」的社會形象。

所謂「公是公非」，也就是「大是大非」。西諺有云：「吾愛吾師，吾尤愛真理」，真理就是「公是公非」；佛說：「依法不依人」，依法就是「公是公非」。

「公是公非」是評論世間一切好壞、對錯、正謬、善惡的法則與智慧；有智慧才有「公是公非」。「公是公非」是檯面上的，不是私下的；是天下人的，不是個人的；是普遍法界的，不是片面的；是萬眾平等的，不是差別的；是凡事必然的，不是變異的；是亙古永恒的，不是一時的，因為「公是公非」就是般若真理，有般若真理才能證悟解脫。當初佛陀捨棄王位出家，正是感於生命的苦空無常、四姓階級的不平等，以及眾生的顛倒妄想，因此毅然割愛辭親，出家修道；佛陀的證悟真理，就是「公是公非」般若智慧的顯現。「公是公非」不是以自我為中心，而是以公理正

義為依歸；「公是公非」不是以一家一國為對象，而是以全法界眾生的幸福安樂為訴求。所以，佛陀成道時即向普世宣告：「眾生皆有佛性，人人皆得成佛」，而這種「生佛一如」、「眾生平等」的真理，便是「公是公非」的極致發揮。

佛陀所證悟的真理──「緣起性空」，所謂「諸法因緣生，諸法因緣滅」，是在說明宇宙世間一切都是依因緣法則而運行，人有生老病死的因緣，世界有成住壞空的法則。因緣聚則生，因緣散則滅，生生滅滅，讓自然界有花開花謝、宇宙間有生住異滅、人世裡有貧富貴賤等「無常」變化，這不是神明創造，也不是威權左右，這就是「公是公非」。

佛教的「因果業報」講「種如是因，得如是果」，這就是非常公道的「公是公非」；無論達官貴人或販夫走卒，無一不是在「善有善報，惡有惡報」的因果定律下循環。「王子犯法，與庶民同罪」，如果真能做到，

這就是「公是公非」。

古代的帝王貴族，總想把榮華富貴延續到來世，因此陪葬大量的金銀財寶，但是這並不合乎「因果業報」；所謂「萬般帶不去，唯有業隨身」，這才是「公是公非」。

「公是公非」是維繫社會秩序的公義紀律，也是修養個人品德的圭臬指南。一個人的身語言行、舉心動念，不要以為他人不知，所謂「天知、地知、你知、我知」，冥冥之中必然有「公是公非」的準則。

世間上有的人以利害為重，有的人以是非為重；以利害為重的人不講究是非，以是非為重的人不計較利害。古來多少聖賢為了發揚「公是公非」的精神，他們輕利害，甚至捐棄生命也在所不惜。宋朝理學家張載的「為天地立心，為生民立命，為往聖繼絕學，為萬世開太平。」此種「公是公非」的精神，即仁人君子所謂的生命中之生命也。莊子在《天道》

中說：「是非已明，而賞罰次之」，又謂「天地與我並生，萬物與我為一」；義大利天文學家伽利略，為了堅持自己在天文及力學上所獲致的實驗結果，拼死不向神權低頭，這都是具有「公是公非」的大智、大勇的表現。

在一個講究倫理道德的社會裡，群眾都十分重視「有是有非、大是大非、真是真非、公是公非」的道理；反觀今日社會，是非觀念普遍淡泊，可以說在我們周遭的人，大都是「少是少非、無是無非、不是不非、混淆是非」。因為當今人類不肯服膺是非公理，「成者為王，敗者為寇」，造成強權代替「公是公非」、金錢左右「公是公非」，投機的投機，取巧的取巧；是非不彰，真理不明，怎有「天道良心」呢？

自由民主是現代人類引為最好的政治目標，但是用我的自由妨礙你的自由，用我的主張強要你奉行，而又美其名之曰「自由民主」；正如大魚

吃小魚、貓跟老鼠講民主、民眾和獨裁者講民權，會有「公是公非」嗎？

現在的社會動輒主張公投，公投很民主，也符合「公是公非」的精神，但是參與公投的人都懂得「公是公非」嗎？甚至決策者對整個事件都有「公是公非」的觀念嗎？五十一票對四十九票的民主，就是「公是公非」嗎？如果本身公私不分、是非不明，一旦認知有了問題，就沒有「公是公非」。故知「公是公非」要有大智慧、大勇氣，對公理正義要負有道德的責任，要講究公平、講究正直、講究無私、講究無我，若能如此，才是所謂「全民的希望」，能夠達到全民的要求，那才是有「公是公非」的自由民主。

「眾緣所成」、「同體共生」，甚至「公有共管」、「集體創作」都是「公是公非」的原則，如古代的佛教十方叢林「傳位傳賢」、唐堯虞舜的「禪讓天下」，甚至孫中山先生的「天下為公」，這都是「公是公非」。

在佛教史上，不少祖師大德對於毫無師承關係的學僧，只要能堪受大任，莫不欣然傳法授位，例如弘忍傳位於六祖惠能，獦獠也能得法作祖，此皆「公是公非」的行為。遺憾的是後世弟子對「公是公非」的認知不夠，例如有的人「依人不依法」，有的人「依神不依佛」，有的人「依師不依理」，有的人「依假不依真」，致使不能體會祖師的心意，所以禪門才因而日漸式微。

《金剛經》講的「布施無相」、「度眾無我」、「修行無住」、「證悟無得」，這就是「公是公非」。「無我相」、「無我相、無人相、無眾生相、無壽者相」而一切無所不相，如：「無我相」的人，必不自私執著；「無人相」的人，必能平等尊重；「無眾生相」的人，必不外相分別；「無壽者相」的人，則不會一成不變。泯滅四相，必有「公是公非」，凡事必能依法依理。所謂只問是非善惡，不計毀譽得失；「寧教老僧墮地獄，不拿佛法當

人情」，都是發揚「公是公非」的真理大義。

所謂「公是公非」，要經得起良知的認同，更要經得起歷史的評鑑。曹操當初挾天子以令諸侯，有人尊他為亂世英雄，有人譏他為竊世奸賊；武則天的評價，有人肯定她的天才治績，有人唾棄她的荒淫亂政，他們的功過，即使歷史也難以給予「公是公非」的評價。「周公輔佐成王日，王莽禮賢下士時」，假使當時身先死，不知如何定忠奸？」此即所謂「公是公非」不易為人瞭解之處，若無大智大慧，何能有「公是公非」的認知？

世間上，有的人因緣際會，卻無實才；有的人懷才不遇，怨嘆時運不濟。其實，論三世的因果，此中必有「公是公非」。南非總統曼德拉，在被囚禁二十七年之後能坐上總統寶座；中華民國的孫中山，歷經十次的革命終能締造民國，此乃必有「公是公非」的關鍵存在。即如今日工商企業

界投資經營，賺取合理的利潤，本來無可厚非，但不可將社會的發展歸功於自己的貢獻，須知世間上凡一切成就，必有相關的因緣助成，所謂高樓大廈，需要多少的一磚一瓦，所謂開花結果，需要多少的地水火風，對於許多默默助成的因緣，我們若能懂得感恩報答，這才能還給世間一個「公是公非」的公道。

現代舉世提倡環保，重視生態保育，然而以少數的該存，多數的該死，此種不合公平的觀念，也有待重新研討。「公是公非」要放諸四海而皆準；「公是公非」是法界眾生賴以生存的規則。「公是公非」要放諸四海而公非」寄望於包青天，然而我們身邊的包青天在那裡呢？「因緣果報」就是「公是公非」；「善惡業感」就是「公是公非」；「事理圓融」就是「公是公非」；「最後判決」就是「公是公非」。因此，希望今後凡我佛光人，都能以「公是公非」為立身處事的準則，人人都有「公是公非」的

睿智，大家一起發願，共同來創造一個公平正直、法界圓融的祥和社會。

最後祈求佛光加被，祝福大家吉祥如意，大會圓滿成功！

人間與生活

佛陀出生成道在人間
人間佛教就是佛陀的本懷
佛法在哪裡　就在當下
當下在哪裡　就在生活裡
我們要用佛法來指導生活
更要在生活中落實佛法

國際佛光會第三屆第一次理事會議
地點：南非約堡杉騰飯店會議中心
時間：2001年4月19日

**副** 總會長、各位理事、各位貴賓、各位協會會長、各位與會的佛光人代表等，大家吉祥如意！

國際佛光會自創會以來，每年都會固定在世界各地召開一次理事會議，今年是由南非約堡協會承辦；因為這樣的因緣，所以今天大家不遠千里從世界各地齊聚到南非來，首先僅代表約堡協會歡迎大家。

南非是非洲五十三個國家之一，位於非洲的最南端。提起非洲，他不但是世界最古老的陸地，也是人類的發源地，但是長期以來由於受到種族紛爭、政治不安、環境髒亂、社會落後、氣候炎熱、人民知識水準低落等因素影響，因此非洲一向有「黑暗大陸」之稱。尤其自從三十年前第一宗愛滋病例在非洲發生，目前全世界有三千六百萬愛滋病患，其中二千五百萬人在南非。

由於愛滋病肆虐已嚴重威脅到人類未來的生存，因此有人預言：人類

從非洲起源，也可能從非洲毀滅！面對這樣一個令全世界人類同感憂心的問題，誠如一九九九年在南非召開的全球愛滋病會議中，與會專家針對「如何防治愛滋病」的議題進行討論後，大家一致表示：唯有宗教能解救人類此一浩劫，尤其佛教的戒律，更是根絕愛滋病的不二法門。

這項結論說明佛法是今日人類的一道光明，尤其越是黑暗的地方，越需要佛光的照耀。為此，佛光山於一九九二年到南非創建非洲第一間寺院，繼而在一九九四年由我親自到南華寺為五名黑人青年主持剃度典禮，正式誕生了第一批的非洲出家人，從此也讓南非有了佛法的流布。多年來佛光山南華寺及南非佛光協會在南非及史瓦濟蘭、坦尚尼亞等國家所從事的文教弘化與慈善救濟工作，也都深受南非政府的重視。今天國際佛光會理事會議能夠在南非召開，並有來自世界五大洲三十六個國家、五十八個地區的代表及觀察員七百多人與會，自是意義非凡。在這個屬於佛光人最

重要的年度會議中，我僅提出四點意見，期勉佛光會員今後共同努力致之！

# 一、佛法人間化

「人間佛教」是當代最為膾炙人口，也是大家討論最多的議題，佛光山自一九六七年創建以來，就一直以弘揚人間佛教為目標，所以我曾經說過，當初我創立佛光山，不單只有硬體而已，軟體就是人間佛教，人間佛教不但早就在我的心裡、在我的行為裡，也時時在我的思想裡。只是在我最初提出「弘揚人間佛教」的理念時，卻一再遭到教界人士的質疑、反彈，認為「人間佛教」是我個人所自創。其實，佛陀出生在人間、成道在人間、弘化在人間；佛陀說法主要以人為對象，佛教是人本的宗教，佛陀

是人間的佛陀，佛教本來就具足人間性，所以人間佛教不是哪個人所發明的，人間佛教既不是六祖慧能大師，也不是太虛大師，當然更不是我個人的創見，人間佛教是佛陀的本懷，佛教本來就是人間佛教！

既然佛教是人間的，為什麼現在還要強調「佛法人間化」呢？原因是多年來我在佛教界，看到一些很有學問的人雖然進入佛門幾十年，卻不能與佛法相應。譬如佛教講慈悲，但他不慈悲；佛教講忍耐，而他不忍耐。甚至有的人重視佛學玄談，不重視實際修證；有的人重視吃素拜拜，不重視人格道德的增進及日常生活的問題，缺少對人世的責任感；有的人著重自修，不問世事，失去對社會大眾的關懷。

其實，「佛教」與我們的日常生活有著密不可分的關係，我們不可以把佛法全然當成學問來研究，佛教是一種宗教，應該把它融會在我們的日常生活裡。因為人不能沒有生活，而生活需要用佛法來指導，所以我覺得

在信仰的歷程上，應該把所信仰的佛法和生活打成一片，也就是用佛法來指導生活，達到「佛法生活化、生活佛法化」，能夠在生活中修行、落實佛法，這才是人間的佛教。

至於人間佛教如何修行？簡單的說，你吃飯，青菜蘿蔔、粗茶淡飯，你能感到很感恩、很滿足，這就是人間佛教的修行；你穿衣，很樸素、很淡雅，只要乾淨、整齊、莊嚴就好，這就是人間佛教的修行。

人間佛教的修行就是生活的修行，舉例說，你發心，你有慈悲，就是修行；你懂得慚愧、懺悔，就是修行。你慈悲心生起了，你慚愧心修好了，你菩提心萌芽了，這就是修行！所以，人間佛教的修行就是對人要慈悲，對人要尊重，對人要包容；學佛修行不是喊口號，如果不在言行、生活裡落實佛法，那裡有菩提可證？

所以，在人間佛教裡，廣結善緣是修行，與人為善是修行，五戒十善

當代人心思潮

是修行，四攝六度是修行。你舉心動念有道德、有慈悲，就是修行；你的身口意行為裡，身不行好事，口不說好話，心不存好念，沒有三好運動，就是沒有修行！因此，「勤修戒定慧，息滅貪瞋癡」，身口意的淨化就是人間佛教的修行。

其實，在我們的生活裡無一不需要人間佛教，你吃飯、睡覺、走路，乃至交朋友，與人共事，那一樣不需要佛教？佛教不是只在經書裡，佛教也不是只在禪堂裡，佛教更不是只在念佛聲中；佛法是遍於我們的生活，佛法要在行住坐臥之間落實。

再進一步具體來說，佛法在那裡？就在當下！當下是什麼？就是在生活裡。過去有一些人只講究自我的修行、自我了生脫死，因此讓佛教被人詬病為遁世的宗教。現在國際佛光會已經讓佛教從山林走向國際、走上社會、走入家庭，實現了當初我創立國際佛光會的目標「從傳統到現代、從

山林到社會、從遁世到救世、從獨居到大眾、從唯僧到和信、從弟子到講師、從經懺到事業、從行善到傳教、從散漫到制度」，也讓社會大眾認識佛教其實是幸福、安樂、真誠、善美的宗教，這也是人間佛教的真義。

今後舉凡慈悲惜緣、智慧開擴、禪淨戒忍、感恩發願等，都是人間佛教所應推動的佛法，希望我們全體佛光人對於人間佛教還要多花一點功夫去認識，因為人間佛教廣博深遠，平時大家會講《楞嚴經》、《華嚴經》、《法華經》……，但是並不一定會講人間佛教。人間佛教也不一定要靠演說，人間佛教是講究實用，不重清談，所以「佛法人間化」就是凡是人間大眾所喜歡的慈悲、歡喜、金錢、財富，甚至尊重包容、和諧共生等佛光會多年來所推動的人間佛教精神，不但佛光會員能受用，全世界的大眾也都能以「佛法人間化」的理念，促進世界的和平。

甚至，我們不只是要推動佛法走向世界、走向社會、走向家庭，更要

走向人心。人心愛之，佛法與之；人心惡之，佛法去之。真善淨美，人之所愛；真善淨美，皆人間佛法也！邪惡驕慢，人之所惡；邪惡驕慢，佛法應予去之！

總之，在我們的生活中，不管舉心動念皆可修行，我們應本著「自他兩利」的精神，將「佛法生活化、生活佛法化」。希望未來大家都能一起來建設生活樂趣的人間佛教、建設財富豐足的人間佛教、建設慈悲道德的人間佛教、建設眷屬和敬的人間佛教。

## 二、生活書香化

人在世間生活，要懂得營造生活的樂趣，要重視生活的品質，要讓生活過得有意義、有價值。所以生活不能只是為了三餐溫飽，不能只有吃

飯、穿衣，不能只是追求物質、金錢、愛情等五欲塵勞，生活裡應該要有般若、知識，要充實自己的氣質、內涵，要找出自己的真心、佛性，要讓自己的生活過得多采多姿。

如何才能讓生命活得豐富多采，首先必須要多讀書，要讓「生活書香化」。讀書不但能增加我們的知識、智慧，改變我們的氣質、品德；讀書更能開擴我們的思想、見聞，讓我們真正認識宇宙人生。一個不學無術的人，跟一個讀書人在一起，同樣有父母，同樣吃飯生活，可是他們的品德、氣質就是不一樣，所以自古聖賢都會鼓勵青年子弟要多讀書，唯有多讀書，才能博學多聞，才能提昇心性、品質、人格，不讀書的人，膚淺無知，全身充滿俗氣，所以我們要建立書香的世界、書香的家庭，要過書香的人生。當然，這一切要從每一個人都能過著書香的生活開始，因此國際佛光會與佛光山合作，成立「人間佛教讀書會」，積極推動全民讀書的風

當代人心思潮　　　122

氣。

近年來台灣的文建會和教育部也在積極倡導讀書會，國際佛光會提出的「生活書香化」，一方面是為了響應政府的政策，同時希望透過讀書會，提倡書香人間，推動全民閱讀，希望人人本著「學海無涯，學無止境」的認知，養成「活到老，學不了」的精神和習慣，人人多讀書，從個人精神生活的充實，進而提昇社會的和諧，促進人間的和平與美滿。

談到「讀書會」，既是「讀書」而不是「看書」，當然就應該講究「讀」的方法，例如可以全讀、段讀，或是對讀、隨讀、齊讀。讀書不是「默讀」，而是要朗朗上口的讀，甚至要像唱歌一樣的讀。

讀書要「讀活書、活讀書」，不要刻板的死讀書，同時要勤於做筆記。平時我們讀完一本書，常常很快就忘記書的內容，但是當你把重點記下來，偶爾翻閱一下自己的筆記，所有往事就會再度呈現在你眼前，如此

不斷的溫故知新，不斷的用心深思，日久書本上的知識就會融入到自己的身心血液裡，成為自己的養份。

讀書還要慎選有益的書來讀，在我自己這一生中雖然沒有受過完整的正規教育，所幸中日抗戰期間，在棲霞山有一座小小的圖書館，我利用管理圖書的機會，拼命的讀書、寫筆記，如此日復一日，一年一年過去，我覺得自己深深受用。記得當時由於佛教的書我讀不懂，因此就讀中國的歷史小說，如《岳傳》、《荊軻傳》、《三國演義》、《七俠五義》等，我覺得閱讀歷史小說對我的人生助益很大。例如，看過歷代多少英雄好漢，歷經多少艱難困苦，最後終於有所成就，無形中都在激勵自己要立志，要奮發；乃至歷史上多少正人君子、俠義之士的行儀，也啟發我懂得做人要有情有義，要有正義感，要能正派做人。

甚至後來因為小說讀多了，認的字也多了，我便開始把自己所學的知

識講給別人聽。回想我這一生之所以能教書，是因為我一直很樂於把自己看到、聽到的故事複述給別人聽，另一方面也是由過去不會教書的老師教我的，因為有些老師一到講台就只寫黑板，直到打下課鐘，他就帶著書本離開，沒有講一句話。我認字，也是隨著不識字的母親學習的，因為我從小常常念書給母親聽，但因為自己識字不多，凡是不會唸的字，就取半邊來唸。例如「紐約」、「洛陽」等地名我把它唸成「丑」約、「各」陽，這時母親就會指正我、教導我。

　　當時雖然外在的條件欠缺不足，但是我相信只要有心讀書，情況就會改觀。我從歷史小說，後來進而讀佛教的《高僧傳》，因為經論讀不懂，但《高僧傳》有故事、有事蹟，所以各種版本的《高僧傳》我都讀過，而且不止讀一遍。從閱讀「高僧傳」讓我懂得效法高僧的行儀，懂得見賢思齊，我覺得現代的年輕人心中應該樹立起偶像的觀念，要讓心中有好多的

偶像，如一般的老子、莊子、孔子，都是我們的偶像。乃至《古文觀止》裡，文學八大家的文章寫得那麼好，固然是我們學習的對象；佛教裡翻譯經典的唐玄奘、鳩摩羅什，他們艱難困苦的奮鬥精神，也都是我們的模範。

讀書要靠日積月累，要持之有恆，而且不能把讀書當兒戲，不能輕描淡寫、不能輕忽為之；讀書是很認真的事業，讀書是每日必做的功課，所謂「三天不讀書，言語乏味」，其實我自己從小就養成讀書的習慣，如果三天不讀書，會覺得連吃飯都沒有滋味。在我的生活裡，平時除了做事、講話以外，所有時間都是用來讀書，如果出門在外，身邊沒有一本書，日子真不曉得怎麼過。所以我在世界各地雲遊弘化，承蒙侍者總是幫我在箱子裡裝了一堆書，好讓我在飛機上看，使長途的旅行得以解除寂寞。

讀書也應該有所規劃，在青年階段可以多讀文學的書，包括中國文

學、外國文學及傳記文學。像台灣出版的《傳記文學》、《中外雜誌》雜誌，我每期都會用心細讀。有一次，有位八十多歲的老記者與我談話，談到民國初年的人物，乃至抗戰時期有什麼人、清朝有什麼人、明朝末年有什麼人，我都能應答如流，令他大為吃驚，這是因為我看過他們的事蹟。

我覺得名人傳記是文學，也是傳記，它有史蹟可考，也有人好事的內容，值得我們回味、觀摩。

另外，中國的《西遊記》、《西廂記》、《水滸傳》，我幾乎無所不讀。不過學生時代光看文學的書是不夠的，文學之於人生只是增加文字的美感、意境。從二十歲到三十歲，在文學以外還要學習歷史，如《二十四史》等史書，我也幾乎全都翻閱過，因此對於歷代發生的史實，過去雖然也是一知半解，但現在再把讀過的史書細細回味，對於歷史人物錯綜複雜的關係就會慢慢清晰，而且再經自己整理一番，感覺真是美好。

從四十到五十歲，要從閱讀歷史進而研讀哲學。基本上，文學就像美麗的外衣，歷史只是知識，哲學則是內容涵義。文學的外衣要有歷史、哲學的內涵來充實，甚至這還不夠，到五、六十歲更要看宗教的書。年輕時我看佛書常是怎麼看都看不懂，老師上課時我也聽不懂；不過現在我不用看、不用聽，不管什麼書，只要信手一翻，一切自然了然於心，書中的義理自然清楚浮現腦海。

所謂「讀書如同金字塔，要能廣大要能高」，讀書比吃飯要緊，每日三餐的飲食能增加身體的營養；不時的讀書則能增長我們的智慧。讀書就像商店要經常進貨，否則如何出貨？讀書也有精讀、略讀之分，有的書必須用心細讀，有的書只要大略看過即可，但最重要的是要能廣讀。記得四十幾年前，我曾問過一位法師：「怎樣看大藏經？」他回答：「我亂看。」這個道理當時不容易瞭解，後來終於慢慢體會到，所謂「亂看」，

就是找自己懂得的書看，書看多了自然能融會貫通，自然會豁然有悟。所以關於讀書，希望佛光會員要廣讀，要多讀文學、歷史、哲學，乃至宗教的書籍，甚至科技知識等，都應該廣泛的涉獵。

今日要想提昇人類的生活品質，必須鼓勵人人多讀書，人人讀好書、讀善書、讀佛書；唯有讀書，才能變化氣質，才能昇華人格。因此，希望佛光會的會員大眾，不但人人擁有收藏書、床頭書、桌上書，更能人手一書，每一個佛光會員都是讀書人，都能在行住坐臥之間實踐書香生活，建立書香人生，透過讀書來提高我們的素質，昇華我們的人格。因此，所謂「生活書香化」，就是要我們大家今後都能努力讀書，希望我們都能建設「書香人生」，甚至全世界都能成為「書香的社會」。

## 三、僧信平等化

國際佛光會在成立之初，我曾為佛光會員寫了一首四句偈：「慈悲喜捨遍法界，惜福結緣利人天，禪淨戒行平等忍，慚愧感恩大願心。」此中「平等」就是一切佛法，佛教主張「生佛平等、事理平等、自他平等、空有平等」，佛法就是一個平等法，沒有平等，就沒有佛法，所以不能尊重平等的，都是外道。

在佛教的僧團裡，男眾、女眾要平等，出家眾、在家眾要平等；唯有平等，互相尊重，互相包容，這才是佛法。當初佛陀提倡一切眾生平等，現在我們倡導「四眾平等」、「僧信平等」、「男女平等」，凡是有人提倡女性至尊至上，或是心存男性優越感、大男人主義者，都是有違佛法。

「眾生平等」這是佛法的真諦，不由得我們違背佛法，各自另彈別調。但是多年來令人慨嘆的是，佛教界有一些人在掌握教權以後，始終不肯交棒，例如中國佛教會理事長一任多年，直到老死還不肯讓位，甚至理

當代人心思潮　　　　130

事長只能由比丘擔任，比丘尼、在家居士永遠沒有機會。這是因為中國佛教會比丘佔比較多數，他們訂下來的條文經過眾議決定，就成為規矩。這種落伍、自私、不公平、不平等的制度，在今後的時代必定不能存在。佛法要現代化，必須從我們自己的思想現代化，從我們的制度現代化。其實，佛教裡不管那一本經、那一部論，都是主張眾生平等，人人都能成佛，為什麼我們要曲解佛法呢？

在佛教界，一般在家信徒縱使學佛幾十年，儘管他的學問、道德、佛法足以為人師表，但他永遠都是三寶「弟子」，從來不敢以「老師」自居。為了提倡「僧信平等」，國際佛光會的章程裡就規定，在家信徒可以做檀講師、檀教師，唯有讓在家眾參與傳教的行列，授給他們傳教的權利，佛法才能普遍弘傳。試想，全台灣總共只不過才有幾千個出家眾，如果每一個鄉鎮由一人主持，也不夠分配；假如能把全台灣的信徒，乃至全

世界幾億的信徒，都能提昇做老師，都能到全世界弘法，「佛化全球」必然有望，必然有成功的一日。

多年前我曾經寫了一首「佛教青年的歌聲」：

「聽啊！真理在呼喚，光明在照耀，

這是佛教青年的興教歌聲，響徹雲霄，

青年為教的熱誠，掀起了復興佛教的巨浪狂潮，

成功的一日，就要來到。」

現在聽來還是感動不已。我相信只要我們立志努力，放大眼光，有遠見、有包容，對一切眾生尊重、平等，誠如我在第三期的《普門學報》發表的〈論佛教民主自由平等的真義〉一文中說：「佛教的皈依三寶，就是皈依人人和佛陀共有的佛性，這就是民主的精神；受持五戒，就是對人尊重，不任意侵犯，這就是自由的意義；眾生生權的提倡，是因為諸佛與眾

生一如，一切眾生都能成佛，這就是平等的主張。」

所以，我們能尊重一切眾生都有生命的自主權，都有生存的權利，這就是佛教的主旨所在；我們不能再有「在家眾這個不能，那個不可以；比丘尼這個不行，那個不容許」的論調了，因為不僅佛教的教義不允許，今日時代的潮流已經走上自由民主，也容不得我們再走回頭路。所謂「四姓出家，同一釋氏；百川入海，同一鹹味。」江河溪湖，流入到海洋裡，都是一樣的味道，所以我們看未來的社會，「平等」的世界就要來到，這是必然的。

甚至現在社會各界都在提倡「生命教育」，所謂「生命」，舉凡一花一草、一沙一石，乃至一件衣服、一張桌椅，都有生命。一件衣服本來可以穿上三、五年，你不愛惜它、糟蹋它，二、三個月就壞了，它的生命就結束了。所以不光是人有生命，動物、樹木花草等植物也有生命，乃至山

河大地都有生命，甚至時間就是生命，因為生命是時間的累積，所以浪費時間如同殺生。相同的，隨便浪費物品也是廣義的殺生，尤其現在提倡環保，重視生態，唯有尊重生命，平等對待一切生命，才有資格活在現代，如果不重視生命的尊嚴，就沒有資格稱為現代人。

「平等」與「和平」是一體兩面的真理，今日世界所以不能和平，就是因為不平等，舉凡政治上的以強欺弱，經濟上的貧富不均，宗教、種族的排擠，男女、地域的分歧，這些不能和平解決的問題，莫不是因為彼此不能平等共存所引起。再如現在海峽兩岸，因為不平等，所以不容易統一。我們希望未來的世界都能從平等、和諧上發展，今後世界上的國家與國家平等、民族與民族平等、宗教和宗教之間都應該像兄弟姐妹一樣，尤其國際佛光會是由四眾弟子所組成，凡是參與佛光會者，正如江、河、溪、湖，一旦流入海洋，均為一味，沒有誰高誰低、誰大誰小。為了實踐

佛陀「眾生平等」的理念，在佛光山的僧團與佛光會的教團裡，出家眾可以弘揚佛法，在家眾也能主持寺院行政。佛光山和佛光會如同人之雙臂、鳥之雙翼，都是同等的重要，凡是佛光人都應該明白「同體共生」的意義，都應該與人間和平相處，共同實踐真正的平等，共同創造平等的世界。

## 四、寺院本土化

因此，國際佛光會的會員大眾，大家不可以有差別的觀念，凡是佛光山派下的寺院，都是僧信所共有，由出家眾管理法務，在家眾可以協助寺院行政，甚至出家眾以弘法為家務，佛光會檀講師亦可登台說法。我們希望所有佛光會員不管出家、在家，都能做到「僧信平等化」，達成理事平等、空有平等的真理，讓佛法普遍，光明普照。

過去華人走到世界任何地方，不管做事或傳教，都要強調「發揚中華文化」，這種言行思想有待修正。因為世界上亞洲有亞洲的文化、歐洲有歐洲的文化，美洲有美洲的文化，澳洲有澳洲的文化，非洲有非洲的文化，我們應該尊重各地的文化，要用中華文化與當地的文化融和交流，而不是用自己的文化去侵略別人的文化。就如有一次我到美國康乃爾大學講演，該校一位約翰麥克雷教授在跟我談話時說道：「你來美國弘法可以，但是不能開口閉口都是中華文化，好像是故意為征服美國文化而來的。」

當時我聽了心中就有一個覺悟：我應該要尊重別人的文化，我們來到這裡只是為了奉獻、供養，如同佛教徒以香花供養諸佛菩薩一樣。

由這件事例可以看出，美國乃至世界各國，他們雖然吸收他國文化，但其實他們也害怕被人征服，所以不管佛光會乃至今後的佛教，一定要發揚「本土化」。因為佛教不是用來做為一個國家侵略他國文化的工具，而

是要同體共生，共同發展，共存共榮，所以佛光會奉行人間佛教，只要在人間，都要發展具有當地特色的本土化佛教。

所以，所謂「本土化」就是要讓佛教依各地的文化思想、地理環境、風俗民情之不同，發展出各自的特色。就如當初佛教從印度傳到東土，印度比丘到中國都只是從事經典翻譯，建寺的責任則讓給中國比丘負責，因此才有現在的中國佛教；如果當時印度的迦葉摩騰、竺法蘭等人都不回印度，而移民到中國建寺弘法，何來現在中國佛教的特色？甚至當初達摩祖師東來，將大法傳給慧可，也只是為了落實「本土化」。所以佛光山在多年前，我把住持之位傳給心平和尚繼承；心平和尚是台灣人，這也是在落實本土化。

「本土化」必然是未來佛教發展的方向，「本土化」只會增加力量，唯有「本土化」才能更深耕，才能更擴大，才能更發展。因此，提出「寺

院本土化」，主要就是為了幫助佛教的發展，假如現在佛光山海外的分別院，西來寺是由美籍的出家人當住持，南天寺、中天寺由澳洲籍的出家人當住持，南華寺由非洲籍的出家人當住持，其他的各個地方也都是由當地的人士住持；如果佛光山現在把佛教發展到這個程度，那將是一個怎麼樣的盛況呢？所以我希望從現在起，二十年到三十年之間，我們要輔導當地本土的出家人來負責本土的道場，如此佛法必定能更加快速的發展。

現在佛光山分布在南非、澳洲、印度、馬來西亞、香港、巴西等地的十六所佛教學院，也都在負起接引當地青年學佛的責任，以為未來落實「本土化」儲備人才。甚至目前在佛光山佛學院受教育的學生，各國弟子都有，未來希望更擴大種族的吸收，使他們都能成為佛光人，將來組織寺院，發展佛光普照，使佛法真正流傳於三千世界。

以下四點：

一、佛法人間化，

二、生活書香化，

三、僧信平等化，

四、寺院本土化。

希望未來全體佛光人都能建立共識，不但落實在生活裡，並且以此為依循的方向與目標，共同弘揚人間佛教。

# 發心與發展

幫助自己要「發心」
發心，就是開發我們的心地
發心，就是建設自我

幫助世間要「發展」
發展，就是開發我們的世界
發展，就是建設世界

國際佛光會第九次世界會員代表大會
地點：日本
時間：2002年4月

各位貴賓、各位會員：

大家好！國際佛光會創會已然邁入第十一年了，今天大家不遠千里，從世界各地前來日本東京參加第九次世界會員大會，實在非常難得殊勝。

聯合國曾訂定一九六五年為「國際開發年」，「開發」是個時代大家共同的任務。尤其廿一世紀是個科技進步，資訊發達的時代，一般人莫不以汲汲開發世間的經濟生活為要務，而我們佛教徒則以開發內心的真如佛性為根本。

國際佛光會是一個佛教的團體，因此我們不但要有「內在」的開發；我們同時也要有「外在」的開發。內在的開發就是開發我們的心地；外在的開發就是開發我們的世界。

例如，現在舉世矚目的太空總署，長期以來一直積極地開發外太

空，人類不但登陸了月球，甚至發現火星、木星裡也有水源，也能提供植物的生存；甚至蘇聯和平號的衛星，在太空服務人類十多年後，才在去年於南太平洋功成身退。現在的開發公司，更致力發展都市建設、開發山海新生地等工程。目前世界上著名的機場，包括香港過去的啟德機場、現在的大嶼山機場，還有新加坡的樟宜機場、曼谷的廊曼機場等，不就是興建在海埔新生地上的建築物嗎？

此外，現在的學校教育，有將「開發潛能」列為教學計劃者，還有文學家開發文學的領域，創作許多優美的詞章、動聽的詩歌，以及哲學家發揮對未來學的思惟、對人類慈悲心的提倡等，這些都是在開發我們的精神世界。由此可知我們人類文化一直都在不斷地進步中。

國際佛光會的會員也和社會大眾一樣，時時都在開發自己，以求自

度；念念開發社會，以期度他。例如「佛光會員四句偈」說：

「慈悲喜捨遍法界，惜福結緣利人天；

禪淨戒行平等忍，慚愧感恩大願心。」

從這四句偈中，我們希望會員大眾能開發自己的慈悲心，開發自己的喜捨心，開發自己惜福結緣、慚愧感恩的心，甚至開發自心本性裡大願力的禪心佛性，以期自利利他，自度度人。

此亦說明，本會自從十一年前創會之初，就在提倡自他開發、內外開發、事理開發。主要的是希望我們的家庭，不只是開發財富能源，更要重視開發人際關係的和諧；不只是希望升官發財，更要以福利社會人群為心志之所歸。

今年是國際佛光會創會屆滿十一周年，又值二十一世紀人類新紀元的初始，所以我們特別在國際佛光會第九次世界會員代表大會在日本召開的

此刻，提出「發心與發展」的主題，希望今後人人在「發心」方面，要能發四種心：

一要「發慈悲心，怨親平等」；

二要「發增上心，定慧等持」；

三要「發同體心，人我一如」；

四要「發菩提心，自在圓滿」。

「發心」之外，還要有四種「發展」：

一要「發展人性的真善美好」；

二要「發展世間的福慧聖財」；

三要「發展人際的和樂愛敬」；

四要「發展未來的生佛合一」。

發心，就是建設自我；發展，就是建設世界。幫助自己要「發心」；

幫助世間要「發展」。茲略述其義如下：

## 一、發心

佛教的百千法門中，「發心」最為重要。發心就是開發我們的心地。

佛教將「心」比喻為「田」、為「地」；田地不開發，如何能播種？心地不開發，如何長養菩提？所以在佛門的修持裡，都要我們發「四無量心」，發「四弘誓願」，並且實踐「四攝法」、「四加行」，以期自度度人。

省庵大師說：「入道要門，發心為首；心發，則佛道堪成。」因此，希望我們會員大眾要發四種心。

(一)、發慈悲心，怨親平等

「慈能與樂，悲能拔苦。」娑婆世間最大的缺陷，就是愛與恨的分歧、怨與親的疏離。其實，愛恨、怨親都是主觀的分別，例如自己身上的一塊爛肉，由於是自己的，因此就會好好的加以洗滌、治療、保護。本此心理，如果我們對於自己不喜歡的人，能夠「以愛止恨」、「以親處怨」，懂得人我乃是「同體共生」、「人我一體」，把你我的立場相互融和，進而開發自己的慈悲心，所謂「無緣大慈，同體大悲」，則一切眾生都是我們的父母親眷，都是我們的羅睺羅。

所以佛經說：「以慈止怨，以忍息諍」，基督教也說：「愛你的仇敵」；儒家則有「泛愛眾而親仁」的精神。佛陀更以叛徒提婆達多為自己的逆增上緣，這一切都是慈悲心的展現。

慈悲是佛法的根本。《維摩經》說：「智度菩薩母，方便以為父，一切眾導師，無不由是生。法喜以為妻，慈悲心為女，善心誠實男，畢竟空

寂舍。」佛教的三藏十二部雖然有無量的法門與教義，但是皆以慈悲為根本；《怖魔經》說：「一切佛法如果離開慈悲，則為魔法。」

所謂「慈悲」，如《八大人覺經》說：「生死熾然，苦惱無量，發大乘心，普濟一切，願代眾生，受無量苦，令諸眾生，畢竟大樂。」自古以來，菩薩發心都是甘願為眾生做牛做馬，為眾生服務；如果沒有眾生，何來佛道呢？所以慈悲是通往佛道的一條捷徑。

慈悲不僅是理念上的了解，更應該從身體上付諸實踐。例如：地藏菩薩的「地獄度眾」、韋馱尊者的「三洲感應」、溈山靈祐禪師的「願做眾生的老牯牛」、布袋和尚的「撿拾人間的煩惱」等。歷代的諸佛菩薩、一切聖賢，那一個不是如觀世音菩薩一樣：以慈眼視眾生、以悲心度眾生，以慈悲來示現人間呢？

慈悲是淨化、昇華的愛。人與人之間，如果能換個立場，人我對調，

為對方著想，就能興起慈悲的念頭。一念慈悲可以化除瞋恨，一念慈悲可以化除驕慢，一念慈悲可以化除怖畏。所謂「一人慈悲，眾皆伴侶」；「萬人慈悲，法界一如」。如果一個人實踐慈悲，大家都可以做我們的朋友；如果社會大眾都發起慈悲運動，普天之下自然也都能如兄弟手足一般的相親相愛了。

過去，佛陀的慈悲曾經讓眾生得到庇護安樂；現在希望我們的佛光會員，也能本著佛陀的慈悲心懷，先從自他怨親平等做起，能夠如《法華經》所說：一切男子是我父，一切女子是我母，一切年輕於我者，皆是我的兄弟姊妹；即使是冤家仇敵，我也可以化他、愛他，但不能恨他。以此慈心來引導全世界人類，邁向光明幸福的康莊大道。

（二）、發增上心，定慧等持

「增上」就是增勝上進的意思。《成佛之道》說：「下求增上生，現樂後亦樂。」對於世間的物用，我們並不排斥、否定，因為人在世間上生活，自然就需要眷屬的愛敬、淨財的增長，以及福樂富貴的不斷增上，這才是人間生活的要求。

但是，我們光有外在的富有，這是不夠的，我們對於內在的精神，還必需透過「定慧等持」、「止觀雙修」，不斷的自我提昇，以期如「佛光會員信條」所說：「我們現證法喜安樂，永斷煩惱，遠離無明。」

談到「定慧等持」，在《六祖壇經》的「定慧品」中，惠能大師說：「定慧一體，本是不二。」「定」，就是要我們遇境不動心、不氣惱；「慧」，就是要我們運用得體，凡事如法，那就是智慧的妙用。如大顛禪師的侍者告訴大顛禪師說：對付韓愈要「先以定動，後以智拔」。

定與慧，離一非道。《涅槃經》說：「定多慧少，增長無明；慧多定

少，增加邪見。」六祖大師則說：「常生清淨心，定心而有慧；於境上無心，慧中而有定；定慧等無心，雙修自性證。」

定與慧的關係，如金與器、如水與波、如燈與光，都能相互為用，不即不離。定與慧，如鳥之雙翼，如人之雙臂；如果「定慧等持」、「體用一如」，還有何事不能成辦呢？

因此，我們希望佛光會員，人人發增上心，定慧等持。

至於「發增上心」，在佛教裡認為，「五乘佛法」也是從人、天進入到聲聞、緣覺，而到達菩薩的目標，這就是增上；「四羅漢果」也是從須陀洹、斯陀含，而到阿那含、阿羅漢，依序增上；菩薩的五十一階位，也是從十信、十行、十住、十回向、十地，而到等覺、妙覺的佛果。所以，修行絕非一蹴可及，而是逐漸增上的。

現在的佛教，以在家信眾為多，信眾以家庭眷屬的愛敬為根本，如果

把家庭的日用、社會的名聲、物質的利養，都排除在佛法之外，則信徒以何而生存呢？

所以，本會一直強調，出家僧眾應以發「出離心」為要；在家信眾只要發「增上心」即可。如果能夠從發「增上心」，漸漸的看破放下，而能激發菩提心，達於「定慧等持」，則何愁慈悲不能圓滿呢？

### （三）、發同體心，人我一如

世間上，最煩惱的事就是「差別」，諸如男女、貧富、知見、中外等各種差別。因為有差別，就有諸多的矛盾；有矛盾就會產生抗拒；彼此抗拒的世間，人我怎能和諧一如呢？因此，吾人要求世間的和平幸福，就必須泯除人我分別，發同體心，人我一如。

佛法昭示我們：「同體平等，人我一如」。黃山谷在「戒殺詩」說：

「我肉眾生肉，名殊體不殊；原同一種性，只為別形軀。」想到如此，大地眾生皆和如來一樣，具有智慧德相，只因我人妄自分別，故而才從差別中生出世間的一切苦相。

世間上的眾生有種種性、種種相；然而相上雖有白種人、黃種人和黑人等種族的分別，但是「人同此心，心同此理」。例如，人人對於安全、和樂、平安、順遂，都是一樣的需求；既然如此，我們就不應該把自己的幸福建築在別人的痛苦之上，就不可以把自己的成就建築在別人的渺小上面。

孔子說：「己所不欲，勿施於人。」佛教主張要把禪悅法喜與世間大眾共同分享，要把世間上的一切眾生，都看成是自己的伴侶，都是我自己身心的一部分，都是我自己的生命所有。

說到眾生，在類別上，有「胎生、卵生、濕生、化生」；在形相上，

有「若有色、若無色」；在精神思想上有「若有想、若無想」等等。眾生雖有千差萬別，但性靈和吾人都沒有分別。即使是大地山河、樹木花草，因吾人成佛，它也可以跟我們的自性連為一體。所以，一切眾生，自性真如都是平等的。

人類，與自己愈近者愈親，與自己愈遠者愈疏。你看，舉世的芸芸眾生，同國、同黨、同派、同事、同學、同鄉、同姓、同一家；所以有夫妻之情，有兒女之情，有父母之情。愈是近親，愈是感到和自我的關係密切，所以要建立同體的觀念，先要建立舉世人類都和我有相互的關係。例如，農夫種植米穀，我才有飲食；工人織布，我才有衣穿；甚至我們生活中的一切，那一樣不是社會大眾所供給的呢？如果沒有他們的心意、精神、勞苦，則我們便無法得生。所以離開了眾生，離開了因緣，「我」就不能單獨的存在；能夠建立人我眾生一如的思想，則在同體共生的理念

下，還愁世界不會和平嗎？

## (四)、發菩提心，自在圓滿

菩提心就是犧牲奉獻，就是成就眾生，因此菩薩道的精神，就是發起「上弘下化」的菩提心。

實踐菩薩道的大乘行者，受持菩薩戒除了有防非止惡的攝律儀戒以外，更有勤修善法的攝善法戒，以及度化眾生的饒益有情戒。這顯示了菩薩行者不僅要消極地不作惡，更要積極地修一切善，乃至遍學一切法門，以度無邊眾生。

根據《菩薩善戒經》說：「有二因緣失菩薩戒，一者退菩提心，二者得上惡心。」因為菩薩發心是為廣度眾生，如果不發上弘下化的菩提心，便不能稱為菩薩。

歷代聖賢發菩提心，行菩薩道者，均可作為吾人修行的典範。如《本生經》載，佛陀在往昔行菩薩道時，曾不惜性命「捨身飼虎，割肉餵鷹」，以完成菩薩布施度的宏願；作忍辱仙人時，為歌利王割截肢體，以不生瞋恨而圓滿忍辱的修行。

此外，目犍連「為教殉難」、富樓那「蠻邦興化」、摩訶男「自沉河底救族人」、法珍比丘尼「斷臂募資刻藏」等，若非靠著菩提心發起的力量，如何能有此大願大行！如果沒有歷代的古德們捨身捨命行菩薩道，佛法命脈如何延續於後世？

菩提心不是一時的情緒，而是從生活中點滴的受持奉行；菩提心是不放棄一個眾生，不輕視一點小善；菩提心是以佛道為依歸，以真理為法侶。

佛光會的宗旨目標，就是要帶給眾生佛法，尤其是歡喜的佛法；是要

讓每個人能夠改善自己，從煩惱的枷鎖中解脫出來，享受人生的歡喜，從物質和自我的束縛中解脫出來，享受群我共生的喜悅。

人生一期一期的生命，過去世、未來世因有隔陰之迷而無法掌握，但是一定要能掌握現世的歡喜。一個人如果擁有再多的金銀財寶、功名富貴，乃至美貌、學識等，卻不快樂、不歡喜，這樣的人生也是沒有意義的。因此在佛法裡提倡禪悅、提倡法喜，諸佛菩薩中更有歡喜佛、禪悅藏菩薩、歡喜地菩薩等。這說明在佛法裡如果沒有體會到佛法的歡喜，就是沒有宗教的體驗，這樣的信仰就有了危機。如果有了法喜的人，即使給人批評、漫罵、欺負，也不會失去歡喜，即使苦行，乃至誦經、拜佛、布施助人，也都會充滿了快樂歡喜。

所以，布施、修行，都是法喜、快樂的事；如果布施很苦、修行很苦，就不自在；不自在，就不是菩提心。人生如果不自在，也不圓滿；觀

世音菩薩「遊諸國土」，遊，就是自在。因此，希望吾等佛光會員，人人都能效法諸佛菩薩的廣發菩提心，能夠「上求佛道」，也能「下化眾生」；能夠在菩提心中自在解脫，才能圓滿。

## 二、發展

國際佛光會自一九九一年二月一日在台灣創會，繼而翌年的五月十六日在美國成立世界總會。十年來佛光會一直本著既定的宗旨、目標、方向在發展。

佛光會的發展方向，就是希望我們每個人，從做好一個「佛光會員」，繼而建設「佛光人家」，接著發展「佛光社區」，到最後創造「佛光淨土」為終極目標。

創造佛光淨土既是佛光人努力發展的目標，因此我們希望未來的佛光

會，應該加強檀講師、檀教師、檀導師的訓練，加強佛光會員的國際宏觀，大家一起來開發世間的能源，更一起來開發內心的寶藏，希望大家朝著下列四個方向，努力實踐。

## (一)、發展人性的真善美好

佛光會自創會以來，一再的提倡文化、教育、慈善、共修，尤其在有關信眾的教育方面，我們在各地舉辦讀書會、短期出家修道會、各種講習會、各種成長營，甚至青少年的進修班、交響樂團，還有佛光青年團、佛光成人禮等。

我們在文化、教育、公益上給予信徒的教育，主要就是要大家開發真善美的品德。因為現在的世間，家庭裡的份子，彼此缺乏真情，所以家不成家；社會上，群我之間缺少善行，所以產生人我決裂。由於人類不把真

如佛性裡的美好，表現到人間來，大家共榮、共有、共好，反而到處充滿了貪瞋嫉妒，猙獰醜陋，失去了真善美好的因緣，這個世間還有什麼可愛的呢？

真善美好，是人間最重要的目標，也是人間最需要開發和建設的境界。《妙法聖念處經》說：「眾善應可愛，如父復如母；美善體安然，能離於喧諍。美善人天喜，美善增勤勇；美善眷屬多，美善三塗離。美善息諸惡，美善離煩惱；能棄語過非，應修諸眾善。」

真善美好的人生，是天上、人間，大家一致共同追求的目標。為了開發人間的真善美好，我們希望本會大眾，今後應該在身口意上，依循佛陀的開示：

一、說話時，要說真語、實語、如語、不異語、不誑語等令人受用的好話。（《金剛經》）

二、做事時，要做善行、懿行、美行、利行等有益於人間的好事。

三、存心時，要存慧心、道心、悲心、願心等祝福別人的好心，這也正是本會所提倡的「三好運動」。

（《阿含經》）

說好話、做好事、存好心，這也正是本會所提倡的「三好運動」。本會長久以來雖然一直都以推動三好運動來發展人性的真善美，並且將此視為發展的重要任務，但是總覺得還是不夠。因此，我們更希望政府當局，乃至全世界的有識之士，對於有關開發人性真善美好的建設，都應該給予獎勵，給予宣揚。以期風氣所及，讓我們的人間社會，到處所聽到的都是美好的聲音，到處所見到的都是真誠感人的事情；到處所想到的都是為人服務的善事。

我們希望全體佛光會員，大家率先動員，大家一起來學習發展，讓我們推己及人，創造一個和諧美好的人間，讓大家都能擁有一個真善美好的

人生。

## （二）、發展世間的福慧聖財

世間上，人人都希望發展自己的事業，發展自己的財富。但是，我們尤其希望大家能重視福慧事業的發展，重視共有聖財的發展。

說到財富，有「狹義的財富」，諸如金錢、房屋、土地、股票等；有「廣義的財富」，例如健康、智慧、人緣、信用、道德等。

除此以外，還有「有價的財富」，譬如聲望、名譽、成就、歷史；也有「無價的財富」，比如人格、良知、真心、本性等。乃至有形的財富、無形的財富；現世的財富、來世的財富；個人的財富、大眾的財富；物質的財富、精神的財富；一時的財富、永遠的財富等等。

所有的財富，要能與福慧建立關係；福慧是人生最究竟圓滿的財富。

佛陀是福慧具足的兩足尊；福慧事業不能發展，人生就不能圓滿。所以我們呼籲大家，為了要福慧具足，要發展聖者的財富。

所謂聖者的財富，例如般若禪定的財富、法喜禪悅的財富、慚愧感恩的財富、慈悲智慧的財富；也就是淨財、善財、法財。

《諸法集要經》說：「珍寶有散壞，法財用無極；唯所修善法，百千生相逐。」真正的財富，不一定要看銀行裡的存款，也不一定是指土地、房屋、黃金、股票，這些都是五家所共有，個人無法獨得；人生唯有發展信仰、滿足、歡喜、慚愧、人緣、平安、健康、智慧等，才是真正的擁有世間的福慧聖財。這些財富不但現世受用，來世還可以受用；不但一時受用，還可以終身受用；不但一人受用，還可以大眾受用。

因此，人不要只看重個人的財富，也要創造、發展共有的財富。甚至，你固然可以擁有私有的財富，但你更要懂得享受共有的財富，例如陽

當代人心思潮　　　　162

光、空氣、淨水等。你懂得的話，宇宙山河、公園道路，都是我們能享有的財富，我們還會貧窮嗎？

人為什麼來到人間？人不是為了受苦而來，也不是為了鬥爭而來；是為了享受人間的福慧，享受人間的資源，享受自心的平靜而來。但是這一切，也要靠我們自己來發展，才能獲得。

### （三）、發展人際的和樂愛敬

世間不是我們任何一個人的，世間是由很多個人所共同組織成的社會，大家在社會裡共求營生。

世界上幾十億的人口，大家要想和樂愛敬的共同生存，當然就要培養人際之間的關係，發展人我之間的共同需要。所以就有人在物質上發展富麗堂皇的都市，在經濟上發展銀行貨幣的流通，在感情上發展婚姻眷屬的

關係，在生活上發展衣食住行的需要。

但是，在社會的各種建設當中，也有一些不當的發展，例如，舞廳、酒家、賭場、幫派等場所或組織的設立，提供人們在追求五欲之樂，追求感官刺激的同時，也讓內在深層的性靈生活跟著墮落、沉淪了。所以社會出現了畸形的發展，人際之間也造成了許多的矛盾、許多的糾紛；也因此使得和樂愛敬的人際關係，在此世風日下、世道紛雜的混亂時刻，更加顯示出它的重要性，更加的需要吾人去為它重新估定價值。

過去，基督教發揚博愛，墨子發揚兼愛，儒家發揚仁義，歷代諸子百家、宗教學者，莫不希望在思想、學術上發展出另外的一套方案，以充實人際之間和樂愛敬的關係。

但是，從各種發展的結果看來，開發人類賴以維持社會秩序的和樂愛敬之美德，還是有待佛教來負擔起責任，因為佛教講「心」，心才是一切

善美品德的源頭。

一般開發世間的能源，那只是物質上的發展；發展內心的寶藏，那才是真正給人超脫的方便。例如，國際佛光會為了淨化人心，多年來一直發展「把心找回來」系列活動；為了促進社會的健全和諧，我們推展「七誡運動」；為了找回人性的尊嚴，我們提倡「慈悲愛心人運動」；為了群我關係的互助，我們舉辦「三好運動」等。

歷屆的佛光會世界會員大會，我們相繼提出「歡喜與融和」、「同體與共生」、「尊重與包容」、「平等與和平」、「圓滿與自在」、「自然與生命」、「公是公非」等主題演說，目的就是希望發展一個和樂愛敬的社會人間。

此外，我們主張「尊重會員大眾，來時歡迎去時相送」；我們提倡「實踐生活修行，隨時隨地心存恭敬」，也都是為了和諧美好的人我關

係。

我們更希望會員大眾，人人學習佛陀「示教利喜」的精神，不斷開發自己內在的能源。我們要學習《法華經》中常不輕菩薩「我不敢輕視汝等，汝等皆當作佛」的尊重；我們要實踐普賢菩薩「隨喜功德」等深弘誓願；我們要效法古德先賢們「為大法也，何惜生命」之堅忍不移的精神。希望我全體佛光會員，都能朝此目標發展，並臻完成。

### ㈣、發展未來的生佛合一

現在的時代，對人間的發展可以說一日千里，大家對未來的發展，更是寄以殷切的關注。

「未來學」是這個時代的熱門學科，大家的眼光都望向未來，注意未來。例如，現在的青少年都懂得要有「生涯規劃」，現代的長者也在計劃

如何「安渡餘年」，以及各國政府也有五年計劃、十年計劃，甚至有人在研究十年後、百年後的世界。可見對未來的發展，已經成為這個時代重要的任務。

過去，佛教也總是鼓勵信徒要修好來生；來生就是未來。現在的科學家，已經在預備未來要佔領太空，因此現在不但有人到月球預購土地，甚至有人計劃移民其他星球。人類對於宇宙世界，愈來愈有更大的發展，愈來愈具有宏觀的思想。

自古以來，一般普通的民眾，都希望開發天堂，以供自己長住久安；佛教徒也開發兜率內院，寄望親近彌勒尊佛，時常聽經聞法，以期成佛。還有許多佛教大乘行者，立志開發東方琉璃淨土，開發西方極樂世界，以期能夠「生佛一如」。

所以，佛教對「未來」，已經有數百千年的發展經驗，現在經過科技

的文明，經過各種文化的啟發，對於發展未來的理想，更是愈來愈濃厚。像佛教徒的合掌、禮拜，都是希望藉此與諸佛菩薩接心，但現在的佛教弟子，他的願望不只是接心，而希望與諸佛菩薩長相左右，達到生佛合一的目標。

我們閱讀經文，都看到東方世界、南方世界，各處世界裡的諸佛菩薩和他的子民如何和諧、如何安樂。這已經不是經文上的記載，這也是我們人類應有的發展理念。

在《佛性論》有一段記載：「由般若故，成就佛法；由大悲故，成熟眾生。由二方便，住無住處，無有退轉，速證菩提，滅五過失，生五功德，是故佛說一切眾生皆有佛性。」

生佛合一，這不但不是遙不可及的夢想；甚至心佛眾生，本來就是等無差別的真理。所以，我們希望佛光會員們，能夠在現世的人間，開發我

們的慈悲智慧，開發我們的真如佛性；只要我們能夠時時擁抱真理，只要我們能夠永作佛國的一員，那就是與佛合一了。

綜上所說，「發心與發展」實在是每一個現代人，不僅對自己、對家庭、對社會、對國家，甚至是對全宇宙人類應有使命。

因此，我們希望從今以後，大家不要辜負了佛教裡「發心」這麼美好的用語，不要讓它成為老生常談的空話，希望人人都能真正的「發慈悲心，怨親平等」；「發增上心，定慧等持」；「發同體心，人我一如」；「發菩提心，自在圓滿」。

「發展」，也不要讓它成為社會上發展物欲的專屬，希望人人真正做到：「發展人性的真善美好」；「發展世間的福慧聖財」；「發展人際的和樂愛敬」；「發展未來的生佛合一」。

發心，人人要發，刻不容緩；發展，即時行動，期能早日圓成。

# 自覺與行佛

行佛就是依照佛陀的教法去實踐奉行
真正的修行人　必須解行並重
有了慧解才能自覺　透過行佛才能覺他；
自覺是自我開發　覺他是行佛之行
能夠自覺與行佛
必然心中有佛　時時與佛同在

國際佛光會世界總會第十次世界會員代表大會
地點：台灣
時間：2004年9月3日

各位貴賓、各位會員，大家好！

今天是國際佛光會創會以來第十次召開世界會員代表大會，也是第三次回到台灣佛光山舉行，感謝大家從世界各地不遠千里而來參加。

今年是我出家六十六年、弘法邁入第五十六個年頭；去年出版《雲水三千》時曾有人問我：什麼叫雲水三千？也有人問我：為什麼要經常在五大洲來回奔忙？我回答：天上的白雲飄來又飄去，地下的河水流去又流回來；出家人行腳就是雲水。雲水到哪裡去呢？三千大千世界。所以，雲水就是「行佛」。

這數十年來，看到佛教在台灣乃至世界各地蓬勃發展，不但信仰佛教的人口逐年增加，尤其佛教所辦的各種弘法活動，也都普遍受到社會各界人士的熱烈參與，這真是值得可喜的現象。但是另一方面，卻又感於這麼多年來，一般佛教徒的信仰始終停頓在「信佛」、「拜佛」、「求佛」的

階段，不免想到過去佛教之所以衰微、沒有力量，就是因為佛教徒沒有在生活中落實佛法。例如，佛教要我們的慈悲，多少佛教徒有真正的慈悲？佛教要我們喜捨，多少佛教徒具有喜捨的性格？佛教要我們有般若，多少佛教徒是真正的明理、有智慧？身為佛教徒而沒有佛法，佛教怎麼不衰微呢？

為了提昇佛教徒的信仰層次，最近我提倡「行佛」運動，並且訂定今年為佛光會的「行佛年」，希望大家在日常生活中都能確實實踐佛法。例如佛要我們慈悲，則不可輕易傷害生命；佛要我們忍辱，則不可瞋心怒罵；佛要我們廣結善緣，則不可以自私自利……。唯有大家真正落實「信仰生活化」、「生活佛法化」，在二六時中，不管行住坐臥都能自動自發、自覺自悟的「行佛所行」，如此自己才能得到佛法的受用，佛教也才能根植人間。所以今年的大會我以「自覺與行佛」為主題，提出四點意見，希望做為大家未來努力的目標。

# 一、用自覺心昇華自我

人，從小就有父母來教育我們；及長入學，必須接受學校老師的教育；走出家庭、學校，則有社會教育。在很多的教育當中，以「自覺」的教育最為重要。

「自覺」就是一種自我教育，佛經講：「自依止、法依止、莫異依止」，就是自我教育；「觸類旁通、舉一反三、聞一知十」，也都是自我教育。

自我教育的「自覺心」是修學佛法的一個重點，當初佛陀所說的教法，無非是為了讓眾生悟入「覺」的境界，導引有情悟入佛的知見，而與佛平等；就是佛陀自己本身也是因「自覺」而成道。佛陀因證悟宇宙人生的真理（自覺），而又本著無盡的慈心悲願，以真理來教化眾生（覺

他），所以是「自覺」、「覺他」、「覺行圓滿」的覺者。佛陀以他自己名號的意義，就是要我們效法他，學佛要靠自己覺悟；一個人能夠「自覺」，繼而「覺他」，才能成就「覺行圓滿」的功德。

自覺的教育，考之於西方社會，他們從小就訓練學生要懂得自己思考、懂得發覺問題、懂得解決問題。老師平時只是啟發、引導學生找資料、寫報告，甚至課堂上也由學生自己講說，而不是由老師講給學生聽，讓老師來幫學生讀書。反之，中國的填鴨式教育一直為人所垢病的，就是受囿於老師在台上講，學生在台下聽，都是由老師單方面的上對下傳授，這是一種框框，讓學生失去自我教育的本能。

所謂「自我教育」，就是要自我要求、自我學習、自我充實、自我反省，而不是只想依賴別人；平時自問、自覺、自發、自悟，透過自我的觀照而能找到自己，這就是自我教育成功。

佛教的自我教育，諸如懺悔、認錯、反省、禪思、自我觀照等。佛教的教育有時用聞思修來受教，有時用參訪來受教，有時用冥思來受教，有時用悟性性來受教。甚至，有時候一個人自己學不來、讀不來，如果你發心教人，所謂教學相長，反而能教得會，這就是自我教育。

自我教育就是凡事要反求諸己。禪宗有一則公案，道謙禪師與好友宗圓結伴參訪行腳，途中宗圓不堪跋山涉水之疲困，幾次三番鬧著要回去。道謙安慰他說：「我們已發心出來參學，而且也走了這麼遠的路，現在半途放棄回去，實在可惜。這樣吧，從現在起，一路上如果可以替你做的事，我一定為你代勞，但只有五件事我幫不上忙。」宗圓問道：「哪五件事呢？」道謙非常自然地說：「穿衣、吃飯、屙屎、撒尿、走路。」意思是說，你要自己解決問題，才能一起上路。

人要靠自己自知、自覺、自悟，才能成功，別人的幫助終究有限。因

為別人吃飯，我不能當飽；別人走路，我不能到達目標。自己有病了，別人更不能替我痛苦；身體疲倦了，別人也不能替我休息。開悟證果，修行成道，尤其要靠自己來，如趙州禪師說：「像小便這麼簡單的事，還得我自己去做，何況成佛的大事，別人豈能代替得了？」所以凡事自我要求，一切從自我出發，才有成功的一天。

「自覺」的重要，在《宗鏡錄》說：「如人飲水，冷暖自知。如群盲眼開，分明照境，驗象真體，終不摸其尾牙。」其實早在二千五百年前，佛陀於金剛座上菩提樹下悟道時，對人間發出的第一句宣言就是「大地眾生皆有如來佛性！」每一個人都具有成佛的性能，人人都可以成佛；人與佛本來是平等無二，但由於凡夫一念不覺，因此長淪生死。學佛，就是要開發自性，要覺悟自性。

「覺」有發現、察覺的功能，和發明不一樣。發明是透過創新，研究

出一種新的東西，而發現則是就本有的東西加以察覺。如舉世熟悉的英國大科學家牛頓發現「地心引力」，這就是一種「察覺」的功能，因為即使牛頓不發現，地心引力依然存在。甚至當初佛陀證悟成道，他也只是發覺了「緣起」的真理，而非創新，所以《雜阿含經》說：「若佛出世，若未出世，此法常住，法住法界，彼如來自覺知，成等正覺。」

人類生存在地球上的歷史已經相當悠久，但為什麼只有牛頓發現地心引力？因為牛頓比一般人更有敏銳的觀察力，以佛法來說，就是他的「覺性」比一般人高出許多。覺性的高低對一個人智慧的開發影響很深。佛法非常重視對有情眾生之覺性的開發，有了覺性才能開發智慧，才能看出和體驗出解脫之道。

在佛教的「十法界」中，「四聖」之一的「緣覺」，他是「無師自悟」而「不由他覺」；緣覺因為出於沒有佛陀出世，或者沒有佛法的時

代，他是觀十二因緣而覺悟真諦之理，因此稱為緣覺。乃至佛陀的弟子大迦葉，他曾經自豪的說：「如果我不能遇到釋迦牟尼佛，我一樣也能成為獨覺的聖者。」

因為大迦葉尊者的覺性高，所以當初佛陀在靈山會上「拈華示眾」，與會百萬人天大眾皆面面相覷，無法會意，唯有迦葉尊者當下靈犀相應，破顏而笑，於是佛陀把「正法眼藏，涅槃妙心，實相無相，微妙法門，不立文字，教外別傳，付囑摩訶迦葉。」禪也因此在「拈花微笑」、師徒心意相契的剎那之間流傳下來，這就是「自覺」。

在中國的禪門一直講究「覺悟」，凡事要靠自己去參，不能說破。

有一次香嚴智閑因為師兄為山靈祐禪師問他：「未出娘胎前，什麼是你的本分事？」智閑懵然不知應對，他請師兄為他道一句，為山禪師說：「我說了，那是我的見解；對你，又有什麼益處呢？」智閑於是回到僧堂，把

所有語錄經卷搬出來，左翻右翻，竟然沒有一句合乎應對的話，不禁嘆息道：「說食不能當飽，畫餅豈可充飢？」於是把所有典籍付之一炬，發誓說：「這輩子不研究義學了，從今以後要好好做個粥飯僧，免得浪費心神。」

智閑拜辭溈山禪師，來到南陽慧忠國師住過的遺址禁足潛修。有一天，在割除雜草時，無意中瓦礫擊中石子，發出響聲，他廓然頓悟，說偈云：「一擊忘所知，更不假修治；動容揚古道，不墮悄然機。處處無蹤跡，聲色外威儀；諸方達道者，咸言上上機。」

當初如果溈山禪師一語道破，何來智閑的廓然頓悟呢？所以六祖大師說：「與汝說者，即非密也；汝若返照，密在汝邊。」一個人如果忘記了自己，不管修學什麼，都是別人的。此即所謂「從門入者，不是家珍；從心流出，才是本性。」

人生在成長的過程中，有時候需要父母的教導、老師的訓誡、社會大眾的幫助、長官的提攜、朋友的勉勵；但是最重要的，還是要靠自己「自覺」。如果自己不能自覺，光是依靠別人，就如自己的身體，血管裡的血液是自己的，是自發的營養，對增進健康有最大的功效與幫助；如果靠打針、注射營養劑，總是外來的，利益有限。所以平常我們說「皈依三寶」，其實是皈依自己的自性三寶，是為了找到自己、認識自己。人的自性本來清淨無染，因為一念不覺，不能自知，故而忘失自家本來面目，所以沉淪苦海。學佛，就是要開發自己的真心，摘下自己的面具，誠懇的剖析自己、認識自己。但是這一切，不能依靠別人完成，唯有自覺，才能達成目標。

「覺」就是證悟涅槃妙理的智慧，我們常說要發菩提心，要行菩薩道。何謂菩薩？《大智度論》卷四說：「自覺復能覺他，是名菩薩。」如

當代人心思潮　　　　180

果將這一份功德再行提升，再行圓滿，就是成佛的境界。成就佛的功德主要是從自覺、覺他和覺行圓滿中來，意思就是告訴我們，在學佛的過程中，要時常以覺性的啟發來面對當前的生活，以恆常覺性的圓滿來成就佛道。所以，菩提心、菩薩道基本上是在說明，人生的過程其實就是一條覺悟之路。

要開發自己的覺性其實並不是難事，可以說只要留心，處處都是覺悟的表現。儒家的「一日三省吾身」，佛教的「往昔所造諸惡業，一切我今皆懺悔」，都是自覺的功夫。宋朝大慧普覺禪師更說：「學道人逐日但將檢點他人底工夫常自檢點，道業無有不辦。或喜或怒，或靜或鬧，皆是檢點時節。」一個人一旦發覺自己有了過失，必須要有「自覺心」來自我改造。如梁啟超說：「今日之我不惜與昨日之我宣戰。」儒家也有「苟日新、日日新、又日新」的自我改造之言；佛教裡的沙門生活規範是「勤修

戒定慧，息滅貪瞋癡」，因能時時自覺而擁有戒定慧的武器，當然就能降伏貪瞋癡。所以，懂得自覺、自悟，才能自我進步。

自覺是一條趨向自我解脫的道路，自己一句「我會了」、「我懂了」、「我明白了」，比別人的千言萬語教導我，還要管用；反之，如果自己不求覺悟，光靠別人，就如《遺教經》說：「我如善導，導人善路，汝若不行，咎不在導；我如良醫，應病與藥，汝若不服，過不在醫。」又如《金剛經》說：「凡所有相，皆是虛妄。」「若人以色見我，以音聲求我，是人行邪道，不能見如來。」執相而求，終是離道愈遠；唯有自覺，才能找到自己內心的天真佛，才能發掘自己本自具足的真如佛性。因此，希望今後所有佛光會員大眾，大家都能用自覺心來昇華自我，平時要發心聽經聞法，要自我思想來「聞所成慧」、「思所成慧」，進而「解行並重」的精進修行，透過「修所成慧」的實修來體證自我的覺悟，如此才能

圓滿自己。

# 二、用本土化發展佛教

隨著時代進步，在資訊發達、交通便利的帶動下，整個世界的大環境正朝向全球化、國際化的方向發展，「地球村」的時代已儼然成形。然而在此同時，「本土化」的議題卻從來不曾在人類的歷史舞台上消失過，最近台灣的政治圈便對此展開廣泛而熱烈的討論。

其實，在佛教裡，天堂也分三十三天，也有三界之別，所謂欲界六天、色界十八天、無色界四天；甚至佛的國土也有東方與西方之不同。在現實人生裡，世界上有許多國家、種族的不同，這是不爭的事實，而在各種不同當中，彼此最怕的就是被侵略、被征服，不但國土不容侵略，文化

更不希望被征服。

記得過去我在世界各地雲遊弘法，有一次在美國康乃爾大學講演。會後有一位約翰麥克雷教授跟我說：「你來美國弘法可以，但是不能老是拿中華文化來壓迫美國人，開口閉口都是中華文化，好像是來征服美國文化的。」當時我聽了心中就有一個覺悟：我應該要尊重別人的文化，我們來只是為了奉獻、服務，如同佛教徒以香花供養諸佛菩薩一樣。所以對於不同的國家、文化，大家要互相尊重，要容許不同的存在，就如東方琉璃淨土有琉璃淨土的特色，西方極樂世界有極樂世界的殊勝，甚至山林佛教有山林佛教的風格，人間佛教有人間佛教的性向。能夠「異中求同，同中存異」，世界才會多采多姿。

回想當初佛教從印度傳到東土，印度比丘到中國來都只是從事翻譯經典的工作，建寺廟的責任則讓給中國比丘去做，所以才有現在的中國佛

教。假如當時印度的迦葉摩騰、竺法蘭等人都不回印度，而移民到中國來建寺弘法，那裡會有現在中國佛教的特色呢？甚至當初達摩祖師東來，將大法傳給慧可，為什麼？只為了本土化。所以，佛光山在多年前，我把住持之位傳給心平法師繼承，心平法師是台灣人，這也是本土化的落實。

所謂「本土化」，我所提倡的本土化是奉獻的、是友好的、是融和的、是增加的，不是排斥的，不是否決的。例如，過去我看一般華人在美國參加國慶日遊行時，雖然他們都已移民美國，取得美國公民的身份，但是他們的心中並未認定美國是他們的國家，所謂「人在曹營心在漢」，所以我就鼓勵佛光會員在遊行時，高喊口號「我是美國人」，因為我們來到別人的國家，既然身在美國、生活在美國，就不希望一直把自己當成「中國人」，做人家的「國中之國」。

當然，文化是可以互相交流的，但是將心比心，如果我們把立場互

換，自然也不希望在中華民國裡還有「美利堅合眾國」，或是「大日本帝國」的存在。所以現代的新移民，不管走到哪裡，要有「落地生根」的思想，要本土化，要融入當地，不能老是在別人的國家裡還要「國中有國」的發展自己。

因此，對於過去華人走到世界任何地方，不管做事或是傳教，都要強調「發揚中華文化」，這句話是不對的！因為歐洲有歐洲的文化，美洲有美洲的文化，澳洲有澳洲的文化，我們應該尊重當地的文化，用中華文化與當地的文化融和交流，不要用我們的文化去侵略別人的文化。所以每個國家、種族，都要本土化，乃至今後的佛教，大家來自於世界各地，也一定要發揚本土化。

佛教的傳播，雖然其根本教義是不容改變的，甚至戒律也有他的堅持，但是佛教傳到中國、日本、韓國，就是北傳佛教；傳到斯里蘭卡、緬

甸、錫蘭、泰國，即成南傳佛教；傳到新疆、西藏、蒙古，就是藏傳佛教。這是因為氣候、地理、風俗、民情不同，所以要隨順世間。如同天主教的丁松筠神父曾經對我說：「如果你生長在西方，可能會當神父；如果我生長在東方，也可能會去作和尚。」這也是受到當地的地理、文化、教育、民俗、風情等影響所致，就如出產木材之地，人民使用的桌椅等像俱，必定大都是木製的；出產石頭之地，則多數是石材用物。此乃「就地取材」，是受環境影響的關係，不是好或不好的問題。

現在講到用「本土化」來發展佛教，因為佛教不是用來做為一個國家侵略他人文化的工具，而是要同體共生，共同發展，共存共榮。所以佛光會奉行人間佛教，只要在人間，都要發展當地的佛教。就等於美國有五十一州，除了有中央法制外，另外各州有各州的州法。中國三十六行省，也有自治區、特區、少數民族區，因此我們傳播佛教的人，傳承期要

儘量發心落實本土，在很多的不同中，如米穀果疏都有不同的品種，讓佛教在各地也有不同的特色，除了根本教義不變以外，都應該隨順當地風俗民情的需要，容許和歌頌他們的存在。

今年（二○○四年）三月，國際佛光會與大陸佛教界攜手合辦的「海峽兩岸以及中華佛教音樂展演會」，由兩岸漢傳、藏傳、南傳佛教，八大名寺百餘位僧人在臺灣國父紀念館、美國洛杉磯柯達劇院、加拿大英女皇劇院聯合演出佛教梵唄，大家雖然來自不同地方，但是在一起各有梵音嘹亮，才更加美妙。

也就是說，佛教雖有大乘、小乘、南傳、北傳、藏傳等不同，彼此各有特色。特色不要改變；甚至各自的語言、唱腔不同，服裝顏色也不同。儘管不同，但是在同一個佛教下發展，唯有「本土化」才能更深耕，才能更擴大，才能更發展。

有鑑於此，二〇〇一年四月十九日在南非約堡杉騰飯店會議中心舉行「國際佛光會第三屆第一次理事會議」時，我曾在會中提出「四化」的主張，即：「佛法人間化」、「生活書香化」、「僧信平等化」、「寺院本土化」。所謂「寺院本土化」，就是凡佛光山的信徒和佛光會的會員，在世界共創的數百間寺院道場與弘法事業，不為某一人所有，此乃大家的共財；然而佛光人有一心願，即在二十年、三十年之間，將使世界各地的寺院予以「本土化」。

當時我告訴大家，假如現在佛光山海外的分別院，西來寺是由美籍的出家人當住持，南天寺、中天寺由澳洲籍的出家人當住持，南華寺由非洲籍的出家人當住持，其他的各個地方都是由當地的人住持；如果佛光山現在把佛教發展到這個程度，那將是一個怎麼樣的盛況呢？

所以我希望從現在起，二十年到五十年間，讓我們輔導當地本土的出

家人來負責本土的道場，如此佛法必定能更加快速的發展。尤其目前在佛光山佛學院受教育的學生，各國弟子都有，未來希望更擴大種族的吸收，使其都能成為佛光人，將來組織寺院，發展佛光普照，使佛法真正流傳於三千世界。我想，這也是最好的「行佛」之實踐。

## 三、用新事業增廣淨財

人生在世，必須要有正當的事業，透過勤奮經營，使得衣食豐足，生活安定，然後才能從事種種的善事，此即所謂「衣食足，然後禮樂興」也。

衣食住行不但是一般人日常生活中不可或缺的要件，即使成了覺行圓滿的佛陀，也離不開衣食住行的生活。因此，修學佛法不一定要以窮苦為

清高，佛教鼓勵在家信眾可以聚財營生，可以擁有正當的資用生活，甚至可以榮華富貴。如《大寶積經》說「在家菩薩如法集聚錢財，非不如法。」只要「平直正求」，而且有了財富以後要「給事父母妻子，給施親友、眷屬、知識，然後施法。」

意思是說，在家營生，要積聚有道，要合乎八正道的正業與正命，如《雜阿含經》說：「營生之業者，田種行商賈，牧牛羊興息，邸舍以求利。」只要能將本求利，勤勞賺取，無論是農牧收成，或是經商貿易、企業經營、投資生息所得等等，都是佛教所認可的經濟營生。

佛教所謂的「正業」，又叫作「正行」，即指離殺生、不與取等行為，也是指正當的職業；「正命」，就是正當的經濟生活和謀生方式。據《瑜伽師地論》卷二十九：「如法追求衣服、飲食，乃至什物，遠離一切起邪命法，是名正命。」正常而合理的經濟生活是生存的基本要素，舉凡

不會危害社會大眾的士農工商等職業，佛教認為都可以從事。佛教主張應該存財於百姓，百姓富足了，國家才能強盛，佛教有了淨財也才能興隆，因此合理的經濟生活是佛教所認可的。

然而遺憾的是，過去一些弘法的大德法師們，常常用出家人的修行標準來要求在家信眾。譬如談到金錢，就說「黃金是毒蛇，好可怕哦！」談到夫妻，則是「不是冤家不聚頭」；講到兒女，都是一群討債鬼；論及世間，凡事都是苦空無常。這種度化的方式可以說完全悖離人性，不契合眾生的根機，難怪有一些不懂佛法的人，一聽到要他信仰佛教，莫不避之唯恐不及。

其實，過去一般人都以為佛教講四大皆空，應該只重視精神生活，而不重視物質生活。但是根據《阿彌陀經》之說，極樂世界不但「思衣得衣」、「思食得食」，而且黃金鋪地，宮殿樓閣皆為七寶所成，另有七重

欄楯、七重羅網、七重行樹，皆是四寶，周匝圍遶；四邊階道，亦以金、銀、琉璃、玻璃等寶合成，所有菩薩莫不寶冠頂戴，瓔珞披身，可以說極盡莊嚴堂皇，富貴無比。

不過，長久以來有一點令人疑惑不解的是，許多佛教徒輕視當前的福樂財富，而把希望寄託在琉璃淨土或極樂世界；今生貧窮不要緊，只願未來能生到他方世界，享受福樂財富。因此不少佛教徒以苦行為修行，以貧窮為有道，在此理念之下，也使得佛教的傳播受到很多的障礙。

記得多年前有一次在歐洲各國參觀博物館，看到天主教的教堂都是金碧輝煌，他們講究富有，極力發展事業。反觀三四十年前的臺灣，舉凡教堂、銀行都建在十字路口、三角窗、大街小巷的出入口等精華地段；但是如果你要到某一間寺院訪問，只要走到無路的陌巷，環境衛生最差的地方，寺院道場就到了。

事實上，人間化的佛教，主張今生就可以擁有無限的福樂財富，佛教不是叫人不要錢財、不可以享樂；佛教要我們獲得淨財越多越好，享受禪悅越妙越好。即使世間上的福樂財富有限，我們也可以體會佛法裡的法喜，探索信仰裡的財富，享受心裡的世界，擁有全面的人間，這才是建設真正福樂財富的人間。

再說，佛教最初從印度傳到中國、韓國、日本等地，之所以能在當地社會普遍被接受，其中一個很重要的原因，是因為佛教能重視資生利眾的事業，正確解決民生的問題。佛教寺院不僅是傳法、辦道的地方，往往是結合宗教、文化、藝術、教育的文化中心，並與農業生產、商業經濟以及社會福利事業相聯繫，具有多種社會功能。

甚至自古寺院建築，朱簷碧瓦，雕樑畫棟，富麗莊嚴；亭台樓閣、廊院相接，重重疊疊，幽遠深邃，因此有謂「佛門淨土」。佛門其實就是一

個清淨莊嚴的世界，一個安樂富有的世界。佛教雖然主張淡泊物質，反對過份耽迷於物質享受，但在普通社會裡，適度的擁有物質文明的享受是合乎道德的；佛教雖然不太重視資用生活，但是世間還是要藉物質來表達莊嚴。一個寺廟裡，大雄寶殿如果不是巍峨堂皇，怎麼會有人來參拜？佛像如果沒有裝金，怎麼會有人尊敬？西方極樂世界因為黃金鋪地，七寶樓閣，富麗堂皇，所以才能接引眾生，欣然往生其國。

因此，佛教雖然講究個人的生活要簡單樸素，但對大眾則建廣單，接納十方大眾掛單。正如杜甫的《草堂詩》說「安得廣廈千萬間，庇蔭天下寒士俱歡顏。」佛教雖然主張出家人可以清茶淡飯，所謂「三衣一鉢」、「衣單二斤半」、「頭陀十八物」，但對廣大的佛教徒要給予新的求生觀念。因為「巧婦難為無米之炊」、「貧賤夫妻百事哀」，一個在家修行的人不能沒有錢財，否則如何孝養父母？如何安頓家庭的生活？何況修行辦

道、布施救濟，都需要錢財作為助緣資糧。即使是國家社會的各項發展，也需要豐實的國庫作為後盾。而佛教本身必須提供弘法利生、醫療慈善、教育文化等服務來淨化社會，造福人群，如果沒有淨財，又怎能成辦這些佛教事業呢？因此，佛教不排斥錢財，只要是來路明白、用途正當的「淨財」、「善財」、「聖財」，都是佛教所容許的。

在佛教裡常常講「發心」，若照佛教的發心來說，發增上生心的在家居士，在社會上營求功名富貴，並且過著妻子兒女的倫常生活，這是佛法所允許的。如《維摩經》裡，維摩居士在世間奉行佛道，他和世俗的人一樣，開商店、做生意、種田耕地、賺錢營生，但是金銀財寶在他手中，一點也沒有妨礙，他身帶金錢，到各種不同的場所隨緣度化眾生，使得這個世界成為淨化的人間淨土。

在佛教教團中，本來就包括僧信二眾，維摩居士以在家優婆塞的身分

經營事業，獲取利益，這是說明治生事業與佛法並不相違背，因為有充份的經濟能力，才有辦法推動佛教的法輪。

我們看現在的社會，集團有集團的事業，個人也有個人的跨國公司，甚至黨派有黨產、教會有教產，這就是企業化。企業化不是只為賺錢，要有組織、任用人才、為人服務、拓展管理方法。佛教徒為了光大佛法，遠紹如來家業，常有一句話說：「弘法是家務，利生為事業。」出世的佛教雖然不以營利為弘法事業的目標，卻不能因此否定佛教事業的成就和貢獻，因為人間佛教是「以出世的精神，做入世的事業」，特別注重信徒現生的幸福安樂。因此佛光山一向本著「非佛不做」的原則，發展文化、教育、慈善等佛化事業。因為我們認為，雖然過去的佛教重視道業、學業，不重視事業，但是山林比丘可以透過閉關修行，用道業的成就來受人供養；人間比丘則應該透過說法著作，用宣揚來教化、推廣佛教。

除此之外，佛教還需要有在家信眾從事佛光事業，例如設立滴水坊、文物流通處、素食館、交通旅遊、顧問公司等，藉以發展結緣的事業，提昇服務的品質。或是開辦工廠、農場、電力公司、自來水廠、百貨公司、大飯店等民生所需的事業，以及保險、報紙、電台、電視台，乃至安養院、育幼院、兒童之家、幼稚園、托兒所等。甚至將來佛教有辦法，也可以發展電腦、網路，讓全球共享佛法與資訊。

另外，過去寺院培養山林，給人休憩，現在佛教也可以發展園林觀光之無煙囪工業。現在的時代，「受益者付費」的觀念已經普受社會人士所認同，一般參觀博物館、風景名勝等都要付費買門票，這在全世界早已成為慣例。未來佛教設立的文物陳列館、園林景觀也可以酌收維護費，只是信徒如果是到寺院禮佛參拜則不可以收費，因為信徒自然會添油香，兩者要有所分別，這個問題目前在大陸、韓國、日本等地，都有檢討的必要。

當代人心思潮　　　　198

現在佛教辦學校、醫院，也如過去的寺院收租一樣。過去寺院都是用田產、房屋來收取租金，現在也可以開設大旅社、會議室，一樣可以收租金。甚至可以開銀行，為信徒貸款，如過去寺院也開設當舖，並非沒有先例。

在古代經濟活動尚未發達之際，寺院經常以暫時閒置的善款、餘糧來幫助信徒周轉、救急，例如北魏的僧祇粟與僧祇戶，幫助政府解決了人民的飢饉；南北朝的寺庫、唐代三階教的無盡藏院、宋代的「長生庫」、元代的「解典庫」等金融機構，資貸財物，供人民周轉之需。以及歷代所從事的油坊、磨坊、碾米坊、當舖、旅店、製硯、製墨、紡織、印刷、藥局、義塾、書院、養老、濟貧、賑飢、慈幼、醫療、漏澤園（公墓）、義塚、浴室、道路橋樑維修等等，都是繁榮經濟、便民利國的福利事業。

經濟是民生命脈之所繫，佛教的經濟來源，在過去印度佛陀時代提倡

供養制度，傳到中國以後，歷代禪門提倡農林生產，到了近代太虛大師又再提倡工禪合一，現在則有基金制度；未來，以原始佛教的供養制度，結合農禪、工禪生產而發展出適合現代的經濟制度，例如：果菜園林、房租田佃、生產事業、佛書出版、書畫流通、佛像法物、法會油香、經懺佛事、餐飲素食、推廣社教、弘法贊助、參觀門票、慈善服務、安單靜養、互助標會、護法委員等，則為時代發展的必然趨勢。

總之，佛教對錢財的看法是「非善非惡」，佛教並不完全否定錢財，黃金是毒蛇，黃金也是弘法修道的資糧，是一切佛化事業的基礎。佛學院、禪堂、念佛堂、學校、醫院、電台、雜誌社等，都需要金錢才能推動。所以，金錢並不完全是毒蛇，佛經所謂「淨財」、「善財」、「聖財」，只要能善用金錢來弘法利生，其功德比裝窮學道更大，更有意義，更有智慧。是以佛教應該重新估定經濟的價值，只要是合於正業、正命的

淨財，應是多多益善；只要能對國家民生、對社會大眾、對經濟利益、對幸福快樂生活有所增益的事業，佛教徒都應該去做。因為有錢並不可恥，貧窮才會招來罪惡。

未來，希望佛光會員都能發心從事佛教的新事業來增廣淨財，藉此建設莊嚴堂皇的人間淨土，這才符合人間佛教的思想。

## 四、用大願力行佛所行

我們做任何事情，一定要先訂定目標，有了目標才有努力的方向，有了方向，做事才能著力。訂定目標就是「立志」，在佛教稱為「發心立願」。

在社會上，一個人將來的事業成就有多大，就看他童年的志願如何？

在佛教裡，一個修行者的功行有多深，也看他的願力大小。根據佛經所載，所有佛菩薩都是靠願力而成就，沒有一位佛菩薩不是由發願所成。如《無量壽經》卷上記載阿彌陀佛四十八大願、《悲華經》卷七所說釋迦牟尼佛五百大願、《彌勒菩薩所問本願經》所載彌勒奉行十善願、《藥師如來本願功德經》中藥師如來為滅除眾生病苦而發十二大願等。乃至文殊菩薩十八大願、普賢菩薩十大願、觀音菩薩十大願、地藏菩薩發願「地獄不空、誓不成佛」等，都是諸佛菩薩的偉大行願。

此外，古來多少高僧大德為「正法能久住，眾生得離苦」而發下弘願。譬如：玄奘大師「寧向西天一步死，不回東土一步生」，終於完成西域取經的大願；鑑真大師「為大事也，何惜生命！」終於將佛法弘傳於日本。乃至近代慈航法師的「我今發心，不為自求，人天福報，聲聞緣覺，乃至權乘，諸位菩薩，唯依最上乘，發菩提心，願與法界眾生，一時同得

當代人心思潮　　　　202

阿耨多羅三藐三菩提。」都是後世佛子學習的典範。

發心立願是學佛的根本，發心立願可以堅定信心與毅力，可以增長菩提心、提昇信仰，使我們的道德、人格臻於至善。因此我們每日要不斷發願，把發願當成是一種修行的功課。例如：我願意孝順父母，和睦鄰里；我願意奉獻自己，造福社會；我願意犧牲小我，成就大眾；我願意促進世界和平，人民安樂。乃至我願意當一座橋，讓大眾通行；我願意是一棵大樹，供人乘涼；我願意是一滴小水滴，滋潤眾生；我願意當大地，乘載一切眾生；我願意如日月，給人光明；我願意如和風，吹拂人心開意解。甚至我願意從善如流，我願意與人為善，我願意如花朵般給人歡喜，我願意如山水般給人欣賞，我願意如甘泉般解人饑渴……。

立願如同時鐘上緊了發條，汽車加足了汽油，能產生前進的動力；又如船隻裝了羅盤，學生訂了功課表，有了前進的目標。學佛首重發心

立願，《勸發菩提心文》說：「入道要門，發心為首；修行急務，立願居先。願立則眾生可度，心發則佛道堪成。」《大智度論》卷七說：「作福無願，無所標立；願為導御，能有所成。譬如銷金，隨師而作，金無定也。」「莊嚴佛國事大，獨行功德難以成就，須藉願力方能達成。如牛力雖能挽車，亦須御者方有所至。」

此外，《大集經》說：「發願能摧伏煩惱魔軍。」《發菩提心經論‧誓願品》說：「菩薩發心，先建至誠，立決定誓，立誓之人，終不放逸、懈怠、緩慢。」由此可見，入道之由，莫不行願，因為「果」雖然是由「行」所招感，但是如果沒有「願」力，即使是行，也無法到達所期望的目的，所以發心立願是成就一切事業的重要助緣與動力。

一般學佛的人，經常勸人要發心、要立願。其實，發心立願不是佛教徒的專利，社會上任何一個人都應該發心立願。發心，才能把事情做好；

立願，做事才有目標。發心立願就像開採能源一樣，心裡的能源是每個人取之不盡，用之不竭的最大財富。《勸發菩提心文》說：「金剛非堅，願力最堅；虛空非大，心王最大。」一個人的心量有多大，成就便有多大；願力有多堅，力量就有多強。心發則佛道堪成，所以，學佛一定要發心立願，發心立願才會有成就。

發願也如讀書，要不斷升級，剛開始只發小小的願不妨，但漸漸的要發大願，要讓願力不斷昇華。例如，我發願在這一生中，能誦多少經，能念多少佛，能為眾生做多少善事，能傳播佛法度多少眾生；我發願，一生做道場的護法，做眾生的馬牛，做家庭的保母，做社會的明燈。能夠發願

「行佛」，確實「行佛所行」，更是了不起。

談到「行佛」，曹仲植先生是臺灣「生命線」的創始人，她的夫人是個虔誠的佛教徒。四十年前，她在「普門精舍」皈依佛教，對我所提倡的

人間佛教思想極為推崇，所以她時常鼓勵曹居士親近佛教，聽經聞法。向來沒有信仰的曹居士原本十分為難，但由於深愛太太，也就勉強陪她出入佛教寺院。

有一次法會結束，曹夫人拉著先生的手，走到我面前，說道：「師父！請您度我的先生信仰佛教，教他拜佛。」

只見曹居士一臉尷尬的表情，我連忙打圓場道：「曹先生不必拜佛，行佛就好了。」

曹居士一聽，高興極了，此後逢人便說：「星雲大師講的，我不必拜佛，我是行佛的。」

此後，曹居士從事社會慈善公益活動，不遺餘力，例如他創辦臺灣「生命線」，援助無依無助的人走向光明之路；成立曹氏基金會獎助清寒學生，捐助殘障人士輪椅數十萬部；每年災害，捐助千百萬元賑災。此

外，對於佛光山、美國西來寺、法國巴黎道場的建寺工作及國際佛光會的銅牌，介紹佛教史蹟。

弘法活動，他也發心資助；在印度、錫蘭等佛教聖地，他設中、英、梵文

當別人讚美他善名遠播時，他總是說：「念經不如聽經，聽經不如講經，講經不如實踐。我只是『行佛』而已。」

「行佛」就是依照佛陀的教法去實踐奉行。平時我們稱呼學佛的人為「行者」，就是要去「修行」佛法，要如佛陀所說、所行去做，所以真正的修行人，是要「行佛」，而不只是「學佛」而已。

在佛教的經典裡，每部經都是以「如是我聞」為開頭，最後則以「信受奉行」作為結束；能夠信受奉行佛法，就是行佛。所以佛弟子應以「行佛」為修持的標準，例如：

1、慈悲喜捨是行佛

2、救苦救難是行佛

3、奉獻服務是行佛

4、義行仁道是行佛

5、端正身心是行佛

6、生活密行是行佛

7、尊重包容是行佛

8、與人為善是行佛

9、慚愧感恩是行佛

10、吃虧委屈是行佛

11、忍耐接受是行佛

12、四不壞信是行佛

13、與時俱進是行佛

14、胸懷法界是行佛

15、同體共生是行佛

16、佛化人間是行佛

經云：「心、佛、眾生三無差別。」佛陀是已經證悟成佛的眾生，眾生是未修證的佛陀；佛陀是「所作已辦，不受後有」，眾生是「所作未辦，流轉生死」。因此，如果我們能「行佛所行」「學佛所學」，則必定可以離苦得樂，解脫自在。

修學佛法，需要「解行並重」，不重慧解，盲修瞎練容易走火入魔；但是光在慧解上著力，在修持上沒有實證的功夫，所謂慧解也只是知識，和研究哲學差不多，不能獲得宗教裡的真正利益。學佛的人，必須「解行並重」，解是信佛、行就是行佛。有了慧解，才能自覺；透過行佛，才能覺他。我們既然信佛，又再發心修持，就要在生活裡每日受用佛法。例如

嘴邊常掛著讚美別人的言詞，就是奉行佛法言語布施；常體會出人我之間的因緣關係，就會悟出眾生原是一體不可分的；勤勞服務，看起來是為別人，其實是為自己的；感恩恭敬，看起來是對人的，其實是自己受益的。

中國自明清以來，佛教大德們都非常理解佛法，談玄說妙，差不多都能把佛法說得頭頭是道。遺憾的是大都沒有實證的功夫。一個對於宗教沒有實際體驗的人，其言行難免不會走樣。比方說，念佛，你曾有過一心不亂的境界嗎？參禪，你曾有過心境合一的時際嗎？禮拜，你感到莊嚴的人格昇華嗎？誦經，你對佛法有大信心，生大尊敬嗎？除了這些形式的修持外，你對橫逆境界有大忍耐，能不生退心嗎？你對芸芸眾生能慈悲喜捨，毫不慳吝嗎？在五欲之前，能去除貪念；在氣憤之時，能去除瞋心嗎？可以說多少會講佛法的人，自己就是不能實踐佛法。所謂「說到一丈，不如行到一尺」，由此愈發突顯「自覺」與「行佛」的重要。

當代人心思潮　　　　210

自覺是自我開發，覺他是行佛之行；能夠「自覺」與「行佛」，必然「心中有佛」，而時時與佛同在。如果一個人「心中有佛」，眼裡看到的必定都是佛的世界，耳朵聽到的必定都是佛的音聲，鼻中嗅到的必定都是佛的氣息，口裡所說的必定都是佛的語言，身體所做的必定都是佛的事情；如果人人如此，這就是一個佛的世界，家庭怎能不幸福安樂呢？治安怎能不安全良好呢？國家怎能不富強康樂呢？

所以，讓我們每一個人從今天開始，都自我期許「我是佛」吧！

化世與益人

一個人如果沒有自覺
即使給你再好的東西
教你再多的道理都沒有用
唯有自覺
才能不斷進步　自我健全　化世益人

國際佛光會二〇〇六年世界會員代表大會
地　　點：台灣佛光山
時　　間：2006年10月4日-8日

**副**總會長、各位長者、各位理事、各位協會督導、會長、各位貴賓、各位佛光人，大家好！

今年是國際佛光會創會第十五年，也是佛光山開山屆滿四十週年，在這別具意義的時刻裏，很高興看到這麼多來自全球的佛光人，大家不遠千里回到總本山，共同在這裏召開二○○六年國際佛光會世界會員代表大會，心中無比欣慰。

回顧過去十五年來，所有佛光會員分佈在世界各地化世益人，大家不辭辛苦的弘法傳教、成立分會、舉辦各類活動，乃至護持佛光道場所推動的各項弘法事業等，不但在生活中參與奉獻，增加很多宗教體驗，同時也為自己與社會寫下無數的歷史，尤其見證了佛光會的成長以及「佛教全球化」發展的成就，因此今天在這裏首先要對大家表示由衷的讚嘆，同時藉由這次的因緣，提出「化世與益人」，做為今年大會的主題，也是表示對

各位佛光會員的一份期許與希望。

談到「化世」與「益人」，我想到自己這一生，從十二歲出家以來，心中始終只有一個念頭，那就是「為了佛教」。

「為了佛教」，雖然自己從小就在叢林裏過著清苦淡泊的歲月，但是我一點也不覺得辛苦或委屈，因為「為了佛教」。為了佛教，我出家；為了佛教，眼看著同道中有人熱衷於供養優渥的經懺事業，但是我一點也不心動，因為「為了佛教」我立願將來一定要從事弘法利生的工作。甚至為了佛教，儘管年輕時就不斷有一些來自教內教外的誘惑，例如有人想要請我擔任當家、住持，有人希望我從事有名位、有權利的職務，但是我都斷然拒絕，因為我有另外的想法，那就是「為了佛教」。

什麼是「為了佛教」？其實在當時我只知道為了佛教我要讀書，為了佛教我要參學，為了佛教我要勤勞，為了佛教我要發心，為了佛教我要結

緣，為了佛教我要興辦各種佛教事業。所以後來創辦第一所佛教學院時，平常不趕經懺的我，不但主動到太平間為人誦經，甚至通宵念佛，目的就是希望多增加一些辦學的經費，那時我心裏很清楚知道，這才是「為了佛教」。乃至後來為了建設佛光道場，為了推動佛教的文教、慈善等各項弘法事業，雖然種種辛苦，但是「為了佛教」我從來不曾心生退卻，甚至在虛度八十年歲月後，至今仍然雲水行腳於全世界，到處講經說法、隨緣度眾，這一切無非都是「為了佛教」。

為了佛教，我把自己的一生奉獻給「化世」與「益人」，因為這才是真正的「為了佛教」。所以，今天我僅針對「化世與益人」這個主題，提出：一、以自覺健全來化世益人；二、以發心動力來化世益人；三、以隨眾參與來化世益人；四、以菩提願力來化世益人等四點意見，提供給佛光會員共同勉勵，希望大家未來都能朝此「化世益人」的方向努力。

# 一、以自覺健全來化世益人

佛教是個重視「覺悟」的宗教，不只佛陀本身因為「自覺」、「覺他」、「覺行圓滿」而成就佛道，就是佛陀所說的教法，無非也是為了引導有情悟入佛的知見，讓眾生「覺佛所覺、悟佛所悟」而能與佛平等，所以學佛主要的目的就是要開智慧，求覺悟。

所謂「覺悟」，「覺」就是證悟涅槃妙理的智慧，「悟」就是生起真智，反轉迷夢，覺悟真理實相。學佛雖然是要向佛陀學習，但是「覺悟」必須要靠自己，不能依賴別人；凡事靠別人幫助終究有限，尤其開悟證果、修行成道，一定要靠自己自覺。例如，自覺人生憂悲苦惱，自覺生死無常，自覺人情多變，自覺世間國土危脆，難以安身立命；有了自覺，才會努力想方法去克服這許多的煩惱妄想，才會發心健全自己，才能獲得自

在安樂，如果自己不懂得自覺自悟，即使佛陀慈悲，也不能幫助我們自覺覺他，不能幫助我們開悟成佛。

談到「成佛」，所謂「佛」者，如《佛地論》說：「於一切法、一切種相，能自開覺，亦開覺一切有情，如睡醒覺，如蓮花開，故名佛也。」佛陀雖然是覺悟宇宙真理的覺者，也是徹知宇宙真相的智者，但其實「佛是已覺悟的眾生，眾生是未覺悟的佛」，佛是人成，所以人人都有成佛的性能，每一個人的清淨自性本來就與佛無異，只是因為被無明煩惱所覆而不能顯發，就如明鏡蒙塵，又如明月為烏雲所遮蔽，因此《法華經》說「懷珠作丐」、「藏寶受貧」，這是眾生最大的遺憾。

吾人發心學佛，最主要的目的就在於去除煩惱、開顯佛性。人的根本煩惱就是貪瞋癡，因此要「勤修戒定慧，息滅貪瞋癡」，只要三毒息滅，三慧明朗，就能破除無始以來的無明，這就是「自覺」，也就是禪宗所說

的「開悟」或「見性」。

在中國的禪門一直很著重「自覺」，凡事要靠自己去參，不能說破。當初佛陀在靈山會上「拈華示眾」，迦葉尊者靈犀相應，破顏而笑，於是佛陀把「正法眼藏，涅槃妙心，實相無相，微妙法門，不立文字，教外別傳，付囑摩訶迦葉。」禪因此就在「拈華微笑」、師徒心意相契的剎那之間流傳下來，這就是「自覺」。

「自覺」就是一種自我教育，佛經講：「自依止、法依止、莫異依止」，這就是自我教育。人要靠自我教育才能成功，因為自己的缺陷、自己的無知、自己需要教育的地方，只有自己最清楚，因此要做自己的老師，自己教育自己。也就是說，人要懂得自我要求、自我學習、自我充實、自我反省；凡事能夠反求諸己，不斷自問、自覺、自發、自悟，透過自我的觀照才能找到自己，否則如《遺教經》說：「我如善導，導人

善路，汝若不行，咎不在導；我如良醫，應病與藥，汝若不服，過不在醫。」自己不覺，不但佛陀幫不了我們的忙，即使佛教的出版品多如汗牛充棟，佛教的大藏經再怎麼精闢的闡述般若真理，都不能幫助我們覺悟，一定要自我閱讀、深入經藏，透過聞思修才能自覺自悟。

《圓覺經》說：「譬如銷金，金非銷故有；雖復本來金，終以銷成就；一成真金體，不復重為礦。」學佛就如開採金礦一般，雖然佛性人人本具，但若不經過修行，則如金礦未經開採，終不能得。所以，關於如何自覺健全？下列的問題可供大家自我審查：

（一）、我對皈依三寶的信心具足嗎？

（二）、我對受持五戒的觀念清楚嗎？

（三）、我對因緣果報的見解正確嗎？

（四）、我對自己的服務助人真心嗎？

（五）、我對護持正法的方式正確嗎？

（六）、我對參與活動的心地清淨嗎？

（七）、我對佛法的進修日有進步嗎？

（八）、我對佛法道理有融入身心嗎？

以上八點，如果你都有正面而肯定的答案，就表示你有自覺，證明你對佛法的信心堅固，你在學佛的道路上也會自我健全，甚至還懂得發四無量心、行六度波羅蜜，乃至發奮加行，饒益有情，廣度眾生；否則光陰虛度，徒有學佛之名，沒有得到學佛的實益，實在可惜。故此首先提出「自覺健全」的呼籲，因為一個人如果沒有自覺，即使給你再好的東西、教你再多的道理都沒有用，唯有自己自覺才能不斷進步，唯有自己自覺才能自我健全，唯有自己自覺才能化世益人。

## 二、以發心動力來化世益人

佛教的百千法門中，「發心」最為重要，如《勸發菩提心文》說：「入道要門，發心為首；心發，則佛道堪成。」發心就是開發我們的心地，就是建設自我。佛教將「心」比喻為「田」、為「地」；田地不開發，就無法播種；心地不開發，也無法長養菩提，所以在佛門的修持裏，發心第一，例如發「四無量心」、發「四弘誓願」等，發心才有動力去實踐「四攝法」、「四加行」，才能自度度人。

講到「發心」，十五年來的佛光人，大家在國際佛光會這個教團裏，有的人發心當會長、幹部、檀講師，乃至榮任督導、長者，有的人發心參與讀書會、訂閱佛書、參與印經、推廣福報、勸募會員、捐獻淨財、參與救災、護持道場、帶領朝山、參加法會，或是推動臘八粥運動、雲水布

教、托鉢興學等，甚至有的人到學校、監獄去做公民教育、心靈諮商、佛法開示等，你們以自己的行動，表達今日廿一世紀的佛教徒全部都動員起來了，大家都懂得要走出自我、走出家庭，進而走入社會來與大眾結緣、聯誼。就拿十五年來，國際佛光會召開的世界會員大會、理監事會議、青年會議、金剛會議、婦女會議、童軍會議等，大家就不只十幾次的東西方相互往來、洲際之間彼此互動。這樣的情誼交流，帶動了佛法的傳揚，促進了人際的和諧，這都是由於各位的發心所產生的動力而成就。

發心就是開發心田，學佛首先要學會發心，心的田地如果不開發，縱使外緣具足，福德具足，也不能長出菩提之苗。就像一粒種子，如果沒有好的田地，它就不能結出好的花果，所以我們要開發心中的財富，開發心地的能源，必須從「發心」開始。

世間上，發心有多大，成就便有多大，發心的力量不可思議。過去儒

家的學者一直叫人要立志，佛教的行者則要人發願；立志、發願，就是發心，心一發，則志可立，心一發，則願可成。

發心的力量真是微妙，例如：你發心吃飯，飯菜不但可以吃飽，而且味道更加美妙；你發心睡覺，覺會睡得更加甜蜜、更加安然。只要一發心，所做的事情，品質就都不一樣了，正是所謂「平常一樣窗前月，才有梅花便不同。」只可惜世間上的人大多心外求法，不知道自家裏有無限的寶藏，所以一般人只懂得要把荒地、山坡地，開發成為農地、建地，卻不知道我們的心裏有無限的寶藏、無限的能源。因此，聰明的人應該反求諸己，應該由外向內來開發我們自己心裏的能源和寶藏。

發心是一本萬利的投資，在佛教裏都鼓勵人要發慈悲心，要發菩提心，要發增上心。我們究竟要有什麼樣的發心呢？茲提供幾點方向如下：

（一）、我們要有「慚愧自己所學有限」的發心：比方說：很多的文學典故我不懂，很多的科技常識我不知道，很多的哲學理論我不明白，甚至於做人處事的道理我都不健全，因而感到慚愧。因為慚愧自己的才疏學淺，才會激勵自己發心學習，所以要廣學多聞，要博覽一切常識，不會駕駛的就去學開車，不會電腦的就去學習電腦資訊管理，不會記帳的就去學習會計帳目，不會音樂唱歌的就去學習各種樂器等。

（二）、我們要有「慚愧自己能力不足」的發心：譬如：我做事不周全，我教書不能盡職，我領導人不盡圓滿；因為慚愧自己的無能，因此要發心增強自己的能力，以便更能擔當，更能負責。

（三）、我們要有「慚愧自己心地不淨」的發心：例如：心裏常常充滿貪瞋煩惱，常常有侵犯別人的意念，常常心懷陰謀詭計；因為慚愧自己心地

不清淨，因此要發心來改善自己、淨化自己。

（四）我們要有「慚愧自己善念薄弱」的發心：譬如：自己不能常常心存善念，不能盡心盡力廣做善事，所以今後要發心多做一點善事，多布施一些善財，多帶給別人一些歡喜。

此外，我們尤其要開發如海、如空、如地、如性的真心：

（一）、開發如海的真心：大海不但是魚蝦的宮殿，大海也蘊藏了無限的寶藏，現代人要開採石油能源，不都是往大海裏探勘嗎？大海的資源，往往可以成為國家的財富，所以各個國家都要保護海域，就是保護國家的資源。我們的真心也像大海一樣，蘊藏著慈悲、菩提等豐富的寶藏，所以要開發他。

（二）、開發如空的真心：我們的心可以用「虛空」來比喻，所謂「心如

虛空，量周沙界」，虛空裏有日月星辰，虛空裏有雷電雨露，虛空裏容納宇宙萬有，所以現代各個國家都想探索太空，希望能在太空裏找到寶藏。我們的心也如虛空，充滿了歡喜、滿足等無窮的寶藏，我們要經過開發，才能找到寶藏。

（三）、開發如地的真心：大地是我們的母親，大地孕育了我們的生命，人類不但靠天吃飯、靠海過活，而且靠地維生。大地能成長萬物，地底更蘊藏著金銀銅鐵等各種寶礦。我們的心也如大地，埋藏著佛性、真如等無限的寶藏，懂得開發心地，才能讓寶藏出土。

（四）、開發如性的真心：每個人都有一顆自性真心，當我們開發了如海的真心、如空的真心、如地的真心以後，如果能再開發自己的性天，把本性的天地加以開發，就能發掘自己的真如自性，就能見到自己的本來面目，就能找到自己的家鄉，就能尋回自己的所有了。

當代人心思潮　　　　226

總之，凡能幫助我們完成「自利利他，自覺覺他」之學佛最高目標的願心，諸如感恩心、慚愧心、向道心、功德心、深信心、尊敬心、廣大心、忍耐心等，都是學佛者不可一刻或忘的發心。

發心，就是立志，就是發願；發心是動力，無論什麼機器都要講究它的動力有多少。我們每一個人也要自問自己的能量、動力有多大？能量、動力來自於發心，你所發的心願有多大，動力就有多大，所以關於如何「化世益人」的第二點，我希望未來全體佛光會員都能以「發心動力」來化世益人。

## 三、以隨眾參與來化世益人

世間萬法，都靠因緣和合才能成就，所謂「緣聚則成，緣滅則散」，

缺少因緣，不但諸事難成；離開因緣，個人也無法生存，所以人不能離開大眾。大眾就是我們的因緣，大眾就是幫助我們生存的條件，故而佛教講究「緣起」，講究「集體創作」，講究「眾緣所成」。

佛教把人稱為「眾生」，意即「眾緣和合而生」。世間上沒有個人單獨存在的時空，要存在，一定要靠大眾相互依存；有了大眾的因緣成就，個人才能存活。因此，我們要把這些因緣聚集起來，再分享、利益給大眾，千萬不要做離群的自了漢，因為「佛果在眾生身上求」，離開大眾，固然生命無法生存，失去大眾，也無佛道可成。

眾，實在是一個非常美好的意思，像「眾生平等」、「以眾為我」、「大眾第一」、「眾志成城」、「眾望所歸」、「眾擎易舉」、「眾星拱月」等，乃至佛經所說，任何一個法會，任何一個事業，都需要「眾成就」，因此和合隨順眾生才能成事，這是不容置疑的真理！

談到「眾」的重要，在自然界裏，樹木都要叢生成林，花草也講究簇生聚集，動物也都是「物以類聚」。人也不例外，我們每個人來到這個世間，都是雙手空空而來，雖然在世間建設了家庭，有了眷屬、家人、財產、事業，最後還是得空空而去，因此人生最好就是擁有佛法、擁有功德、擁有福田、擁有大眾、擁有未來，這些才是永恆持續的資產，才是生命的最高價值。

尤其，世間上最寶貴者，並非黃金白玉，也不是汽車洋房；最可貴的是「緣份」。人與人要有緣份才能和好；人與事要有緣份才能成功；人與社會，乃至事事物物、你、我、他等等，都要有緣份才能圓滿功德。因此，在人世間有許多的好事值得我們去做，例如布施、守法、奉獻、服務等；在眾多的善法之中，沒有一樣比「給人一些因緣」更為重要。

「緣」不是佛教的專有名詞，緣是宇宙人生的真理，緣是屬於每一個

人的。人的一生都是在「緣」中輪轉，例如機會就是機「緣」；世間凡事要靠眾「緣」和合才能成功，建房子少個一磚一瓦，都不算完成。在人生的旅途上，有的人碰到困難就會有貴人適時相助，這都是因為曾經結緣的緣故，所以今日結緣就是為來日的患難與共做準備，「結緣」實在是人世間最有保障的投資。

人既然是依靠因緣而生存在這個世界上，因此今後佛光人應該隨眾參與各種活動，多多廣結善緣，因緣愈多，成就愈大；尤其我們要創辦各種佛光事業，有了事業才能利益大眾。過去一般人以為佛教的事業，無非就是誦經祈福，喪葬超渡；或是深入山林，農耕自足，過著離欲清淨的生活。事實上，千百年來佛教一直為人間提供各種醫療救濟、社會公益、教育文化等事業，不遺餘力的造福社會，利濟群生。

例如：北魏的僧祇粟與僧祇戶，幫助政府解決人民的飢饉；南北朝的

寺庫、唐代三階教的無盡藏院，以及歷代所從事的油坊、當舖、旅店、茶館、食堂、碾磑業等，都是繁榮經濟、便民利國的福利事業。尤其隋唐佛教之所以興盛蓬勃，寺院發展佛教事業來利濟蒼生，可以說是主要的原因之一。其中磨坊、碾廠、倉庫促進民生的發展，宿坊、車坊便利商旅的往來，義學、私塾、藏經閣、譯經院提昇社會的文教，僧衹粟、寺庫穩定國家的金融，病坊、當舖照顧貧者的需要。

其實更擴大開來看，歷代的寺院無不興辦許多利濟群生的事業，包括植樹造林、墾荒闢田、鑿井開渠、興建水利、維護泉源、築橋鋪路、興建公廁、建立涼亭、利濟行旅、經營碾磨、設置浴室、賑饑濟貧、施醫給藥、養老育幼、急難救助，乃至開辦義塚、義學等。也可以說，佛教自從傳入中國之後，一直隨著時代的發展，從農業生產到工業參與，從旅遊服務到臨終關懷，從當舖油坊到倉庫碾磑，從慈善工作到文教事業，不但帶

動經濟的蓬勃發展，更是提昇了社會的人文素養。

一直到了現在，我們以實踐「人間佛教」為目標的佛光會員，更要有計畫的興辦各種佛教事業來化世益人，福利社會。例如可以設立佛教文物流通處，讓佛教徒及社會人士方便獲得各類佛書、法物、佛教錄音帶、錄影帶等，以帶動佛教文物流通，使佛教文化得以弘揚。或者在各地成立佛光緣美術館、滴水書坊、語言翻譯中心、醫療護理中心，乃至成立讀書會、推動人間音緣、提倡心靈環保、重視生態保育等，透過語文、講說、音樂、藝術、護生、救濟、醫療等，都可以提供廣大群眾接觸佛教的因緣，藉此利樂十方眾生。

甚至佛光人為了發展慧學，將來你們也可以進入佛光山創辦的各級學校教書，或是加入佛學研究中心來深入經藏，專心研究、推動人間佛教的思想、經論，或是到佛光山的禪堂、淨業林，體驗禪淨雙修，落實解行並

重，乃至加入佛光教團，支薪工作等。

以下茲就適合佛教徒從事的事業，列舉數十種，提供佛光會員發展事業之參考：

**‧文化事業**：報社、電台、電視台、書局、唱片行、佛教文物流通處、美術館、文化廣場、出版社、印刷廠、翻譯社、劇場、音樂廳、會議中心等。

**‧教育事業**：各級學校、幼稚園、補習班、外籍新娘識字班、長青學院、才藝中心、信徒大學、社區大學等。

**‧社會福利**：醫院、復健中心、洗腎中心、療養院、安養院、老人俱樂部、托兒所、育幼院、兒童之家等。

**‧服務業**：旅行社、葬儀社、花店、托運公司、顧問公司、律師事務所、保險公司、職業介紹所、技能訓練班等。

・**工商類**：超級市場、佛教百貨公司、大飯店、素食館、物流中心、室內設計公司、園藝設計公司、電力公司、自來水廠、農場、工廠等。

以上所舉之外，只要是能化世益人，只要對國家民生、對社會大眾、對經濟利益、對幸福快樂生活有所增益的事業，佛光會員都可以視自己的專長、興趣和經濟能力，實際投入參與。另外，未來佛光會員還應致力於傳統與現代的融和，要將古老的東西改良成為現代人可以接受的方式，例如集會的改良、共修的改良、活動多元化的舉辦等。尤其要鼓勵青年團、童軍團的發展，以便接引更多的青年人共同參與佛教事業，相信必能更有助於發揮佛教化導俗世、利益大眾之功。

# 四、以菩提願力來化世益人

佛教講究智慧，但尤重慈悲；重視慈悲，更重行願。佛教的諸佛菩薩，都是依靠悲智願行而成就道業，因此前面提到，學佛首重發心立願，如《大集經》說：「發願能摧伏煩惱魔軍。」《大智度論》也說：「作福無願，無所標立；願為導御，能有所成。」由此可見，入道之由莫不行願，因為「果」雖然是由「行」所招感，但是如果沒有「願」力，即使是行，也無法到達所期望的目的，所以學佛要發菩提心，立菩提願。

菩提心就是指自覺覺他，就是「上求佛道、下化眾生」的大願心。過去佛教所以衰微，就是因為佛教徒悲智願行的力量不夠，例如「四弘誓願」，大眾敢唱不敢講，敢講不敢做，敢做做不到。所以今日佛教要興隆，佛教徒必須要有悲智願行，應該要效法古聖先賢，發大菩提心，例如佛陀在菩提樹下金剛座上立願「若不成佛，誓不起座」，阿彌陀佛發四十八大願成就極樂淨土，藥師如來發十二大願莊嚴琉璃世界，乃至文

殊、普賢、觀音、地藏，也是以慈悲行願做為實踐的行門。

此外，玄奘大師西天求法，鑒真大師東渡日本弘法等，他們化世益人的精神都值得我們學習；乃至「四弘誓願」更是每一位大乘行者所應奉行的功課，所以發心奉行菩薩道的佛光會員，都應該以「菩提願力」來化世益人，因為「人間佛教」一旦離開了菩提心，那就是世間法，就會遠離佛道。

因此，我們要如何發菩提心，如何發大願才有力量呢？如《楞嚴經》說：「因地不正，果遭迂曲。」發心立願要合於《大乘起信論》的「大」、「正」、「圓」、「真」，要有「假使熱鐵輪，於汝頂上旋，終不為此苦，退失菩提心」的發願，如此才不會偏離正道。

以下茲舉數例，提供佛光會員發願之參考：

（一）、我願做一個正信的佛子，用佛法分享世人。

（二）、我願將正信佛教，傳之於世界。

（三）、我願到邊遠落後的地方，傳揚佛法。

（四）、我願到苦難的地方，施與愛心。

（五）、我願將產業交給佛教團體，永續經營；我願將遺產交與佛教團體，利益群生。

（六）、我願建立正知正見的佛化家庭，重視信仰傳承。

（七）、我願奉行一師一道，護持正法。

（八）、我願發心著書、說法、修行、傳教。

此外，現代佛教徒應該以現實人生的需要，幫助社會解除苦難為自己的願行，例如：

1．成立「電話法語中心」，讓求助無門的苦悶者，用電話訴說心事，給予一些佛法的指導和慰問。

2・成立「救苦救難中心」，讓徘徊在人生十字路口的人，及時得到救助，免於誤入歧途。

3・成立「佛法諮詢中心」，為社會上一些有疑難的人，給予佛法的心理輔導，助其解決生活、職業、家庭、感情上的問題。

4・成立「老人俱樂部」，提供一般老人聚會、喝茶、下棋、閱報、念佛等，不但藉機聯誼，同時可以從佛法裏獲得身心的安頓。

5・成立「大同養老之家」，發揮「老吾老以及人之老」的精神，照顧社會上許多獨居老人，使其免於孤單無依之苦。

6・成立「收容之家」，對於一時因故無家可歸的貧病孤弱，給予暫時收容，以便重新調整身心，再創前途！

7・成立「婦女求職中心」，提供鄉村婦女到都市求職時，解決其求職前的食宿問題，讓他有一個緩衝時間，以免遭到壞人所騙。

8.成立「病患慰問團」，有組織、有計劃的到醫院，或到病患家裡慰問，為其誦經祝福，贈送佛書，以慰病苦。

9.參加「送醫藥到偏遠地區」活動，如佛光山雲水醫院，讓健康的人出錢，為窮苦的人看病。

10.組織「急難扶持會」，對一些遭受重大天災人禍而流離失守、生活無著的人，及時施以救濟，此即一般所謂「救急不救窮」也。

11.發心將個人薪水所得，撥出十分之一作為布施之用。

12.每週安排數小時的時間，為信仰或慈善而加入義工服務。

其實發心立願並不是佛教徒的專利，社會上任何一個人都應該發心立願，發心，才能把事情做好，立願，做事才有目標。尤其今日社會亂象紛陳，很多人在為世風日下、道德淪喪而感到憂心不安之際，如果人人都能發心立願，例如：身為警察的，發願克盡職守，除暴安良，打擊犯

罪，消除社會的歪風邪道；身為家庭主婦的，發願孝順公婆，教育兒女，體貼丈夫，確保家庭的倫理道德、和諧美滿；身為學生的，發願用功讀書，孝順父母，尊敬師長，和睦朋友，做個品學兼優的好學生。甚至舉國上下，如果人人都能發願，願於每日把歡喜布施給別人，把快樂分享給大眾，相信必能使社會充滿祥和之氣。

總之，發願就像開採能源一樣，心裏的能源是每個人取之不盡，用之不竭的最大財富。唯有人人經常立志發願，才能為自己留下歷史，為家庭留下貢獻，為社會留下慈悲，為世界留下光明！

因此，希望未來所有佛光人等，不分男女老幼，人人都能擁有悲智願行，都能以菩提願力來化世益人，則佛教普及社會，深入人心，自是指日可待。

國際佛光會的成立，不但有助於提升信眾信仰的層次，同時也是佛教史上革命性的創舉。十五年來，在佛光會員們共同推動「人間佛教」的努力下，已逐漸實現佛教的生活化、現代化、本土化、國際化。未來更期許每個會員，都能本著佛教慈悲、智慧的特質，人人自覺健全，同時以發心為動力，隨眾參與、護持佛教的弘法事業，更以菩提願力為後盾，一起為佛法的弘傳，為世界的淨化，為人類的幸福與安樂而奉獻心力。

# NOTE

# NOTE